God's Programs:

An Introduction to Understanding the Bible

But now being made free from sin, and become servants to God,
you have your fruit unto holiness, and the end everlasting life.

For we preach not ourselves, but Christ Jesus the Lord; and
ourselves your servants for Jesus' sake. For God, who
commanded the light to shine out of darkness, has
shined in our hearts, to give the light of
the knowledge of the glory of God
in the face of Jesus Christ.

For all who love the LORD Jesus Christ,
desire to understand the Scriptures,
and look for the blessed hope
of His glorious appearing.

Amen.

God's Programs:

An Introduction to Understanding the Bible

By

Don Samdahl

Thy word is a lamp unto my feet,
and a light unto my path.
Psalm 119.105

A Doctrine Publication
Doctrine.org

First Edition: October 2017
Printed in the United States of America
ISBN: 978-0-9994689-2-0

Table of Contents

Many ask the following questions. The answers to these questions and many more are answered in this book. If the answers to these questions are of interest to you, this book is for you.

1. Why did Jews have no idea of dying and going to heaven?
2. Where is the kingdom of God? In heaven? On earth?
3. Why did God choose the Jews?
4. Why is the Old Testament "old" and the New "new?"
5. How did God save men and women in the Old Testament?
6. What did the Jews understand about the Messiah?
7. What were the great themes of Jewish theology?
8. What is the Gospel?
9. Has the Gospel always been the same?
10. Why is there disagreement about faith and works?
11. What was the meaning of animal sacrifices?
12. Why did God choose Paul when He had Twelve apostles?
13. Why did Paul rarely associate with the Twelve?
14. Did Jesus, the Twelve, and Paul preach different things?
15. Can one know one is saved? What does saved mean?
16. Why did Jesus not have a ministry to Gentiles?
17. Why did Jesus command the Twelve not to go to Gentiles?
18. Why did Jesus send Paul to Gentiles?
19. What is the Rapture and why do people believe it?
20. What is the meaning of the book of Revelation?
21. What is the Church, the Body of Christ?
22. When did the Church begin?
23. Why does evil exist and how will God defeat it?
24. Why do Peter and the Twelve disappear after Acts 15?
25. What is the "Great Commission?" Is it for the Church?

Prologue

The Bible is a story—a grand drama composed of multiple dramas. The cast includes men and women, spiritual beings, and God Himself. The Bible is the Word of God. God is its author and He is its chief character. The plot is God's revelation of Himself and what He has set out to do. Like all dramas, it has misunderstandings, crises, victories, setbacks, reversals of fortune, failures, regrets, good and evil. The Bible is a love story. It tells of God's love for mankind. And the Bible is a war story. God has enemies—serious enemies. They hate Him and are more wicked than the villains of any novel. But when God fights, He fights to win. And He will. While wounded, He utterly defeats His adversaries.

The characters in God's drama express wills. They obey or rebel against Him. And, as an author of a novel knows, the wills of the characters end the story as the author intended. Make no mistake, the wills in God's drama are free. God's genius allows billions of wills to operate yet have His story end as He planned. God offers each person the choice to ally with Him and join the fight against the powers of darkness. To choose wisely means love, joy, peace, and eternal life. To choose unwisely means receipt of just deserts.

The story ends with God resolving the problem of good and evil and winning the angelic conflict. He will sum up all things in Christ (Ephesians 1.10) who will hand over the kingdom to God the Father (1 Corinthians 15.24).

To a secular world, God is rarely considered and the Bible is seen as passé. Its worldview is diametrically opposed to that which is presented in the Bible. But what is in the Bible has happened. What was to happen has. And what is yet to happen will. The Bible is true. It is all going to happen, just as the Bible says.

Preface

Hundreds of millions of copies of the Bible exist. Multitudes of books have been written about it. Despite this plentitude, most people do not understand or misunderstand it. They include churched and unchurched, believers and unbelievers, laymen and clergy, professors and seminarians. The numerous denominations and churches in Christendom evidence this truth. Each has its view and interpretation of the Scriptures. The Bible is not difficult and should be understood by the vast majority. This is not the case.

The primary reason for the great confusion in Christendom is the failure to recognize and understand, what I call in this book, God's Programs. They are the key to understanding God's revelation. Specifically, the primary reason for Christendom's confusion is its failure to recognize Paul's unique apostleship. Paul was *not* a 13th apostle appended to the Twelve. Paul was the apostle of a whole new program: the Church, the body of Christ.

The perplexity that exists in Christendom has roots which go back 1,950 years. Paul wrote these sad words to Timothy shortly before his execution: "This you know, that all they which are in Asia be turned away from me; of whom are Phygellus and Hermogenes" (2 Timothy 1.15). Paul spent several years and worked tirelessly ministering in Asia Minor (Turkey). Despite his labors, it abandoned his teachings. The great progress he had made with the Asian churches—Ephesus, Colossae, Galatia, Iconium, Derbe, Lystra, Antioch Pisidia, and Laodicea—proclaiming Christ's death and resurrection, teaching salvation by faith alone, instructing believers about their relationship to Christ and living the Christian life—all these churches abandoned his teachings. How this occurred and what occurred with be examined more closely in Chapter 3, which discusses God's great program, the Church.

Only when one understands the differences in God's programs and the unique apostleship of Paul does the Bible become easy to comprehend. If you desire to understand God's revelation, this book is for you.

The Framework of Scripture

Theologians recognize God did not reveal everything at once but that He revealed His plan systematically and progressively. The most basic divisions of the Bible are called the Old and New Testament. This division, however, is an arbitrary construct and provides little help for understanding the Bible. The "Old Testament" is the "Old Covenant," the Mosaic Law, given in Exodus. Technically, the "Old Testament" does not begin until Exodus 20. The "New Testament" is the "New Covenant," prophesied by Ezekiel and Jeremiah, and inaugurated by Christ at the end of His earthly ministry. Thus, the Gospels are Old Testament but are called "New Testament."

Augustine stated, "the New Testament is hidden in the Old, the Old Testament is revealed in the New" (*Novum Testamentum in Vetere latet, Vetus Testamentum in Novo patet*). This axiom, known and quoted widely, fails to recognize that the Old Testament never even hinted of the organism known as the Church, the body of Christ. Its creation was unforeseen.

A better approach is required. The Scriptures reveal five distinct periods, administrations, or programs. This framework reveals how God has structured His progressive revelation. Every believer in Christ should understand this layout or framework since it is the foundation for understanding the Scriptures and one's place in them. The five programs or periods in God's plan noted in the chart are Mankind, Israel, Church, Kingdom, and Eternity.

Framework of the Divine Programs Through the Ages

Program	Mankind	Israel	Church	Israel Redux	Kingdom	New Heavens and New Earth
Key Figure	Adam	Abraham	Paul	Antichrist	Christ	God the Father
Length	Adam to Abraham	Abraham to Paul	Paul to Rapture	7 Years	1,000 Years	Eternal
Revelation	Revealed by the Prophets		Unrevealed by the Prophets	Revealed by the Prophets		

See doctrine.org/chart-of-gods-programs/ for a detailed chart.

God began His program with all mankind. After 2,000 years, He revealed Himself to Abraham and established a new program. The covenant God made with him laid the foundation to create a new race (Israel) through whom God would reveal Himself. After Israel rejected their Messiah, God interrupted this program and began another new program, the Church, the body of Christ. God saved and commissioned Paul to be its founder and architect just as he had saved Abraham to begin His covenant program, Israel. God's Church program will continue until its resurrection, the Rapture. After this, God will finish His program with Israel with the Day of the Lord, the Tribulation (Matthew 24.21, 29). At its end, the Lord will return and establish His next program, the long-promised Messianic kingdom in which He will fulfill His covenant promises to Israel. After it has run its 1,000-year course, God will establish His final program, Eternity, with the creation of a New Heavens and a New Earth.

Within this framework, one must master a basic concept:

All Scripture is FOR us, but all Scripture is not TO us.

An example may be helpful. David asked God not to remove His indwelling Holy Spirit from him after his sin of adultery and murder (Psalm 51.9-11). Believers in this age, members of the Church, the body of Christ, need not pray such a prayer. In David's day, the Holy Spirit indwelled individuals to guide and empower them to accomplish various tasks and responsibilities. His indwelling presence was not guaranteed. But in our age, Paul wrote God the Holy Spirit indwells believers *permanently* (1 Corinthians 12.13; 2 Corinthians 1.22, 5.5; Ephesians 1.13-14). For believers today, the indwelling Holy Spirit is God's down payment (ἀρραβών), our guarantee of salvation.[1] Members of the Church, the body of Christ,

[1] The word ἀρραβών means a pledge, "earnest money," a down payment of the full amount.

live under a different administration than David. We live in a different *program*. What David wrote is FOR us, but not TO us.[2]

Paul expressed this principle in the following words:

> For whatsoever things were written aforetime were written for our learning, that we through patience and comfort of the scriptures might have hope (Romans 15.4).
>
> Now all these things happened unto them for examples: and they are written for our admonition, upon whom the ends of the world are come (1 Corinthians 10.11).

This book will reveal what is TO us and what is FOR us.

---

[2] Understanding the Bible also requires a sound foundation of investigative principles. These include: 1) Recognizing the Scriptures are God-breathed (θεόπνευστος, 2 Timothy 3.16); 2) Employing a sound methodology of interpretation (a hermeneutic with rigor); 3) Understanding how we know what we know (the means of perception of knowledge). These principles are examined in the Appendices.

Chapter 1

Mankind: Program One

And I will put enmity between you and the woman, and between your seed and her seed; it shall bruise your head, and you shall bruise his heel (Genesis 3.15).

Genesis, as its name states, is a book of beginnings. God's first program encompasses Genesis 1-11 and focuses upon all mankind. Genesis provides the record of God's creation of the heavens and earth, His framing of the earth and creating life, and mankind's first 2,000 years of history. Much of the content of these eleven chapters—six chapters—reveals the spiritual warfare that began between Satan and man and the consequences of that warfare. The chart below outlines this revelation:

Spiritual Warfare in Genesis 1-11	
Genesis 3	Introduction of Satan Temptation and Fall of mankind[1] Warfare: God and Man vs. Satan
Genesis 6-9	Fallen angels corrupt human genome Flood as judgment
Genesis 11	Tower of Babel Reintroduction of false religion

[1] Theologians term the beginning of mankind's sin and death "the Fall."

Creation and Dominion

The first two chapters of Genesis reveal God's creation of heaven and earth, plant, animal, and human life.[2] The Genesis account of creation reveals the following:

1. God created the heavens and earth (Genesis 1.1).
2. God fashioned earth into a habitable residence (Genesis 1.3-2.4).[3]
3. God created plant and animal life (Genesis 1.11-12, 20-28).
4. God created life according to "kinds" (Genesis 1.11-12, 21, 24-25).[4]
5. God created mankind (male and female) in His image (Genesis 1.26-27, 2.7).[5]
6. God created woman from man to be his complement and companion (Genesis 2.18, 21-25).[6]

---

[2] God has no beginning. Genesis 1.1 reads, "In the beginning, God created the heavens and the earth." God is outside space and time—nature. God is Spirit, supernature, metaphysical—above and beyond nature. The question, "Who created God?" is meaningless. He is Creator of all reality and phenomena. The Scriptures reveal the Lord Jesus Christ is the Creator (John 1.3, 10; 1 Corinthians 8.6; Ephesians 3.9; Colossians 1.15-16; Hebrews 1.2).

[3] The language of the text, "evening and morning were the *x* day" indicates literal, 24-hour days.

[4] The word "kind" (מִין) approximates "species." God created life, each "kind" fully formed. All life reproduces according to its kind. No exceptions exist. This is the bedrock of all biology. No new "kinds" have come into existence since creation. Science observes extinctions of kinds but none coming into existence. "Kinds" evolve but God has programmed boundaries in the genetic code which cannot be crossed. Science is a discipline which acquires knowledge through observation, experimentation, replication, and reason. Science has never observed macro-evolution. No *scientific evidence* exists for evolution.

[5] Mankind was God's crowning creation. God breathed into Adam the "breath of life," literally, "breath of lives," נִשְׁמַת חַיִּים. God breathed (Spirit) life and man became a "living soul" לְנֶפֶשׁ חַיָּה. (Genesis. 2.7).

[6] Man and woman were "Adam" (Genesis 5.1-2).

7. God established Saturday as the Sabbath, a day of rest (Genesis 2.1-3).

Free Will

God placed man in a garden with pleasant, light, and joyful responsibilities. Adam was to dress and keep the garden (Genesis 2.15)[7] and only one prohibition existed. God told Adam he could eat from any tree except the Tree of the Knowledge of Good and Evil (Genesis 2.9, 16-17). If he partook of it, he would die.[8] God gave man free will. He could obey God or disobey Him.

God created man to participate in resolving the problem of evil and the angelic conflict.[9] Love requires free will. God created mankind in His own image and wished His creation to choose Him, to love Him, for who He is. Free will is essential to God's war against evil and in mankind's salvation.

Temptation, Sin, and Death

God gave Adam and Eve dominion, not only over the Garden of Eden, but over the entire earth (Genesis 1.28-31).[10] How long they lived before their temptation and disobedience is unknown. The

---

[7] A better rendering of "dress and keep it" (KJV) לְעָבְדָהּ וּלְשָׁמְרָהּ is "cultivate and guard it." Implicit in the duty was potential danger.

[8] Genesis 2.17 reads, מוֹת תָּמוּת, "dying you will die," a Qal infinitive absolute and Qal imperfect. The moment Adam ate the forbidden fruit, his spirit died, his soul acquired a sin nature, and the process of physical death began. Adam lived to be 930 years old (Genesis 5.5) and died. Human death is scientific proof the Bible is true.

[9] Evil began with Satan's rebellion against God. The book of Job reveals how God is using man to help resolve evil and the heavenly conflict. Job typified mankind. Satan challenged God that Job trusted Him only because God had blessed him. Despite suffering seemingly irrational evil, Job remained faithful to God and proved Satan wrong (Job 1.8).

[10] Satan occupied Eden and had dominion over the earth before Adam and Eve (Ezekiel 28.11-19).

woman did not converse with a snake.[11] She conversed with a "shining one," Satan. No doubt he observed the couple and concluded an attack upon the woman offered a better chance for success than directly confronting Adam. Eve succumbed to Satan's subtlety and doubted God. Sensing weakness, Satan lied (Genesis 3.1-4) and told her to eat from the Tree of the Knowledge of Good and Evil[12] would not result in death but in becoming like gods, knowing good and evil, וִהְיִיתֶם֙ כֵּֽאלֹהִ֔ים יֹדְעֵ֖י ט֥וֹב וָרָֽע.[13] The "gods" to whom Satan referred were the beings who comprise God's council. This is THE LIE, Satan's great lie to mankind.[14] The woman, deceived, ate. Adam, undeceived, also ate (1 Timothy 2.14). Their disobedience resulted in death, disease, and human misery. The couple now knew good and evil, but not as they had imagined.

Upon eating, a dramatic change took place. Man's spirit died, the part of him which communicated with God. His soul was damaged, gaining a nature in rebellion to God. And physical death began. In

---

[11] The word "serpent" is נָחָשׁ. In Numbers 21.6-7, 9, the Jews were plagued with "fiery serpents" and Moses made a bronze "serpent" שָׂרָף (fiery, burning, shining) called נְחֹשֶׁת or נְחֻשְׁתָּן (Numbers 21.9; 2 Kings 18.4). These words have the root נחשׁ and have the sense "burning," "fiery," "shining." Another related word is נָחַשׁ "divination," "enchantment" (Leviticus 19.26). Eve spoke with a "shining enchanter."

[12] The Tree of the Knowledge of Good and Evil provided knowledge of good and evil apart from God. This knowledge came at great cost: loss of innocence, sin, and death.

[13] The word אֱלֹהִים is translated "God" or "gods" depending on the context. The text of Genesis 3.5 reads, "For God knows that in the day you eat thereof, then your eyes shall be opened, and you shall be as gods, knowing good and evil." The first אֱלֹהִים should be translated "God" and the second, "gods," for the divine beings who attend God. This indicated the couple knew something of their activities.

[14] The Beast of Revelation will again deceive mankind by "the lie," τῷ ψεύδει (2 Thessalonians 2.11). Jesus called Satan "the father of lies" (John 8.44).

the area of the soul, shame attended nakedness.[15] The couple reacted by trying to clothe themselves with fig leaves. Adam and Eve's fig leaf solution was archetypical of mankind's attempt to hide sin and shame. All such attempts fail. Man cannot solve the problem of sin and its penalty, death, through his own efforts.

God knew the couple's attempt was inadequate. Since He loved them, He provided "garments of skin" כָּתְנוֹת עוֹר (Genesis 3.21). This clothing required God to kill an animal (the first instance in which blood was shed in God's creation). By this act God began to reveal that blood was required to cover sin (Genesis 4.4-5, 8.20, 22.7-8; Exodus 10.25; Leviticus 17.11; Hebrews 9.22).

The Scriptures declare blood is the source of fleshly life. Moses wrote, "the life of the flesh is in the blood" (Leviticus 17.11, 14).[16] Animal sacrifices provided a temporary remedy and substitute for the penalty of sin (Romans 6.23) but could not remedy the problem.

The Curse, the Promise

Life had been pleasant and easy for Adam and Eve. Now, everything became difficult. Childbirth became stressful and painful. God cursed the ground and it produced thorns and weeds. Working the soil and harvesting became arduous (Genesis 3.16-19). Despite this unhappiness, God gave the couple hope. Addressing Satan, He said:

---

[15] The essential nature of Adam and Eve's nakedness may have been the loss of attendant glory. The Scriptures provide several examples of it: Moses' face shown while with the Lord (Exodus 34.29-30); the Lord shined in the transfiguration (Matthew 17.2); Stephen's face was shining before the Sanhedrin (Acts 6.15). Believers regain this glory with resurrection bodies (2 Corinthians 3.18).

[16] The diagnostic value of blood has been discovered through advances in the life sciences.

> And I will put enmity between you and the woman, and between your seed and her seed; he shall bruise you on the head, and you shall bruise him on the heel (Genesis 3.15).[17]

God cursed Satan (Genesis 3.14) and declared war between mankind and Satan. The cryptic "bruising of the serpent's head" and "bruising of the man's heel" revealed man would defeat Satan but that Satan would wound man. While neither the couple nor Satan understood the full implications of God's decree, they knew it was a declaration of war between humanity and Satan. Satan desires two things concerning mankind: his worship or his death.[18] After God established the Abrahamic Covenant, the Jewish people became the center of gravity in Satan's war against mankind.

Major Strategic Satanic Attacks	Passage
Adam and Eve	Genesis 3.1-7
Fallen Angels (genetic warfare)	Genesis 6.1-4
Haman's plan of genocide of the Jews	Esther 3.7-11
Herod's murder of the children	Matthew 2.12-18
Christ's crucifixion[19]	Matthew 27.22-23

The Necessity of Blood

The record of the birth of the first human, Cain, is found in Genesis 4. Upon his birth, Eve stated, "I have gotten a man from the Lord" (Genesis 4.1). Eve (and Adam) probably thought this child was the promised one who could undo the curse. They had no idea how long

---

[17] Theologians call this announcement the protevangelium, "first gospel."

[18] This becomes a reality during the Tribulation (Revelation 13.7-8).

[19] Satan thought Christ's crucifixion would be His defeat. He had no idea Christ's death would solve the problem of sin and death or that He would rise from the dead. God keeps critical information hidden from him just as He does from men (Luke 18.31-34). The heavenly host, including Satan, is ignorant of much of the information God has revealed to us in the Bible.

sin and death would reign. Eve's second son was Abel. Abel was a shepherd and Cain was a farmer (Genesis 4.3).

Cain brought an offering of his produce from the ground to God (Genesis 4.3). Undoubtedly it was beautiful. But it was not what God required. Cain's offering, like Adam and Eve's fig leaves, was bloodless. Abel brought an offering from his flocks, i.e., an animal sacrifice. God accepted Abel's offering but rejected Cain's (Genesis 4.4-5). Paul wrote:

> By faith Abel offered unto God a more excellent sacrifice than Cain, by which he obtained witness that he was righteous, God testifying of his gifts: and by it he being dead yet speaks (Hebrew 11.4).

John wrote regarding Cain:

> [11] For this is the message that you heard from the beginning, that we should love one another. [12] Not as Cain, who was of that wicked one, and slew his brother. And wherefore slew he him? Because his own works were evil, and his brother's righteous (1 John 3.11-12).

Cain was a man of Satan. He refused to believe God's revelation of the necessity of a blood sacrifice. His rebellious nature became manifest when he killed his brother, Abel. John stated his works were evil, while Abel's were righteous. The essential nature of evil is unbelief. Abel believed God. As a result, he obeyed what God had revealed. Cain refused to believe God. He rationalized God would accept his sacrifice because he had worked hard to produce it. Cain typified those who think God will accept them on the basis of their works. Abel typified those who believe God.

The essential nature of goodness is *faith*—believing God. Good is doing what God has revealed. Evil is the refusal to believe God. John recorded the Lord's words on this subject in his Gospel:

> [28] Marvel not at this: for the hour is coming, in the which all that are in the graves shall hear his voice, [29] And shall

> come forth; they that have done good, unto the resurrection of life; and they that have done evil, unto the resurrection of damnation (John 5.28-29).

Those who obtain eternal life have done good—they have believed God. Those who will experience eternal doom have done evil—they have disbelieved God. The Scriptures state it is *impossible* to please God apart from faith (Hebrews 11.6).

The Sons of God

Genesis 6 records Satan's attempt after the Fall to corrupt the human bloodline. This plan involved fallen angels intermarrying with human women. The text reads:

> [1] And it came to pass, when men began to multiply on the
> face of the earth, and daughters were born unto them, [2] That
> the sons of God saw the daughters of men that they were
> fair; and they took them wives of all which they chose.
> [3] And the LORD said, My spirit shall not always strive with
> man, for that he also is flesh: yet his days shall be a hundred
> and twenty years. [4] There were giants in the earth in those
> days; and also after that, when the sons of God came in
> unto the daughters of men, and they bore children to them,
> the same became mighty men which were of old, men of
> renown (Genesis 6.1-4).

Several questions attend this passage, e.g., Who were the "sons of God?" Were they angels or righteous men? What did God mean about His spirit striving with man? What were the 120 years? Who were the "mighty men?"

Some have argued the "sons of God" were righteous men from the offspring of Seth. The foundation of this argument is based primarily upon Jesus' statement that angels do not reproduce (Matthew 22.23-33; Luke 20.34-39; Mark 12.18-27). Significant problems attend this interpretation.

The first problem is a lack of parallelism. In Genesis 6.1, the subject is "men" and born to them are "daughters." In Genesis 6.2, instead of "men" marrying "daughters," "sons of God" marry "daughters." Why the phrase, "sons of God," if men were meant? Nowhere in the Old Testament are men called "sons of God."[20] If righteous men were meant, we would expect the text to read "sons of men," "righteous men" or "sons of Seth" to parallel "daughters of men." This imbalance should give the interpreter pause.

Genesis 6.1-2		
Verse 1	Men	Daughters
Verse 2	Sons of God	Daughters of men

The linguistic evidence of the Old Testament only supports the view the "sons of God" (בְנֵי־הָאֱלֹהִים) were heavenly beings (Genesis 6.1-4; cf. Job 1.6, 2.1, 38.7). A similar phrase, בְּנֵי אֵלִים, "sons of the mighty," is also used of divine beings (Psalm 29.1, 89.6).

Early Hebrew commentators and apocryphal writings indicated these "sons of God" were fallen angels.[21] The pseudepigraphical *Book of Enoch* related how angels left heaven, took the form of men, chose wives, and produced giants as offspring. Enoch prophesied the destruction of man by a great flood and announced everlasting doom of these "sons of God."

Jesus stated angels do not marry or reproduce, not that they were *incapable* of sexual activity. A careful reading of the passage reveals He qualified his statement by stating the angels *in heaven* did not engage in sexual activity. This is precisely the point. The

---

[20] The phrase "sons of God" is not used of men in the Old Testament. Nebuchadnezzar saw one like the "Son of God" (לְבַר־אֱלָהִין) in the fiery furnace (Daniel 3.25). This was God the Son in His pre-incarnate form.

[21] The view the "sons of God" were fallen angels was held almost unanimously by ancient writers prior to Augustine of Hippo (354-430 A.D.).

angels, "sons of God," of Genesis 6, *left* heaven and came to earth. Jude made this point in his letter: "the angels which kept not their first estate, but left their own habitation" (Jude 6). They came to earth to have sexual relations with women.

With regard to God's spirit striving and 120 years (Genesis 6.3), the context of Genesis 6 involves God's judgment of evil on the earth with the Flood. The word "spirit" is the normal Hebrew word for "spirit," רוּחַ, introduced in Genesis 1.2. The Hebrew דִּין means "strive," "contend," "judge." Some have taught the 120 years referred to a limit of man's lifespan. A better view is this number was a prophetic timeframe for judgment. God gave the world 120 years to repent. Noah was 500 when he began to have his sons, Shem, Ham, and Japheth (Genesis 5.32) and 600 when he entered the ark (Genesis 7.11). It is reasonable the 120 years corresponded with this timeframe.

The text of Genesis 6.9 states, "Noah was a just man and perfect in his generations." The word "just" is צַדִּיק, the normal word for "righteous," but the word "perfect" is more intriguing. It is תָּמִים and means "sound," "healthy," "unblemished." The Scripture is revealing that Noah's bloodline was uncorrupted by the angelic genome.

Lastly is the matter of the "giants" or "mighty men." The Septuagint (LXX)[22] translated the Hebrew הַנְּפִלִים, "the Nephilim,"[23] as γίγαντες "giants."[24] The "Nephilim" were the

---

[22] The Septuagint (LXX) was a translation of the Hebrew Bible into Greek by Jewish scholars between the 3rd and 2nd century B.C. It was designated LXX because 70 scholars attended the work.

[23] The etymology of "Nephilim" is uncertain.

[24] Harkins, Angela Kim. 2014. *The Watchers in Jewish and Christian Traditions*. Minneapolis: Fortress Press, p. 33. As early as the 8th c. B.C., γίγαντες appears in Greek mythology as the monstrous, belligerent progeny of Gaia, (fertilized by the blood of Uranus' castration) who strove to supplant the Olympian gods until the latter were aided by Heracles, who defeated and destroyed the upstarts (e.g., Hesiod, *Theogony*, 183-187, 954; cf. frag. 43a 65; Homer, *Od.* 7.59-61, 205.

"giants" and "mighty men of old," גִּבּוֹר. The Hebrew scholars understood these offspring were not normal human beings. Apparently, all were men since the Scriptures mention no women giants. And when angelic beings appear in human form in the Bible, they always appear as men. A couple possibilities exist for this fact: the angelic genome may only be capable of producing males or these "sons of God" may have manipulated the genetic code to produce only males.[25]

Who knows the level of civilization these beings created? It may have surpassed our present technology. Whatever their achievements, the world became increasingly evil. The text reads,

> Then the LORD saw that the wickedness of man was great on the earth and that every intent of the thoughts of his heart was only evil continually (Genesis 6.5).

Genesis 6.4 reveals the Flood destroyed all human life except Noah and his immediate family. This included the offspring of the fallen angels. But Genesis 6.4 states giants again came into existence after the Flood. More incursions occurred with angels having sexual relations with women.[26] They appeared in Abraham's day (2000 B.C.) and did not disappear until David's time (1000 B.C.). The giants the Jews encountered after they escaped Egypt and came into the land of Canaan were the product of these unions.[27]

These giants terrified the Jews. After the Jews had escaped Egypt and enter the land of Canaan, the spies sent to examine the land returned from their reconnaissance and stated, "we are like grasshoppers to them" (Numbers 13.33). God had promised He

---

[25] The ancient mythologies in which gods came to earth, had children with women, and produced demigods, e.g., Herakles (Hercules) are consistent with the Biblical record.

[26] The physical bodies of the Nephilim died in the Flood but their spirits lived and became demons according to the *Book of Enoch*. This explains their desire to inhabit physical bodies (Matthew 8.28-31).

[27] The continued unions explain God's harsh commands to slaughter the Canaanites and other related peoples (Deuteronomy 7.1-2; 20.16-18).

would drive them out with hornets but they refused to believe Him and could not enter the land.[28] As a consequence, they wandered in the desert for forty years and died.[29]

Despite the people's fear, Moses waged war against these giants and defeated King Og of Bashan (Deuteronomy 3.1-11). Joshua and Caleb continued this warfare (Joshua 11.21-22, 15.14; Judges 1.20). David became famous for killing the giant Goliath and as king, eliminated all the giants (2 Samuel 21.18-22; 1 Chronicles 20.4-8).[30]

This genetic corruption of the human race was part of Satan's warfare to destroy humanity. He had succeeded in orchestrating mankind to rebel against God in Eden. His next great strategic assault was to corrupt the human genome so God's promised deliverer could not be born through a fully human, uncorrupted bloodline. Satan feared God's declaration of war (Genesis 3.15) and determined to defeat man by any means necessary.

The chart shows the hybrid beings the Jews encountered in the promised land. The Rephaim, Zuzim, Emim, and Anakim, were "cousins" of the original Nephilim. Worship of their "fathers," fallen angels, began at Babel, the source of false religion.[31]

---

[28] What a gracious promise refused (Exodus 23.27-30)!

[29] This sad event occurred at Kadesh-Barnea (Numbers 13.26-33). It was one of the Jews' greatest failures of faith. Paul warned the Jews of his day not to follow their example (Hebrews 3.7-19).

[30] David may have been the greatest warrior-king who ever lived. Goliath was over nine feet tall and carried heavy armament (1 Samuel 17.4-7). David's fearless spirit continued throughout his reign.

[31] Worship of these "sons of God" may have begun before the Flood but became established at Babel, the source of all false religion. This explains why the first two commandments of the Decalogue were that the Jews were to have no other gods before God or make representations of them.

Name	Passages	Meaning
Nephilim נָפִיל	Genesis 6.4; Numbers 13.33	Fallen ones, Giants
Rephaim רְפָאִים	Genesis 14.5, 15.20; Deuteronomy 2.11, 20, 3.11, 13, Joshua 12.4, 13.12, 15.8, 17.15, 18.16; 2 Samuel 5.18, 22, 23.13; 1 Chronicles 11.15, 14.9; Isaiah 17.5	Titans, Children of Rapha
Zuzim זוּזִים	Genesis 14.5	Terrible ones
Emim אֵימִים	Genesis 14.5; Deuteronomy 2.10-11	Terrors
Anakim עֲנָקִים	Numbers 13.33; Deuteronomy 1.28, 2.10-11, 21, 9.2; Joshua 11.21-22, 14.12, 15	Crushing tyrants, Long-necked

The offspring of the "sons of God" died in the Flood and God imprisoned the angels who had left heaven to engage in genetic warfare. Jude and Peter wrote of their judgment. Jude wrote:

> [6] And angels who did not keep their own domain, but abandoned their proper abode, He has kept in eternal bonds under darkness for the judgment of the great day, [7] just as Sodom and Gomorrah and the cities around them, since they in the same way as these indulged in gross immorality and went after strange flesh, are exhibited as an example in undergoing the punishment of eternal fire (Jude 6-7).

Whom could Jude mean by "who did not keep their own domain, but abandoned their proper abode" but rebellious angelic beings? Who "indulged in gross immorality," and went after "strange flesh" (σαρκὸς ἑτέρας) except the fallen angels of Genesis 6? Jude's reference to "strange flesh" was "women." His reference to "strange flesh" with regard to Sodom and Gomorrah was "men," homosexual activity. The meaning of "strange flesh" was unnatural intercourse.

Peter also wrote on this subject:

> [4] For if God did not spare angels when they sinned, but cast them into hell and committed them to pits of darkness, reserved for judgment [5] and did not spare the ancient world, but preserved Noah, a preacher of righteousness, with seven others, when He brought a flood upon the world of the ungodly (2 Peter 2.4-5).

Peter's words agree with Jude's about the imprisonment of these angels.[32] The other fallen angels under Satan's authority are with Satan in heaven.[33] Their final destination is the Lake of Fire.

The Flood

The Flood was a calamitous judgment. It destroyed all human civilization and life with the exception of Noah and his wife, his three sons, and their wives—eight people.[34] God brought about the Flood because of mankind's evil and because the human genome had become corrupted by fallen angels.

Four chapters, Genesis 6-9, deal with the Flood. The change in earth's geography and environment cannot be overestimated. The Scriptures reveal that before the Flood the earth had not experienced rain and that it was watered with a mist or vapor (Genesis 2.5-6). After the Flood, the earth became watered through rain and the water cycle. The topography also experienced tremendous changes. Genesis 2.10-14 states a river flowed out of Eden which branched into four major tributaries: the Pison, Gihon, Hiddekel, and Euphrates rivers. After the flood, only two of the rivers remained, the Hiddekel (Tigris) and the Euphrates. And, of

---

[32] Peter wrote these angels were imprisoned in the chthonic realm of Tartarus, the abode of the wicked dead (2 Peter 2.4).

[33] Satan and his rebellious angels access heaven and earth (Job 1.6-7, 2.1-2). They are expelled from heaven at the mid-point of the Tribulation (Revelation 12.7-9).

[34] The Flood covered the entire earth and destroyed all human and land-based animals except those in the ark. An excellent analysis is Richard M. Davidson's "Biblical Evidence for the Universality of the Genesis Flood." *Origins* 22. no. 2, (October 1995) pp. 58-73. See http://grisda.org/origins/22058.pdf.

course, Eden disappeared. Dramatic changes also occurred in human longevity.

Antediluvian Longevity		Postdiluvian Longevity	
Adam	930	Shem	600
Seth	912	Arpachshad	438
Enosh	905	Shelah	433
Kenan	910	Eber	464
Mahalalel	895	Peleg	239
Jared	962	Reu	239
Enoch*	365	Serug	230
Methuselah	969	Nahor	148
Lamech	777	Terah	205
Noah	950	Abraham	175
*Enoch did not die: "And Enoch walked with God: and he was not; for God took him" (Genesis 5.24).		Isaac	180
		Jacob	147
		Joseph	110

Before the Flood, humans lived about 900 years. After the Flood, (2300 B.C.), until the time of Abraham, (2000 B.C.), longevity dropped from about 600 years to about 200 years. It continued to drop until it settled in a range of 70-100 years.

Before the Flood, men and animals had a vegetarian diet (Genesis 1.29-30, 2.16). After the Flood, in addition to fruits and vegetables, God sanctioned eating meat (Genesis 9.3-4). The one prohibition was against eating blood.[35] God also established capital punishment after the Flood. He declared:

> [5] And surely your blood of your lives will I require; at the hand of every beast will I require it, and at the hand of man; at the hand of every man's brother will I require the life of man. [6] Whoso sheds man's blood, by man shall his blood be shed: for in the image of God made he man (Genesis 9.4).

---

[35] God forbade eating blood for the life of flesh is in the blood (Leviticus 17.11, 14; Deuteronomy 12.23). It is no surprise that Satan worshippers offer human sacrifices and drink blood.

God, not man, established capital punishment. It is a divine institution to restrain evil. Capital punishment recognizes mankind is God's special creation, created in the image of God as God's representative on earth. God also established the fear of man among the animal creation (Genesis 9.2) which apparently did not exist before the Flood. God instituted it to protect both animals and man from one another.[36]

After the Flood, God established a covenant (בְּרִית)[37] with Noah, all of humanity, and all animals in which He promised never again to destroy the world by water (Genesis 9.8-11). As a sign of this promise, God gave the rainbow (Genesis 9.12-17).

Civilization Rebooted

Genesis 10 concerns the table of nations, a record of the sons of Noah, Shem, Ham, and Japheth, their genealogies, and their geographical distributions after the Flood. All races of people descend from these three sons of Noah: Shem, Ham, and Japheth and 70 names are recorded who fathered the primary nations.[38] Any study of ancient civilizations begins with Genesis 10-11 (Genesis 10.32).

A fascinating passage regarding the restart of humanity is Deuteronomy 32.7-9. The text reads:

> 7 Remember the days of old, consider the years of all generations. Ask your father, and he will inform you, your elders, and they will tell you. 8 When the Most High gave the nations their inheritance, when He separated the sons of man, He set the boundaries of the peoples according to

---

36 God removes this fear in the kingdom (Isaiah 11.6-8).

37 The first use of בְּרִית (covenant) is found in Genesis 6.18. God made an agreement with Noah, his immediate family, and the animals that would be upon the ark to save them from the impending Flood.

38 Ross, Allen P. "Studies in the Book of Genesis. Part 2: The Table of Nations in Genesis 10—Its Structure." *Bibliotheca Sacra* 137:548 (October 1980) p. 342.

> the number of the sons of Israel. [9] For the Lord's portion is His people; Jacob is the allotment of His inheritance.

This reading is from the Masoretic Text. According to the last part of verse 8, God set the boundaries of the nations according to the number of the "sons of Israel" (בְּנֵי יִשְׂרָאֵל).[39] The Septuagent (LXX) reads differently. The majority of witnesses read, "according to the number of the angels of God" (ἀγγέλων θεοῦ) and some witnesses read "sons of God" (υἱῶν θεοῦ). The better reading favors ἀγγέλων θεοῦ or υἱῶν θεοῦ rather than "sons of Israel.[40]

Deuteronomy 4.19-20 is another revealing passage:

> [19] And *beware* not to lift up your eyes to heaven and see the sun and the moon and the stars, all the host of heaven, and be drawn away and worship them and serve them, those which the LORD your God has allotted to all the peoples under the whole heaven. [20] But the LORD has taken you and brought you out of the iron furnace, from Egypt, to be a people for His own possession, as today.

Moses warned the Jews not to worship and serve the heavenly host. Unlike the nations, Israel had a special position to God. In the Deuteronomy 32 passage, Moses reminded Israel of this position. When God divided the nations, He set their boundaries according to the number of the "sons of God." In the Table of Nations of Genesis 10, 70 heads of peoples compose the genealogy. God

---

[39] The Masoretic Text ((MT, 𝔐) was the Old Testament text produced by the Masoretes, Jewish scholars, who copied, edited, added vowel points and accents, etc. to the text between the 7th and 10th centuries A.D. It is the basis of translations of the Old Testament in Protestant Bibles.

[40] Heiser, Michael. "Deuteronomy 32:8 and the Sons of God." *Bibliotheca Sacra* 158:629 (January-March 2001): pp. 52-74. Heiser has made a compelling argument for this reading and has also has revealed numerous insights about the divine council. See also Sumner, Paul Byron. 1991. *Visions of the Divine Council in the Hebrew Bible*. Pepperdine University, https://goo.gl/8r1J4Y.

turned control of the nations over to these 70 divine beings, "sons of God," His divine council.[41] Verse 9 of Deuteronomy 32 reads,

> For the Lord's portion is His people; Jacob is the allotment of His inheritance.

The nations belonged to the "sons of God." Israel belonged to God.

Paul wrote the Ephesians that Gentiles were "separated from Christ, excluded from the commonwealth of Israel, and strangers to the covenants of promise, having no hope and without God in the world" (Ephesians 2.12). In Romans 1, Paul stated God "gave them (Gentiles) up." God's "giving up" was precipitated by mankind's desire to worship created beings rather than God (Romans 1.20-23).[42] Paul repeated this language three times (Romans 1.24, 26, 28). The expression "gave up" is παραδίδωμι (3rd person aorist active indicative) and means "delivered up" or "gave over." Paul's first instance (verse 24) governs the next two usages.

> 24 Therefore God gave them over in the lusts of their hearts to impurity, so that their bodies would be dishonored among them. 25 For they exchanged the truth of God for a lie, and worshiped and served the creature rather than the Creator, who is blessed forever. Amen (Romans 1.24-25).

Because mankind "exchanged" (μεταλλάσσω) truth for a lie, the worship of created beings instead of the Creator, God gave them over (παραδίδωμι) to sexual impurity and perversion (homosexuality, Romans 1.26-27). Because Gentile nations

---

[41] The discovery of Ugaritic has been invaluable in understanding Hebrew and ancient near east culture and theology. Ugaritic texts reveal the Canaanite peoples had a pantheon of 70 gods ruled by their supreme god, El and his son Baal.

[42] Nature abhors a vacuum and so does supernature. Rejection of the true God results in worship of pretender gods. God gives man a choice. Each person accepts or rejects God from his own free will.

rejected the true God, God subjected them to the rule of the "sons of God."

Because men desired to remove God from their thinking, He permitted this and gave them up (παραδίδωμι) to a "reprobate mind" (Romans 1.28)—a mind occupied with doing evil (Romans 1.28-32). Man always initiates rejection of God and God will accommodate man's free will.

God has revealed that heavenly beings, fallen and unfallen, operate in the affairs of nations and empires. Daniel, in interpreting Nebuchadnezzar's dream, prophesied the rise of the world powers of Babylon, Medo-Persia, Greece, Rome, and the final empire controlled by the Beast (Daniel 2, 9). In the tenth chapter of Daniel, late in his life, in the third year of the reign of Cyrus, Daniel wrote of a vision of the future. The vision so disturbed the great prophet that he began to fast and pray (Daniel 10.1-2). The text continues:

> [12] Then said he unto me, Fear not, Daniel: for from the first day that you did set your heart to understand, and to chasten yourself before thy God, your words were heard, and I am come for your words. [13] But the prince of the kingdom of Persia withstood me one and twenty days: but, lo, Michael, one of the chief princes, came to help me; and I remained there with the kings of Persia (Daniel 10.12-13).

Three weeks after Daniel began his fast, an angelic being came to him and told him he had heard his prayer when he first prayed but was unable to respond because of opposition from the prince of Persia, a fallen angel with responsibilities over Persia. With Michael the archangel's help, he was able to attend Daniel.[43]

The chapter concludes (Daniel 10.20) with the angel telling Daniel he would leave to continue to fight against the prince of Persia and

---

[43] Michael is an archangel (Jude 1.9) and has a special, protective role towards Israel (Daniel 10.13, 21, 12.1; Revelation 12.7). Gabriel is another angel with a special relationship to Israel (Daniel 8.16, 9.21; Luke 1.19, 26).

revealed the prince of Greece would follow the prince of Persia.[44] This revelation agreed with Daniel's interpretation of Nebuchadnezzar's dream and revealed the reality of a spiritual warfare in which divine beings participate in the spheres of heaven and earth. This truth was confirmed early in Jesus' earthly ministry when He went to the desert and was tested by Satan. The account of His last temptation reads:

> [8] Again, the devil took him up into an exceeding high mountain, and showed him all the kingdoms of the world, and the glory of them; [9] And said unto him, All these things will I give you, if you will fall down and worship me. [10] Then said Jesus unto him, Go, Satan: for it is written, You shall worship the Lord your God, and him only shall you serve (Matthew 4.8-10).

Satan's claim of control over the kingdoms of the world was no idle boast. The Lord did not dispute it for He knew it was true. In the Messianic kingdom, the nations will become Christ's (Psalm 2.6, 8). Until then, they are under the operational control of Satan.[45]

In addition, Paul wrote Satan is the "god of this world" (2 Corinthians 4.4) and we are engaged in a spiritual warfare with Satanic powers:

> [10] Finally, my brethren, be strong in the Lord, and in the power of his might. [11] Put on the whole armor of God, that you may be able to stand against the wiles of the devil. [12] For we wrestle not against flesh and blood, but against principalities, against powers, against the rulers of the darkness of this world, against spiritual wickedness in high places. [13] Wherefore take unto you the whole armor of God,

---

[44] The conquests of Alexander the Great established Greece as the next great world empire after Persia. God revealed this fact to Daniel in Nebuchadnezzar's great dream (Daniel 2.31-45).

[45] Jesus stated Satan was the "ruler of this world" (ὁ ἄρχων τοῦ κόσμου τούτου, John 12.31, 14.30, 16.11). Paul wrote he was the "ruler of the power of the air, the spirit who is working among the children of disobedience" (Ephesians 2.2).

> that you may be able to withstand in the evil day, and having done all, to stand (Ephesians 6.10-13).

Paul identified "the Devil" (τοῦ διαβόλου) as the principal agent of spiritual evil and rule of the earth (verse 11) and enumerated several ranks of spiritual powers: principalities, powers, world-rulers (κοσμοκράτωρ) of darkness (verse 12). Notice these powers operate in heaven. The word ἐπουράνιος, translated above as "high places," means "heavenly places" and is the same word Paul used in Ephesians 1.3, 20, 2.6, 3.10 for the believer's position in Christ, who is seated at the right hand of God (Psalm 110.1). Until the Lord defeats Satan at the end of the age in the Battle of Armageddon, Satan and the spiritual powers allied with him will retain power over the world.

The Tower of Babel

Genesis 11 is the famous story of the Tower of Babel,[46] which was located on the plain of Shinar.[47] The narrative reveals how the human race tried to establish a one-world religious government:[48]

---

[46] This was a ziggurat which the ancient civilizations—Sumerians, Babylonians, Elamites, Akkadians, and Assyrians built. It was a massive structure and the central building of a temple complex. Ziggurats were the earthly representations or correspondences of the "stairway to heaven" Jacob saw (Genesis 28.12).

[47] Shinar was located in Babylonia, in Mesopotamia (אֲרַם נַהֲרַיִם, literally, "Aram of the rivers" or Μεσοποταμία, "between rivers"), i.e., between the Tigris and Euphrates rivers. Genesis 11.19 reads, "Therefore its name was called Babel, because there the Lord confused the language of the whole earth; and from there the Lord scattered them abroad over the face of the whole earth." The text is a pun. Babel, בָּבֶל, referred to the land of Babylonia, but the word "balal," בָּלַל means "confuse."

[48] World government leads to totalitarianism. God's confusion of language led to creation of nation states to protect mankind from absolute statist power. In the Day of the Lord, the Tribulation, (Matthew 24.21, 29), earth will experience world government and religion.

> They said, Come, let us build for ourselves a city, and a tower whose top *will reach* into heaven, and let us make for ourselves a name, otherwise we will be scattered abroad over the face of the whole earth (Genesis 11.4).

These people were not ignorant about heaven and earth thinking they could literally build a tower that would reach to heaven. They were a highly educated and sophisticated civilization and knew about heaven and the divine beings who operated there. They wished to communicate with these beings as mankind had before the Flood. Their desire manifested itself in an attempt to build a tower to serve as a bridge or a platform between heaven and earth.

The revelation of a stairway between heaven and earth is found in several passages of Scripture. Jacob saw it, Moses and the 70 elders of Israel witnessed it, and Jesus spoke about it in His conversation with Nathaniel.

Jacob saw the heavenly stairway at Bethel:

> [10] Then Jacob departed from Beersheba and went
> toward Haran. [11] He came to a certain place and spent the
> night there, because the sun had set; and he took one of the
> stones of the place and put it under his head, and lay down
> in that place. [12] He had a dream, and behold, a ladder was
> set on the earth with its top reaching to heaven; and
> behold, the angels of God were ascending and descending
> on it (Genesis 28.10-12).

Moses wrote about this celestial stairway or ramp:

> [9] Then went up Moses, and Aaron, Nadab, and Abihu, and
> seventy of the elders of Israel: [10] And they saw the God of
> Israel: and there was under his feet as it were a paved work
> of a sapphire stone, and as it were the body of heaven in his
> clearness (Exodus 24.9-10).

Jesus spoke of it in his response to Nathaniel's statement that Jesus was the Son of God, the King of Israel:

> And he said unto him, Verily, verily, I say unto you, Hereafter you shall see heaven open, and the angels of God ascending and descending upon the Son of man (John 1.51).

God judged man's attempt to establish world government by confusing language. Prior to this, only one language existed. The reason the people gave for establishing world governance was, "otherwise, we will be scattered abroad over the face of the whole earth" (Genesis 11.4). This view conflicted with God's command:

> And God blessed Noah and his sons and said to them, Be fruitful and multiply, and fill the earth (Genesis 9.1).

God instructed Noah to reproduce and fill the earth after the Flood. This was a repetition of the original order God had given Adam and Eve (Genesis 1.29). The people rejected God's command and God responded in the following manner:

> [5] And the LORD came down to see the city and the tower,
> which the children of men built. [6] And the LORD said,
> Behold, the people is one, and they have all one language;
> and this they begin to do: and now nothing will be
> restrained from them, which they have imagined to do. [7] Go
> to, let us go down, and there confound their language, that
> they may not understand one another's speech. [8] So
> the LORD scattered them abroad from thence upon the face
> of all the earth: and they left off to build the city.
> [9] Therefore is the name of it called Babel; because
> the LORD did there confound the language of all the earth:
> and from thence did the LORD scatter them abroad upon the
> face of all the earth (Genesis 11.5-9).

God did not want what had occurred before the Flood to occur again. He confused language to force men to divide and scatter throughout the earth. Genesis 10 is the record of how the sons and daughters of Shem, Japheth, and Ham settled throughout the earth after the Tower of Babel.

While nations have waged terrible wars against one another, nation-states protect mankind's freedom. National alliances balance political and military power against aggression and serve to prevent a nation or empire from becoming all-powerful. World government is evil. It is in direct defiance of God's command and it removes God's instituted protection of mankind. God has revealed that at the end of the age the Beast will establish global governance and exercise absolute power. The result will be the loss of all individual freedom and an unprecedented slaughter of the world's population.

Summary of God's Program With Mankind

In this program, recorded in Genesis 1-11, God dealt with all humanity. We learn of God's creation of the heavens and earth, God's framing the world for life, and his creation of all living creatures. God created mankind, Adam, in His image, as His representative on earth. These chapters also reveal how sin and death entered the world and the presence of great evil, led by Satan.

After mankind's disobedience, God declared war between humanity and Satan and prophesied mankind's victory over the Tempter. The emphasis throughout these chapters is upon this spiritual warfare between mankind and Satan. To preserve the human race, God brought about the Flood, and after it, divided mankind into nation-states.

The account in Genesis 1-11, mankind's first 2,000 years of history, is not promising. Mankind repeatedly failed and his livelihood was hampered and corrupted by the powers of darkness as well as his own fallen condition. Given this largely unhappy state, God determined to make a change in His program. That is the next chapter.

Chapter 2

Israel: Program Two

And I will bless them that bless you, and curse him that curses you: and in you shall all families of the earth be blessed (Genesis 12.3).

The British journalist, William Ewer, wrote the epigram: "How odd / Of God / To choose / The Jews." The Jewish writer, Leo Rosten, waggishly rejoined: "Not odd / Of God / Goyim / Annoy 'im." From a Biblical perspective, Rosten's riposte succinctly summed the first 2,000 years of human history.

The age in which God dealt with the entire human race ended in failure. In 2000 B.C., God initiated a new program. No longer would He deal directly with all mankind. Instead, He would mediate His communication through a new, chosen people and establish covenants with them to bless the world.

This new program is known as Israel.[1] God established covenants with the new race who served as His representatives to reveal His will. Two main components constituted Jewish theology. The first was the promise of an earthly kingdom. The second was that God would judge the earth for its evil.

---

[1] The term, "Israel" is technical. It *always* refers to Jews, the offspring of Jacob. For all practical purposes, the terms "Jew," "Hebrew," and "Israel," are synonymous. Abraham is the father of the Jews (Isaiah 51.2; Matthew 3.9; Luke 1.73; John 8.56) and God made all covenants from this point forward exclusively with Israel (Romans 9.4; Ephesians 2.11-13). Gentiles, גּוֹיִם, or the Church are *never* called Israel or included in Israel.

The Covenants: Vehicles of God's Promises

God had established the Noahic Covenant with the entire human race and promised never again to destroy the world by water (Genesis 9.8-17). The covenant God established with Abram was different from the Noahic covenant not only in content but in application. God established the Abrahamic covenant, not with the entire human race, but with one man through whom He would create a new race of people. The Abrahamic Covenant laid the foundation for the promises He would give this new race of people. God would also give other covenants. They were the following:

1. Abrahamic Covenant (foundation)
2. Land Covenant
3. Mosaic Covenant
4. Sabbatic Covenant
5. Davidic Covenant
6. New Covenant

The Abrahamic Covenant

God called Abram (Abraham)[2] from Ur of the Chaldees (Genesis 11.28, 31, 15.7; Nehemiah 9.7) which is located near Nasiriyah, about 150 miles northwest of the Persian Gulf, in Iraq. According to Moses, Abraham's family were idolaters:

> Joshua said to all the people, Thus says the LORD, the God of Israel, From ancient times your fathers lived beyond the River, namely, Terah, the father of Abraham and the father of Nahor, and they served other gods (Joshua 24.2).

Despite his family's idolatry, Abram responded to God in faith. The text records the words God spoke to Abram:

---

[2] When Abram was 90, God changed his name to Abraham (Genesis 17.1-8). Abram, אַבְרָם, means "exalted father" and Abraham, אַבְרָהָם, means "father of a multitude."

> [1] Now the Lord said to Abram, Go forth from your country, and from your relatives and from your father's house, to the land which I will show you; [2] And I will make you a great nation, and I will bless you, and make your name great; and so you shall be a blessing; [3] And I will bless those who bless you, and the one who curses you I will curse. And in you all the families of the earth will be blessed (Genesis 12.1-3).[3]

This divine declaration is known as the Abrahamic Covenant. It was the foundation of God's new program to create a people through whom He would reveal Himself and bless the world. In these three verses, God told Abraham ten things: 1) leave your country, 2) leave your relatives, 3) go to a land God would show him, 4) God would make Abram a great nation (people), 5) God would bless him, 6) God would make his name great, 7) Abram would be a blessing to others, 8) God would bless those who blessed Abram, 9) God would curse the one who cursed Abram, 10) Through Abram, all peoples would be blessed.

God chose Abraham to head this new program. It was a massive theological change from all that had gone before. This new covenant created the program known as Israel. God's blessings to mankind would no longer go from God directly to man but would be mediated through Abraham and his descendants, a covenant line.

One key statement by God made in His covenant promise needs to be examined. Genesis 12.3 reads:

> And I will bless them who bless you, and curse him who curses you. And in you all the families of the earth will be blessed.

A cursory reading of this verse may not reveal anything odd, but it is. One would expect the verse to read, "And I will bless them who bless you / and curse them who curse you." But the text reads otherwise. It lacks parallelism and uses the singular pronoun "him"

---

[3] Stephen recounted this event in his address to the Sanhedrin (Acts 7.2-4).

in the second part, instead of the plural pronoun "them." Why? Who is "him?"

Genesis 12.3	
And I will bless **them** who bless you	and curse **him** who curses you
And in **you** all the families of the earth will be blessed	

Satan attacked the first couple to rebel against God. In Genesis 3.15, God declared enmity, hatred, between the human race and Satan. Satan then attacked the human race to corrupt man's genetic line and orchestrated false religion at Babel. When God called Abraham and established a covenant with him, Satan recognized God had changed His strategic program. The covenant revealed God would now work through a special, covenant people rather than through the entire human race. They thus became the center of gravity in God's plan and the focus of Satan's attacks.

The "him" of Genesis 12.3 is Satan. He is the source of all anti-Semitism.[4] The simplest benchmark to detect good from evil is one's attitude towards the Jews. Those who seek the Jew's ill are under the influence of Satan and God's curse.

By the Abrahamic Covenant, God created a division of the human race into Jew and Gentile.[5] To understand the Bible one must understand the following principle:

---

[4] This explains why Jews have suffered more than any other people and why most nations oppose Israel. The nations of the world belong to Satan and he orchestrates hatred against the Jews (2 Corinthians 4.4; Matthew 4.8-9; Luke 4.5-7; John 12.31, 14.30, 16.11). At the end of the age, with the advent of the Beast, in the last 3½ years of the Tribulation, Satan will indwell the Antichrist and demand mankind to worship him and his image (Revelation 13.4, 8, 15). His last act will be an attempt to destroy all Jews.

[5] The term, "gentile" means a "non-Jew." The word גּוֹי, "goy" and the plural גּוֹיִם "goyim" is translated in the Scriptures as "Gentiles,"

THE ABRAHAMIC COVENANT DECREED ALL DIVINE BLESSING WOULD BE MEDIATED THROUGH ISRAEL

Two Metaphors

God described Abraham's progeny with two illustrations. The first concerned Abraham's earthly descendants.

> [14] The LORD said to Abram, after Lot had separated from
> him, Now lift up your eyes and look from the place where
> you are, northward and southward and eastward and
> westward; [15] for all the land which you see, I will give it to
> you and to your descendants forever. [16] I will make your
> descendants as the dust of the earth, so that if anyone can
> number the dust of the earth, then your descendants can
> also be numbered (Genesis 13.14-16).

The second metaphor revealed Abraham's heavenly progeny:

> [4] Then behold, the word of the Lord came to him, saying,
> This man will not be your heir; but one who will come forth
> from your own body, he shall be your heir. [5] And He took
> him outside and said, Now look toward the heavens,
> and count the stars, if you are able to count them. And He
> said to him, So shall your descendants be. [6] Then he
> believed in the LORD; and He reckoned it to him as
> righteousness (Genesis 15.4-6).

In Genesis 22.17, sand and stars are brought together in one verse:

> Indeed, I will greatly bless you, and I will greatly multiply your seed as the stars of the heavens and as the sand which

---

"heathen," "nations." This two-fold division continued until Paul. To Paul, the risen Lord revealed a new creation, the Church, the body of Christ. God's division of mankind thus became three-fold: Jew, Gentile, and Church (1 Corinthians 10.32).

> is on the seashore; and your seed shall possess the gate of their enemies.

God later repeated this promise to Isaac (Genesis 26.3-5) and Jacob (Genesis 28.13-14).

What is the significance of sand and stars in God's promise? Throughout the Bible, God has kept heaven and earth separate. Genesis 1.1 does not read, "In the beginning, God created the universe." It reads, "In the beginning, God created the heavens and the earth." This is the way the Bible begins and this is the way it ends. The last book of the Bible, Revelation, reveals God will create a new universe but John echoed the language of Moses: "Then I saw a new heaven and a new earth; for the first heaven and the first earth passed away" (Revelation 21.1).

The progeny "sand/dust" is associated with the land promise God gave Abraham. It referred to the covenant line of Jacob who will experience the fulfillment of God's promises in the Messianic kingdom when the Lord rules the earth (Zechariah 14.9; Matthew 6.10).

The progeny "stars" are associated with faith (Genesis 15.6) and with Gentiles. Paul applied this to the Church in Romans 4 and Galatians 3.[6] The terms "sand" and "stars" signify two separate divine programs: Israel and the Church. They remain separate throughout eternity, even as heaven and earth remain separate.

What is the Covenant Line?

With God's call of Abraham, the question arises as to who constitutes the covenant line. Abraham's first child, Ishmael (Genesis 16.15), was born from Hagar, the slave woman, because Abraham's wife, Sarai[7] could not have children. Ishmael, "God

---

[6] Gentiles, the Church in particular, are "children of Abraham" by faith. This does *not* mean Gentiles or the Church are part of Israel.

[7] God changed Sarai's name to Sarah (Genesis 17.15). Sarai (שָׂרַי) means "my princess" and Sarah (שָׂרָה) means "princess." The subtle

hears” had twelve sons who fathered many of the Arab peoples (Genesis 17.20). Later, Abraham and Sarah had a son, Isaac (Genesis 21.3). His son, Jacob (Genesis 25.26), had twelve sons (Genesis 35.22) from whom came the twelve tribes of Israel,[8] the Jews.[9]

God revealed which lineage would fulfill His covenant. When Abraham was 99 years old, he and Sarah were still childless. Nevertheless, God told Abraham that Sarah would have a son, Isaac.[10] The text reads:

> 17 Then Abraham fell on his face and laughed, and said in
> his heart, Will a child be born to a man one hundred years
> old? And will Sarah, who is ninety years old, bear a child?
> 18 And Abraham said to God, Oh that Ishmael might live
> before You! 19 But God said, No, but Sarah your wife will

---

change meant Sarah became a princess of many families instead of one family. God changed Sarah’s greatest unhappiness—barrenness—to joyful plentitude. She became a mother, a princess, of millions.

[8] God named Jacob “Israel,” יִשְׂרָאֵל, after he wrestled with Him. “Israel” means “soldier or commander of God” (שָׂרָה and אֵל). God commended Jacob’s perseverance in wresting and made a prophetic pun. He told Jacob he wrestled like a prince, שָׂרָה. This word has the same root form as Sarai who become Sarah (שָׂרָה). Such language anticipated God’s declaration Israel would be a kingdom of priests (Exodus 19.5-6). Peter echoed these words in writing to Jews who had believed in Jesus that they were a “holy and royal priesthood” (1 Peter 2.5, 9).

[9] The term “Jew,” יְהוּדִי, first found in 2 Kings 16.6, originally meant a member of the tribe of Judah. After the Assyrian invasion of the northern kingdom (8th c. B.C.), members of the 10 tribes escaped and migrated to the southern kingdom and the term began to be associated with any member of the 12 tribes (Jeremiah 32.12, 34.9, 38.19, 40.11, 43.9; Esther 2.5, 3.4, 5.13; Daniel 3.8). Jesus was identified as “the King of the Jews” (Matthew 2.2, 27.29, 37), the King of all Israel, not just Judah.

[10] Isaac (יִצְחָק) means “laughter.” Both Abraham and Sarah laughed at God’s declaration Sarah would have a child (Genesis 17.17, 18.13, 15). God had the last laugh.

> bear you a son, and you shall call his name Isaac; and I will establish My covenant with him for an everlasting covenant for his descendants after him. [20] As for Ishmael, I have heard you; behold, I will bless him, and will make him fruitful and will multiply him exceedingly. He shall become the father of twelve princes, and I will make him a great nation. [21] But My covenant I will establish with Isaac, whom Sarah will bear to you at this season next year. [22] When He finished talking with him, God went up from Abraham (Genesis 17.17-22).

God revealed the covenant line and the promises of the Abrahamic Covenant would go through Isaac, not Ishmael. Circumcision would be the sign of the Abrahamic Covenant (Genesis 17.10, 12-14).[11]

Jacob and Esau

Isaac and Rebekah had twin boys, Jacob and Esau. The birthright of the covenant promise should have gone to Esau since he was the firstborn. But Esau showed little interest in his birthright and sold it to Jacob for a bowl of bean soup (Genesis 25.29-35). Later, Jacob connived with the help of his mother, Rebekah, to deceive Isaac into giving Jacob the blessing intended for Esau. Despite this deceit, Isaac refused to withdraw or reverse his blessing to Jacob. No doubt he remembered the Lord's prophecy at the twin's birth that the elder would serve the younger (Genesis 25.23). Jacob's deceit was wrong but the larger issue was that Esau had no interest in his birthright. He was devoid of faith. Spiritual matters had no appeal to him (Romans 9.13; Hebrews 12.16).

---

[11] Though Ishmael was circumcised, God established His covenant with Isaac, not Ishmael (Genesis 17.19-21). Circumcision was a telling sign. It reminded every Jewish male of their identity and relationship to God. When Israel practiced idolatry, rife with the immorality of the phallic cult, circumcision graphically recalled sin and covenant-breaking.

After Jacob cheated Esau, he fled to Haran because Esau wished to kill him (Genesis 27.41-46). He went to see Laban, Rebekah's brother. While in Haran, he dreamed his famous "ladder" dream.[12] In the vision, God spoke to him. The text reads:

> [12] He had a dream, and behold, a ladder was set on the earth with its top reaching to heaven; and behold, the angels of God were ascending and descending on it. [13] And behold, the LORD stood above it and said, "I am the LORD, the God of your father Abraham and the God of Isaac; the land on which you lie, I will give it to you and to your descendants. [14] Your descendants will also be like the dust of the earth, and you will spread out to the west and to the east and to the north and to the south; and in you and in your descendants shall all the families of the earth be blessed (Genesis 28.12-14).

God reaffirmed His promise that the Abrahamic Covenant would go through Jacob (Acts 7.8; Romans 9.7, 13, 11.26).

The Sovereignty of the Covenants

Paul wrote, "the gifts and the calling of God are irrevocable" (Romans 11.29). The language God used throughout his declarations of the Abrahamic Covenant was *unilateral*. He declared, "I will" (Genesis 12.2, 3, 15.15-17 17.2, 6-8, 19, 21, 22.17, 16.3-4, 28.13, 32.12, 48.4; Exodus 3.17; Judges 2.1; 1 Chronicles 16.18; Psalm 105.11). The fulfillment of all the covenants God made with Israel is based on His character.

---

[12] Jacob saw a "stairway" (סֻלָּם) spanning heaven and earth upon which angels ascended and descended. The word סֻלָּם is a ἅπαξ λεγόμενον (Genesis 28.12). The Akkadian (cognate language of Hebrew) word *simmiltu* may offer some insight into what Jacob saw. It means "stairway" or "ramp," not "ladder." The LORD stood at its top, in the throne complex of heaven. Jacob named this place Bethel, "house of God," (בֵּית־אֵל) and "gate of heaven" (שַׁעַר הַשָּׁמָיִם).

Currently, Israel remains "trodden down of the Gentiles" (Luke 21.24). The nation and the Jewish people do not enjoy the fulfillment of the Abrahamic Covenant or the other covenants. But God has given His word to fulfill His promise to Abraham and His descendants. At the present time, God is blessing believers through His Church, the body of Christ, in which neither Jew nor Gentile exists (Galatians 3.26-29). Our blessings are based upon faith in Christ's death, burial, and resurrection (1 Corinthians 15.1-4). This faith makes all, Jew or Gentile, "Abraham's seed" and "heirs to the promise." The meaning of this will be examined in detail later in Program Three: The Church.

The Land Covenant

In addition to God's promise that Abraham and his descendants would be a blessing to the nations,[13] God revealed He would give Abraham and his descendants a large land grant. The land promise is so intrinsic to Jewish theology that without it the whole program disintegrates. The Jews of Jesus' day knew exactly what John the Baptist meant when he proclaimed, "Repent, for the kingdom of God is near" (Mark 1.15). The kingdom was that kingdom in which Israel would be preeminent among the nations of the earth (Deuteronomy 28.1, 13; Matthew 6.10) and occupy and control the land promised to Abraham.

God told Abraham, "Go forth from your country, and from your relatives, and from your father's house, to the land which I will show you" (Genesis 12.1). A few verses later, the text reads:

> [6] Abram passed through the land as far as the site of Shechem, to the oak of Moreh. Now the Canaanite was then in the land. [7] The LORD appeared to Abram and said, To your descendants I will give this land. So he built an altar there to the LORD who had appeared to him (Genesis 12.6-7).

---

[13] The prophets elaborated specific blessings to the nations (Isaiah 42.1, 60.1-3; Zechariah 8.22-23).

This text reveals the Lord appeared to Abraham and promised him a land and in Genesis 13.14-15 and 17.7-8 the Lord elaborated upon this estate. He told Abraham the land was an *eternal* gift.[14]

Genesis 15.7-21 is the record of the formal confirmation of the Land Covenant. The ceremony was the normal procedure the people of Abraham's day used for legal agreements: the two agreeing parties took animals, cut them apart, and placed the parts on either side of a pathway. Then both parties (party of the first part and party of the second part) walked between the slain animals to signify agreement. But when it came time to confirm the agreement, God put Abraham to sleep. God *alone* moved between the animals. By this action, God revealed He would *sovereignly* fulfill the covenant.

In Genesis 15.18, God specified the boundaries of the land-grant: "from the river of Egypt as far as the great river, the river Euphrates" (cf. Exodus 23.31).[15] Thus, the borders of the land-grant were from the Nile River to the Mediterranean Sea to the Euphrates River. This area would be Israel's possession *forever*.

Israel reached its zenith under the rule of David and his son, Solomon, but never occupied the borders expressed in the covenant and lost the land it held. The Land Covenant will be fulfilled when the Lord returns and establishes His earthly reign (Matthew 6.10; Psalm 37.9). In His hands, the land will become an eternal possession.

---

[14] The text "forever" in Genesis 13.15 and 17.7-8 is עוֹלָם. It was first used by God regarding Adam and Eve's eating from the Tree of Life, "And the LORD God said, Behold, the man is become as one of us, to know good and evil: and now, lest he put forth his hand, and take also of the tree of life, and eat, and live forever" (Genesis 3.22). It can mean a "long time" or "forever" and context determines its particular sense. It is used in reference to God's eternality in Genesis 21.33.

[15] The expression, מִנְּהַר מִצְרַיִם probably meant the Nile River, since נָהָר usually meant a major body of water (cf. 2 Kings 24.7).

God gave the Jews an opportunity to begin to fulfill the Land Covenant immediately after He delivered them from slavery in Egypt.[16] He said:

> 27 I will send My terror ahead of you, and throw into confusion all the people among whom you come, and I will make all your enemies turn *their* backs to you. 28 I will send hornets ahead of you so that they will drive out the Hivites, the Canaanites, and the Hittites before you. 29 I will not drive them out before you in a single year, that the land may not become desolate and the beasts of the field become too numerous for you. 30 I will drive them out before you little by little, until you become fruitful and take possession of the land (Exodus 23.27-30).[17]

God told the Jews He would create fear and confusion among the inhabitants of the land and send hornets to drive them out. The process would be gradual, so Israel would not take more land than they could occupy and settle. From the time Jacob went to Egypt until Moses, God had been preparing the land for Israel to occupy. God told Abraham his offspring would be in a foreign land but in the fourth generation would return, for, "the iniquity of the Amorite is not yet complete" (Genesis 15.13-16).[18] God gave these peoples 400 years to repent.

Once God delivered Israel from Egypt to return to the land, they only needed to do one thing: believe God. According to what God

---

[16] Initially, God told Abraham not to go to Egypt (Genesis 26.2). Later, God told Jacob to go to Egypt (Genesis 46.3). It was in Egypt that the Jews became a great nation.

[17] God promised to send His Angel to guard Israel's entrance into the land and bring them to a place He had prepared. He promised to destroy the Amorites, Hittites, Perizzites, Canaanites, Hivites and Jebusites (Exodus 23.20-26). The nation only needed to believe God.

[18] The term "Amorite" is a metonymy for the Nephilim peoples who inhabited the land, i.e., Canaanites, Philistines, Amalekites, Perizzites, Hittites, etc. (Genesis 6.4). While Israel was in Egypt, the inhabitants of the land built cities, houses, tilled fields, and established vineyards which Israel could have inherited had they believed God.

promised in Exodus 23, no warfare or bloodshed would have occurred. But Moses' generation refused to believe God and never entered the land. They wandered in the wilderness 40 years and died. God then promised the land to a new generation, led by Joshua and Caleb (Numbers 14.26-38). But now, taking of the land would no longer be easy; it would require bloodshed.

God reiterated and amplified the Land Covenant in Deuteronomy 9.1-29, 10.11, 11.8-12, 22-25, 29-31, 12.1, 10-12, 20, 29, 30.1-10. These passages revealed additional information:

1. The nation would return to God and obey Him (Deuteronomy 30.1-2, 8).
2. God would gather Israel from the nations where they were dispersed (Deuteronomy 30.3-5).
3. God would circumcise Jewish hearts to love Him (Deuteronomy 30.6, 19-20).[19]
4. God would curse Israel's enemies (Deuteronomy 30.7).[20]
5. God would bless Israel with abundance in the land (Deuteronomy 30.9).[21]

The record of Jewish history is that when the nation obeyed God, He blessed them and when they disobeyed, He disciplined them. God's discipline came in the form of military defeat and loss of land. One of Israel's greatest problems was idolatry. They mixed what God had revealed to them with the false religions of the surrounding nations. God disciplined the nation through military defeat and showed that without Him, they were no match for the gods of the nations.

When Israel broke the Law by refusing to keep the land sabbaths (Exodus 23.10-11; Leviticus 25.2-7, 18-22), God judged them with Nebuchadnezzar's conquest. For 490 years, the nation had

---

[19] This anticipated the New Covenant (Jeremiah 31; Ezekiel 36; Joel 2).
[20] This anticipated the Day of the Lord, God's wrath upon the nations.
[21] This anticipated the productivity of the Messianic Kingdom.

disregarded the land Sabbaths.[22] God declared He would have His sabbaths and brought the nation into captivity for 70 years (2 Chronicles 36.16-21; Nehemiah 1.8; Jeremiah 25.9-13, 26.6-7, 29.10; Daniel 9.2-20).[23] Moses prophesied this would happen (Leviticus 26.32-35) and during those 70 years, the land became desolate (Nehemiah 1.3, 2.13-17).[24] Despite these failures, God sovereignly decreed Israel will obey Him and receive His promised blessings.

The Mosaic Covenant

Before God gave the Mosaic Covenant, He revealed the nation's grand destiny to Moses. They were to become a holy nation composed of a kingdom of priests. The text reads:

> 3 Moses went up to God, and the Lord called to him from the mountain, saying, Thus you shall say to the house of Jacob and tell the sons of Israel: 4 You yourselves have seen what I did to the Egyptians, and how I bore you on eagles' wings, and brought you to Myself. 5 Now then, if you will indeed obey My voice and keep My covenant, then you shall be My own possession among all the peoples, for all the earth is Mine; 6 and you shall be to Me a kingdom of priests and a holy nation. These are the words that you shall speak to the sons of Israel (Exodus 19.3-6).

God had established His plan to create and set aside a special people for Himself with His call of Abraham. The Abrahamic Covenant passed through Isaac to Jacob who fathered the twelve tribes of

---

[22] God warned Israel if they disobeyed Him, He would remove them from the land and it would lie fallow. He gave this warning 900 years before it happened (Leviticus 26.27-35).

[23] The 490-year lapse required the land to rest 70 years. During this time of the "Babylonian Captivity," God cured Israel's idolatry.

[24] The Bible and secular history reveals that when Jews are not in the land it becomes desolate.

Israel. They became the nation God called a "special treasure."[25] When Moses announced the Law, Israel promised to obey it. Moses wrote:

> 7 So Moses came and called the elders of the people, and set before them all these words which the Lord had commanded him. 8 All the people answered together and said, All that the Lord has spoken we will do! And Moses brought back the words of the people to the Lord (Exodus 19.7-8).

History has recorded their failure. Despite this failure, since the Mosaic Law was built upon the Abrahamic Covenant (as were all Israel's covenants), God's blessings to them have been sovereignly decreed. They will come to pass.

The Nature of the Mosaic Covenant

The Mosaic Covenant required obedience for blessing. God knew Israel would not, indeed, could not keep it—even though the people promised they would (Exodus 19.8).[26] In anticipation of this failure, God promised Israel a New Covenant to replace the Mosaic Covenant or "old covenant." Jesus initiated the New Covenant (Matthew 26.26-29), but its fulfillment with national Israel remains future, like all Israel's covenants.

The Mosaic Law's primary *moral* purpose was to reveal sin. Paul explained this in his letters:

> 19 Now we know that whatever the Law says, it speaks to those who are under the Law, so that every mouth may be closed and all the world may become accountable to God;

---

[25] The word the KJV translated "peculiar treasure" in Exodus 19.5 is סְגֻלָּה and means "possession," "wealth," "treasure." See Exodus 19.5; Deuteronomy 7.6, 14.2, 26.18; Psalm 135.4; Malachi 3.17. Peter and John recognized this in their writings: 1 Peter 2.5, 9; Revelation 1.6, 5.10; 20.6 as did Paul (Romans 3.1-2, Romans 9-11).

[26] Paul stated the Law was "holy, righteous, and good" (Romans 7.12) but no one could keep it (Romans 7.14-25).

> [20] because by the works of the Law no flesh will be justified in His sight; for through the Law comes the knowledge of sin (Romans 3.19-20).

> [8] But we know that the Law is good, if one uses it lawfully, [9] realizing the fact that law is not made for a righteous person, but for those who are lawless and rebellious, for the ungodly and sinners, for the unholy and profane, for those who kill their fathers or mothers, for murderers [10] and immoral men and homosexuals and kidnappers and liars and perjurers, and whatever else is contrary to sound teaching, [11] according to the glorious gospel of the blessed God, with which I have been entrusted (1 Timothy 1.8-11).[27]

Paul wrote the Mosaic Law was to reveal sin. It was not for the righteous, but for the unrighteous (1 Timothy 1.8-11). Good people do not need a moral law.[28]

In addition to the moral Law, primarily the Decalogue (Exodus 20.1-17), were civil and ceremonial laws.[29] These laws governed Israel's daily life and priestly activities. The ceremonial law, i.e., the Levitical sacrifices, dealt with God's mercy in dealing with sin. The civil law dealt with justice in human relationships.

---

[27] Our English word gospel comes from the Old English *godspell* meaning "good news." It is a translation of the word εὐαγγέλιον which is a combination of "good" (εὐ) and "message" or "news" (ἀγγελία). What the "good news" is, is determined by context.

[28] See Jesus' reply to the Pharisees (Matthew 9.11-13).

[29] According to Maimonides (Rambam), the Mosaic Law consisted of 613 commandments. It was a "package" which included the moral, civil, and ceremonial law. James wrote the Jews (James 1.1) that to break one point of the Law was to break it all (James 2.10).

The Levitical Sacrifices

Israel's priests offered animal sacrifices to propitiate (כָּפַר) God.[30] Numerous laws regulated these sacrifices and how they were to be offered. The great day of Israel's calendar was the Day of Atonement (יוֹם כִּיפּוּר). It was a Sabbath (Leviticus 23.28, 30-32) and Israel's high priest offered a sacrifice for the entire nation to deal with its sin (Leviticus 16).[31]

Before this ceremony, the high priest washed (βαπτισμός, Mark 7.4, 8; Hebrews 9.10), put on linen clothing, and went into the Holy of Holies to offer the blood of a bull for a sin offering and a ram for a burnt offering for himself and his household, sprinkling the blood

---

[30] Most occurrences of the word כָּפַר involve a priest "making an atonement." Our word "atonement" was created in the early 1500s by combining at + one + ment to mean a reconciliation. But mankind was not reconciled to God until Christ's death on the cross and His resurrection (Romans 5.10; 2 Corinthians 5.18-19). Animal sacrifices anticipated and portrayed Christ's all-sufficient sacrifice but could not solve the problem of sin and death. They served as a temporary measure for God to deal with Israel in His covenant relationship with them. The verb כָּפַר has been discussed extensively as to its meaning. The LXX translated the word with εξιλασκομαι, "propitiate." The word ἱλάσκομαι is found in Luke 18.13, "be merciful" and in Hebrews 2.17, "to propitiate." Propitiation is mercy and appeasement, not reconciliation. The nouns associated with כָּפַר shed additional light on its meaning: כֹּפֶר was a "ransom," and כַּפֹּרֶת was the "mercy seat," the lid of the Ark of the Covenant.

[31] In the sin offering, a sinner placed his hand upon the head of the animal (identification) and killed it. Then the priest offered the blood to God and placed it on the brazen altar (Leviticus 4.27-31). The individual sin offering covered sins of ignorance, *not* deliberate sins. Unlike individual offerings, on the Day of Atonement, all the sins of the people were propitiated by the animal sacrifices and the scapegoat (Leviticus 16.30, 34).

of the bull upon the mercy seat (כַּפֹּרֶת) seven times (Leviticus 16.14).[32]

For the sins of the people, the high priest chose a ram for a burnt offering and two goats for a sin offering. He then cast lots. The lot that fell on one goat indicated it would be sacrificed as a sin offering. The blood of this goat was taken into the Holy of Holies and sprinkled on and before the mercy-seat. The other goat was presented to the Lord and the high priest would place both hands upon the head of the goat and confess the sins of the nation. A man was then put in the charge of the goat to take and release it in the wilderness. This "scapegoat" (Leviticus 16.10, 20-22), i.e., "escape goat," symbolized removal of sin from the congregation and cleansing (Leviticus 16.30). God declared this an everlasting statute (Leviticus 16.34).

Israel's civil law enforced the moral law. It was an extensive set of laws which covered the everyday life of Jews. Laws governed prayer, treatment of the poor and unfortunate, marriage, divorce, Gentile relationships, diet, business, property rights, oaths, idolatry, tithing and taxes, health, festivals, Sabbath, and many other areas.

The Sabbatic Covenant

The word "sabbath" (שָׁבַת) means "rest." The "sabbath" was a covenant God gave Israel. No record exists that mankind kept the sabbath before Moses. Moses wrote:

> 12 The LORD spoke to Moses, saying, 13 But as for you, speak to the sons of Israel, saying, You shall surely observe My sabbaths; for this is a sign between Me and you

---

[32] The כַּפֹּרֶת "mercy seat" was the "place of propitiation." It was a lid that covered the Ark of the Covenant with a cherub on either side. They represented the beings who attend and guard God's throne. The Tabernacle represented God's throne complex. The mercy seat represented God's throne where He sits between and above the cherubim (Leviticus 16.2; cf. Psalm 80.1, 99.1; Isaiah 37.16; Ezekiel 10-11; Hebrews 9.5).

> throughout your generations, that you may know that I am the LORD who sanctifies you. [14] Therefore you are to observe the sabbath, for it is holy to you. Everyone who profanes it shall surely be put to death; for whoever does any work on it, that person shall be cut off from among his people. [15] For six days work may be done, but on the seventh day there is a sabbath of complete rest, holy to the LORD; whoever does any work on the sabbath day shall surely be put to death. [16] So the sons of Israel shall observe the sabbath, to celebrate the sabbath throughout their generations as a perpetual covenant. [17] It is a sign between Me and the sons of Israel forever; for in six days the LORD made heaven and earth, but on the seventh day He ceased from labor, and was refreshed (Exodus 31.12-17).

Elements of the covenant included the following:

1. A sign between God and Israel (vv. 13, 17).
2. Eternal in length (vv. 13, 16-17).
3. For Israel to know the LORD sanctified them (v. 13).
4. To observe it for it was holy to them (vv. 14-15).
5. The penalty for breaking it was death (vv. 14-15).

The Jewish Week consisted of the following days and the Sabbath was the seventh day:[33]

1. Yom Rishon – יום ראשון "first day" (Sunday)
2. Yom Sheni – יום שני "second day" (Monday)
3. Yom Shlishi – יום שלישי "third day" (Tuesday)
4. Yom Revi'i – יום רביעי "fourth day" (Wednesday)
5. Yom Chamishi – יום חמישי "fifth day" (Thursday)
6. Yom Shishi – יום ששי "sixth day" (Friday)
7. Yom Shabbat – יום שבת "rest day" (Saturday)

---

[33] A Jewish day began at sunset. Thus, "Sunday" begins at Saturday sunset. This is because of God's accounting in Genesis with "the evening and the morning were the *x* day" (Genesis 1.5, 8, 13, 19, 23, 31).

In addition to the normal, weekly sabbath, Israel had other sabbaths. The seven feasts of Israel were "holy convocations" (Leviticus 23.1-4, 37) and all were sabbaths or contained sabbaths except Passover and First-fruits.

Seven Feasts of Israel		
Passover	Leviticus 23.5; Numbers 9.4-5	1st month, 14th day (Nisan)
Unleavened Bread	Leviticus 23.6-8; Numbers 28.17-18	1st month, 15th-21st day, (Nisan)
First-fruits	Leviticus 23.9-14; Numbers 28.26	1st month, 16th day[34] (Nisan)
Weeks (Pentecost)	Leviticus 23.15-22	50 days later, after 7 sabbaths (Sivan)
Trumpets (Rosh Hashanah)	Leviticus 23.23-25; Numbers 29.1	7th month, 1st day (Tishri)
Atonement (Yom Kippur)	Leviticus 23.26-32; Numbers 29.7	7th month, 10th day (Tishri)
Tabernacles (Succoth)	Leviticus 23.33-36; Numbers 29.12	7th month, 15th-22nd day (Tishri)

Israel also had a land Sabbath in which the land was to rest (Exodus 23.10-11; Leviticus 25.1-7; 18-22). Every seventh year, the land was to lie fallow and vines were not pruned. One of the reasons for this was to provide sustenance for the poor and for animals. God told the nation if they were disobedient, He would enforce the land Sabbath (Leviticus 26.27-46). Many years later, Jeremiah warned Israel of its disobedience of not keeping the land sabbath but the nation refused to listen. As a result, God used Nebuchadnezzar "My servant" (Jeremiah 25.9, 27.6, 43.10) to bring the Jews into captivity for 70 years (1 Chronicles 6.15; Jeremiah 25.11-12, 29.10). Nebuchadnezzar elevated Daniel, one of his young captives, to his second in command because he disclosed and

[34] Leviticus 23:11 states on the "day after the Sabbath" he shall wave it. Since the 15th was a Sabbath, First Fruits began the 16th. Josephus, the first-century Jewish historian, wrote, "But on the second day of unleavened bread, which is the sixteenth day of the month, they first partake of the fruits of the earth, for before that day they do not touch them" (*Antiquities of the Jews,* 3.10.15).

interpreted his dream. Daniel read Jeremiah, wrote about the nation's 70-year captivity (Daniel 9.2, cf. 2 Chronicles 36.17-21), and looked for God's restoration of the nation to its land.

The Davidic Covenant

The Davidic Covenant was God's great covenant with Israel's second king, David. God commanded Nathan to deliver the following covenant promise to David:

> [8] Now therefore, thus you shall say to My servant David, Thus says the LORD of hosts, I took you from the pasture, from following the sheep, to be ruler over My people Israel. [9] I have been with you wherever you have gone and have cut off all your enemies from before you; and I will make you a great name, like the names of the great men who are on the earth. [10] I will also appoint a place for My people Israel and will plant them, that they may live in their own place and not be disturbed again, nor will the wicked afflict them any more as formerly, [11] even from the day that I commanded judges to be over My people Israel; and I will give you rest from all your enemies. The LORD also declares to you that the LORD will make a house for you. [12] When your days are complete and you lie down with your fathers, I will raise up your descendant after you, who will come forth from you, and I will establish his kingdom. [13] He shall build a house for My name, and I will establish the throne of his kingdom forever. [14] I will be a father to him and he will be a son to Me; when he commits iniquity, I will correct him with the rod of men and the strokes of the sons of men, [15] but My lovingkindness shall not depart from him, as I took *it* away from Saul, whom I removed from before you. [16] Your house and your kingdom shall endure before Me forever; your throne shall be established forever. [17] In accordance with all these words and all this vision, so Nathan spoke to David (2 Samuel 7.8-17).

The provisions of the Davidic Covenant included the following:

1. God would make David's name great (2 Samuel 7.9).
2. God would ensure Israel's place in the promised land and give them peace (2 Samuel 7.10).
3. God promised David a dynasty and an eternal kingdom (2 Samuel 7.12-13).
4. God stated He would discipline disobedience but the dynasty would continue forever (2 Samuel 7.14-16).

God repeated this covenant throughout the prophets (2 Samuel 23.5; 2 Chronicles 21.7; Psalm 89.3-4; 19-37; Isaiah 9.6-7; Jeremiah 33.19-26; Luke 1.31-33). Like the other covenants, it was a divine promise. The One who would inherit this kingship was the Messiah, the Lord Jesus Christ. He, as the Son of David, would be the eternal King of the Jews. Even before God gave these promises to David, He had revealed through Jacob that Judah would be the ruling tribe with an everlasting reign. The text reads:

> [8] Judah, your brothers shall praise you; your hand shall be on the neck of your enemies; your father's sons shall bow
> down to you. [9] Judah is a lion's whelp; from the prey, my son, you have gone up. He couches, he lies down as a lion,
> and as a lion, who dares rouse him up? [10] The scepter shall not depart from Judah, nor the ruler's staff from between his feet, until Shiloh comes, and to him shall be the
> obedience of the peoples. [11] He ties his foal to the vine, and his donkey's colt to the choice vine; he washes his garments in wine, and his robes in the blood of grapes. [12]
> His eyes are dull from wine, and his teeth white from milk (Genesis 49.8-12).

God knew Israel would disobey Him. However, in His sovereignty, He provided everything necessary to fulfill the Davidic Covenant.

The New Covenant

The "old" covenant was the Mosaic Law. The Mosaic Law was "holy, righteous, and good" (Romans 7.12) but was imperfect in that fallen human nature could not keep it. The New Covenant, however, was "new" and "better" in that it promised divine power to keep the Law. The following passages describe the New Covenant:

> [31] Behold, days are coming, declares the LORD, when I will make a new covenant with the house of Israel and with the house of Judah, [32] not like the covenant which I made with their fathers in the day I took them by the hand to bring them out of the land of Egypt, My covenant which they broke, although I was a husband to them, declares the LORD. [33] But this is the covenant which I will make with the house of Israel after those days, declares the LORD, I will put My law within them and on their heart I will write it; and I will be their God, and they shall be My people. [34] They will not teach again, each man his neighbor and each man his brother, saying, Know the LORD, for they will all know Me, from the least of them to the greatest of them, declares the LORD, for I will forgive their iniquity, and their sin I will remember no more (Jeremiah 31.31-34).

> [16] Therefore say, Thus says the Lord GOD, Though I had removed them far away among the nations and though I had scattered them among the countries, yet I was a sanctuary for them a little while in the countries where they had gone. [17] Therefore say, Thus says the Lord GOD, I will gather you from the peoples and assemble you out of the countries among which you have been scattered, and I will give you the land of Israel. [18] When they come there, they will remove all its detestable things and all its abominations from it. [19] And I will give them one heart, and put a new spirit within them. And I will take the heart of stone out of their flesh and give them a heart of flesh, [20] that they may walk in My statutes and keep My ordinances and do them. Then they will be My people, and I shall be their God (Ezekiel 11.16-20).

> [24] For I will take you from the nations, gather you from all the lands and bring you into your own land. [25] Then I will sprinkle clean water on you, and you will be clean; I will cleanse you from all your filthiness and from all

> your idols. [26] Moreover, I will give you a new heart and put a new spirit within you; and I will remove the heart of stone from your flesh and give you a heart of flesh. [27] I will put My Spirit within you and cause you to walk in My statutes, and you will be careful to observe My ordinances. [28] You will live in the land that I gave to your forefathers; so you will be My people, and I will be your God (Ezekiel 36.24-28).

> [28] It will come about after this That I will pour out My Spirit on all mankind; And your sons and daughters will prophesy, your old men will dream dreams, your young men will see visions. [29] Even on the male and female servants I will pour out My Spirit in those days (Joel 2.28-29).

The provisions of the New Covenant included the following:

1. God would make a New Covenant with Israel (Jeremiah 31.31, 33).
2. God would put His Law into Jewish hearts (Jeremiah 31.33).
3. God would put His Spirit into them (Ezekiel 11.19, 36.27)
4. God would indwell them and cause them to keep His Law (Ezekiel 11.20, 36.27).
5. God would cleanse and sprinkle the nation with clean water (Ezekiel 36.25).
6. God would pour His Spirit upon all mankind (Joel 2.28-29).

God made the New Covenant with Israel. He stated He would cleanse Israel and sprinkle the nation with clean water. This explains John the Baptist's baptizing ministry. To be fit for the kingdom, one must become clean. Water baptism symbolized repentance and the cleansing of the nation from sin. Multitudes came to John to be baptized in water for the remission of sins (Matthew 3.5-6; Mark 1.4, 16.1) but John prophesied One greater than he would baptize the nation with the Holy Spirit (Matthew 3.11; Luke 3.16).

On the Day of Pentecost, God gave His Holy Spirit to those with Peter and the Eleven.[35] Peter quoted Joel that God would pour His Spirit upon all flesh in the last days but Peter only addressed the Jewish nation, not all flesh. Gentiles were not included in Peter's message (Acts 2.14, 22-23, 29, 39). He understood Jews had to come first according to Jesus' instruction, "And that repentance and remission of sins should be preached in his name among all nations, beginning at Jerusalem" (Luke 24.47; cf. Acts 1.8). Pentecost was the *beginning* of the fulfillment of God's promise of the indwelling Holy Spirit and Peter addressed the Jewish people to repent from having crucified the Messiah, be baptized, and believe Jesus was the Christ (Acts 2.36-38). If they would, they would receive the Holy Spirit. Only after Israel repented could the nation fulfill the spiritual aspects of the Abrahamic Covenant to be a blessing to Gentiles (cf. Zechariah 8.20-23).

A Summary of the Covenants

The Abrahamic Covenant was the foundational covenant of all the covenants God made with the nation of Israel. The other covenants were built upon it and provided additional information as to how God would implement His program of blessing to the favored nation and use them to bless Gentiles.

The Abrahamic, Land, Mosaic, Sabbatic, Davidic, and New Covenants were divine promises to Israel (Romans 9.4), each based upon God's sovereign plan for the Jewish people. For the Jews to enjoy God's blessings within their covenant relationship with God required obedience. While Israel has failed to obey, God has declared one day they will and enjoy His promises.

God promised to give His covenant people a land from the Nile, to the Mediterranean, to the Euphrates River, and that this land would constitute an everlasting kingdom ruled by the Messiah (Jeremiah 24.6; 32.36-41; Amos 9.15). If the land promise is not fulfilled, the covenants cannot be fulfilled. Both the Davidic Covenant (2

---

[35] These were the 120 noted in Acts 1.15.

Samuel 7.10) and the New Covenant repeated the Land Covenant (Ezekiel 36.11.17, 36.28).

The Jewish people will obey God. He will enable them through the power of the indwelling Holy Spirit (New Covenant). Redeemed, believing Israel will enjoy God's promises (Romans 9.6-8, 11.26-29).

<table>
<tr><th colspan="4">Jesus the Messiah-King Fulfills Israel's Covenants in the Messianic Kingdom</th></tr>
<tr><td colspan="2">New Covenant
(Spiritual Empowerment)</td><td>Davidic Covenant
(King)</td><td>Land Covenant
(Kingdom)</td></tr>
<tr><td>↑ Mosaic Covenant</td><td>↑ Sabbatic Covenant</td><td colspan="2">The Messiah reigns over the earth as King blessing Israel and the nations.</td></tr>
<tr><td colspan="4">Abrahamic Covenant (Genesis 12.3)
"in you shall all families of the earth be blessed"</td></tr>
</table>

Jewish Theology

The covenants God gave Israel were the vehicles through which He would accomplish His will for Israel and the nations. Within the context of these covenants reside the two great theological themes of Jewish theology: the Wrath of God and the Kingdom of God.

The Wrath of God

Throughout the prophets, God revealed He would exercise His wrath against Israel and the nations. This event was described as the Day of the Lord (Isaiah 2.12, 13.6, 9; Jeremiah 25.30-38, 30.5-11, 46.10; Ezekiel 13.5, 30.3; Joel 1.15, 2.1, 11, 31, 3.14; Amos 5.18, 20; Obadiah 1.15; Zephaniah 1.7, 14; Zechariah 14.1; Malachi 4.5; Acts 2.20).[36] An example passage is Isaiah 2, which is composed of three parts: a) verses 1-4 deal with the kingdom, b)

---

[36] Technically, the Day of the Lord encompasses God's wrath, the return of Christ, and the establishment of His Kingdom on earth. But most references focus upon His judgment of the earth.

verses 5-11 appeal to the nation for righteousness, and c) verses 12-22 deal with the Day of the Lord.

The prophets used the metaphor of a mountain to signify a kingdom with hills representing lesser kingdoms. Isaiah wrote God's kingdom will be above all others with the Lord ruling from Jerusalem (Psalm 2.6; Zechariah 14.9). Israel will become the premier nation on earth (Deuteronomy 28.1, 13) and be a kingdom of priests and a holy nation (Exodus 19.5-6; Isaiah 61.6). Isaiah described this kingdom:

> [1] The word that Isaiah the son of Amoz saw concerning Judah and Jerusalem. [2] And it shall come to pass in the last days, that the mountain of the LORD's house shall be established in the top of the mountains, and shall be exalted above the hills; and all nations shall flow unto it. [3] And many people shall go and say, Come, and let us go up to the mountain of the LORD, to the house of the God of Jacob; and he will teach us of his ways, and we will walk in his paths: for out of Zion shall go forth the law, and the word of the LORD from Jerusalem. [4] And he shall judge among the nations, and shall rebuke many people: and they shall beat their swords into plowshares, and their spears into pruninghooks: nation shall not lift up sword against nation, neither shall they learn war any more (Isaiah 2.1-4).

The following verses reveal Isaiah's appeal to the nation to repent and live righteously in anticipation of the kingdom. John the Baptist repeated this appeal to the nation as the herald of the King. And Peter proclaimed it to Israel on the day of Pentecost after they had crucified their Messiah.

> [5] O house of Jacob, come and let us walk in the light of the LORD. [6] Therefore you have forsaken your people the house of Jacob, because they be replenished from the east, and are soothsayers like the Philistines, and they please themselves in the children of strangers. [7] Their land also is full of silver and gold, neither is there any end of their

> treasures; their land is also full of horses, neither is there any end of their chariots: [8] Their land also is full of idols; they worship the work of their own hands, that which their own fingers have made: [9] And the mean man bows down, and the great man humbles himself: therefore forgive them not. [10] Enter into the rock, and hide you in the dust, for fear of the LORD, and for the glory of his majesty. [11] The lofty looks of man shall be humbled, and the haughtiness of men shall be bowed down, and the LORD alone shall be exalted in that day (Isaiah 2.5-11).

In the following verses, Isaiah described the great Day of the Lord, God's judgment of Israel and the nations.

> [12] For the day of the LORD of hosts shall be upon every one that is proud and lofty, and upon every one that is lifted up; and he shall be brought low: [13] And upon all the cedars of Lebanon, that are high and lifted up, and upon all the oaks of Bashan, [14] And upon all the high mountains, and upon all the hills that are lifted up, [15] And upon every high tower, and upon every fenced wall, [16] And upon all the ships of Tarshish, and upon all pleasant pictures. [17] And the loftiness of man shall be bowed down, and the haughtiness of men shall be made low: and the LORD alone shall be exalted in that day. [18] And the idols he shall utterly abolish. [19] And they shall go into the holes of the rocks, and into the caves of the earth, for fear of the LORD, and for the glory of his majesty, when he arises to shake terribly the earth. [20] In that day a man shall cast his idols of silver, and his idols of gold, which they made each one for himself to worship, to the moles and to the bats; [21] To go into the clefts of the rocks, and into the tops of the ragged rocks, for fear of the LORD, and for the glory of his majesty, when he arises to shake terribly the earth. [22] Cease from man, whose breath is in his nostrils: for wherein is he to be accounted of (Isaiah 2.12-22)?

Peter, on the day of Pentecost, anticipated its soon arrival and quoted Joel 2, another passage that dealt with the Day of the Lord. Peter declared:

> [19] And I will show wonders in heaven above, and signs in
> the earth beneath; blood, and fire, and vapor of smoke:
> [20] The sun shall be turned into darkness, and the moon into
> blood, before the great and notable day of the Lord come:
> [21] And it shall come to pass, that whosoever shall call on the
> name of the Lord shall be saved (Acts 2.19-21).

While the Jews had murdered their Messiah, God's prophetic plan remained intact. Had they repented, God would have initiated the Day of the Lord and Jesus would have returned to establish His kingdom on earth (Acts 2.38-40, 3.19-20).

The Kingdom of God

God's promise of a kingdom began with His promise to Abraham to make him a great nation and give him the title deed of an eternal land grant (Genesis 12.1-2, 6-7, 13.14-15, 15.7, 18, 17.7-8). The promise of a kingdom is therefore associated with a land, a people, and a king. The people are the covenant line, the line of Abraham, Isaac (Genesis 17.21), and Jacob, from whom came the twelve tribes. God told Moses the Jews would be a kingdom of priests. In the Davidic Covenant, God revealed specifics concerning Israel's kingly line (2 Samuel 7). It would come from Judah, the line of David (Psalm 89) and this King would be God Himself. David wrote:

> For the LORD is our defense; and the Holy One of Israel is our king (Psalm 89.18).

> Let Israel rejoice in him that made him: let the children of Zion be joyful in their King (Psalm 149.2).

God declared:

> I am the LORD, your Holy One, the creator of Israel, your King (Isaiah 43.15).
>
> Thus says the LORD the King of Israel, and his redeemer the LORD of hosts; I am the first, and I am the last; and beside me there is no God (Isaiah 44.6).

Zephaniah wrote:

> [14] Sing, O daughter of Zion; shout, O Israel; be glad and rejoice with all the heart, O daughter of Jerusalem. [15] The LORD hath taken away thy judgments, he hath cast out your enemy: the king of Israel, even the LORD, is in the midst of you: you shalt not see evil any more (Zephaniah 3.14-15).

One of the most familiar passages of Bible is Isaiah 9:

> [6] For unto us a child is born, unto us a son is given: and the government shall be upon his shoulder: and his name shall be called Wonderful, Counsellor, The mighty God, The everlasting Father, The Prince of Peace. [7] Of the increase of his government and peace there shall be no end, upon the throne of David, and upon his kingdom, to order it, and to establish it with judgment and with justice from henceforth even forever. The zeal of the LORD of hosts will perform this (Isaiah 9.6-7).

This was an explicit Messianic prophecy describing the birth of the Messiah and His reign upon the throne of David. Its fulfillment is not in doubt: the zeal of the Lord will perform it.[37]

Another famous Messianic passage concerning the coming kingdom is Isaiah 11.

> [1] And there shall come forth a rod out of the stem of Jesse, and a Branch shall grow out of his roots: [2] And the spirit of

[37] The word "zeal" is קִנְאָה, often translated "envy" or "jealousy." It entails intense will and emotional energy.

> the LORD shall rest upon him, the spirit of wisdom and understanding, the spirit of counsel and might, the spirit of knowledge and of the fear of the LORD; 3 And shall make him of quick understanding in the fear of the LORD: and he shall not judge after the sight of his eyes, neither reprove after the hearing of his ears: 4 But with righteousness shall he judge the poor, and reprove with equity for the meek of the earth: and he shall smite the earth: with the rod of his mouth, and with the breath of his lips shall he slay the wicked. 5 And righteousness shall be the girdle of his loins, and faithfulness the girdle of his reins. 6 The wolf also shall dwell with the lamb, and the leopard shall lie down with the kid; and the calf and the young lion and the fatling together; and a little child shall lead them. 7 And the cow and the bear shall feed; their young ones shall lie down together: and the lion shall eat straw like the ox. 8 And the sucking child shall play on the hole of the asp, and the weaned child shall put his hand on the cockatrice' den. 9 They shall not hurt nor destroy in all my holy mountain: for the earth shall be full of the knowledge of the LORD, as the waters cover the sea. 10 And in that day there shall be a root of Jesse, which shall stand for an ensign of the people; to it shall the Gentiles seek: and his rest shall be glorious (Isaiah 11.1-10).

Godly Jews knew these passages. They were the nation's great hope. It was no surprise to find Jews responding to the gospel of the kingdom. They had heard these prophecies throughout their lives. They had lived under the dominance of Gentile powers and longed to be an independent nation again. They looked for the restoration of the glories of David and Solomon. Mary, Zechariah, Simeon, and Anna's declarations in Luke 1-2 reveal Jewish thinking about the kingdom.

John recorded the following conversation between Jesus and Nathaniel:

> 45 Philip found Nathanael, and said unto him, We have found him, of whom Moses in the law, and the prophets,

> did write, Jesus of Nazareth, the son of Joseph. 46 And Nathanael said unto him, Can any good thing come out of Nazareth? Philip said unto him, Come and see. 47 Jesus saw Nathanael coming to him, and said of him, Behold an Israelite indeed, in whom is no guile! 48 Nathanael said unto him, How do you know me? Jesus answered and said unto him, Before Philip called you, when you were under the fig tree, I saw you. 49 Nathanael answered and said unto him, Rabbi, you are the Son of God; you are the King of Israel. 50 Jesus answered and said unto him, Because I said unto you, I saw you under the fig tree, you believe? You shall see greater things than these. 51 And he said unto him, Truly, truly, I say unto you, Hereafter you shall see heaven open, and the angels of God ascending and descending upon the Son of man (John 1.45-51).

This discourse, by any measure, was remarkable. Jesus told Nathaniel He had seen him under a fig tree. This "remote viewing" was enough to convince Nathaniel of Jesus' identity. He declared He was the Son of God, the King of Israel. Such testimony reveals how godly Jews were looking for their Messiah-King.

A Short Course of Jewish Theology

Psalm 2, written by King David, is a summary of God's prophetic program. It revealed mankind's antagonism towards God and His Messiah, God's wrath, and the kingdom on the earth.

Psalm 2 and Commentary	
Passage	Comment
1 Why do the heathen rage, and the people imagine a vain thing? 2 The kings of the earth set themselves, and the rulers take counsel together, against the LORD, and against his anointed, saying,	Verses 1-3 reveal mankind's (Jews and Gentiles) rejection of the Messiah (1st and 2nd advents).

[3] Let us break their bands asunder, and cast away their cords from us.[38]	
[4] He that sits in the heavens shall laugh: the LORD shall have them in derision. [5] Then shall he speak unto them in his wrath, and vex them in his sore displeasure.	Verses 4-5 show God's disdain for and wrath against those who reject His Messiah.
[6] Yet have I set my king upon my holy hill of Zion. [7] I will declare the decree: the LORD has said unto me, You are my Son; this day have I begotten you. [8] Ask of me, and I shall give you the heathen for your inheritance, and the uttermost parts of the earth for your possession. [9] You shall break them with a rod of iron; you shall dash them in pieces like a potter's vessel.	Verses 6-9 reveal the Messiah's reign from Jerusalem, His status (begotten, Acts 13.30-33), His inheritance of the nations, and the nature of His rule.
[10] Be wise now therefore, O kings: be instructed, judges of the earth. [11] Serve the LORD with fear, and rejoice with trembling. [12] Kiss the Son, lest he be angry, and you perish from the way, when his wrath is kindled but a little. Blessed are all they that put their trust in him.	Verses 10-12 reveal God's warning to Gentiles (kings) and Jews (judges) to worship and revere His Son, not anger Him. This warning foresaw His 2nd Advent.

Jewish Theology Revealed in Other Passages	
The Day of the Lord (The Wrath of God)	The Kingdom of God on Earth (Christ is King)
Isaiah 2.20-21, 24.19-23, 34.1-3; Jeremiah 25.15-38, 30.5-7; Zephaniah 1; Joel 2.1-11, 30-31; Zechariah 14.1-7	Isaiah 2.2-5, 9.6-7, 11.1-16; Jeremiah 23.3-8, 30.8-24; Ezekiel 36.21-38, 37.1-28; Zechariah 14.8-11

[38] "Their fetters" and "their cords" is another reference to the plurality of the Godhead found in the Scriptures (Genesis 1.26, 3.22). The rest of the Psalm shifts back to the singular: "He," "Me," "I."

The prophets wrote hundreds of passages about God's promise to establish an earthly kingdom. One can hardly turn a page in the Old Testament without encountering the subject. Similarly, many passages declare God's judgment upon Israel and the nations. The Messiah is the One who will both judge the earth and reign upon the earth.

An Even Shorter Course of Jewish Theology

The shortest course in Jewish theology is one verse: Isaiah 61.2. If one can remember one verse, one can understand Jewish theology.

> 1 The Spirit of the Lord God is upon me, because the Lord has anointed me to bring good news to the afflicted; He has sent me to bind up the brokenhearted, to proclaim liberty to captives and freedom to prisoners; 2 To proclaim the favorable year of the Lord and the day of vengeance of our God; to comfort all who mourn (Isaiah 61.1-2).

Isaiah 61.2: God's Program For Israel and the Nations		
a	To proclaim the favorable year of the Lord	Announce Kingdom is near[39]
b	The day of vengeance of our God	Day of the Lord
c	To comfort all who mourn	Establish Kingdom on earth

Verse 1 is included for context but everything concerning Jewish theology can be found in verse 2. Verse 1 revealed Christ's 1st Advent. Verse 2 elaborated on His 1st Advent and revealed the rest of Jewish theology. Verse 2a described the Lord's 1st Advent which Jesus read in His visit to the synagogue in Nazareth (Luke 4.16-21). What was striking about His reading (which His listeners noted)

[39] Had Israel accepted Jesus as their Messiah, the Day of the Lord (Tribulation) would have followed after His crucifixion and He would have returned at its end to establish His kingdom.

was He stopped after verse 2a. He rolled up the scroll and told the Jews the prophecy was fulfilled that day.

Verse 2b described God's wrath, the "day of vengeance of our God," the Day of the Lord. The Lord called this time the "Tribulation" (Matthew 24.15-16 cf. Daniel 9.27, 11.31, 12.11). It will last seven years according to Daniel's prophecy (Daniel 9.24-27) and Revelation. At the end of this period, the Lord will return. Verse 2c, "to comfort all who mourn" is the Messianic kingdom which lasts 1,000 years.[40] In this future earthly kingdom, God will smooth out life's inequities (Isaiah 40.3-5; Matthew 6.10) and the Messiah will rule the earth from Jerusalem (Psalm 2.6; Zechariah 14.9). God will fulfill His covenant promises and Israel's national hopes will be realized (Deuteronomy 28.1, 13). Israel will fulfill its destiny to be a kingdom of priests and a holy nation (Exodus 19.4-6; Isaiah 61.6; Zechariah 8.20-23).

<table>
<tr><th colspan="6">Israel's Theology: God's Prophetic Plan</th></tr>
<tr><td colspan="6">The Messiah's Death and Resurrection Prophesied but Veiled
(Isaiah 53; Psalm 16.10)</td></tr>
<tr><td colspan="3">The Day of the Lord
(Zephaniah 1; Joel 2)</td><td colspan="3">The Kingdom of God
(Isaiah 2.1-4; Matthew 6.10)</td></tr>
<tr><td colspan="3">The Messiah Exercises Wrath Upon Israel and the Nations
(Psalm 2)</td><td colspan="3">The Messiah Returns as King to Reign
(Zechariah 14.9)</td></tr>
<tr><td colspan="6">God's Covenant Promises to Israel</td></tr>
<tr><td>Abrahamic Covenant</td><td>Land Covenant</td><td>Mosaic Covenant</td><td>Sabbatic Covenant</td><td>Davidic Covenant</td><td>New Covenant</td></tr>
</table>

[40] Revelation 20.2-7 indicates the Messianic Kingdom will last 1,000 years on the earth. Those 1,000 years are a preview of eternity, which begins with God's creation of a new heavens and new earth (Revelation 21.1).

The Messiah in the Old Testament

What did the Jews understand about the Messiah from the Old Testament? The Old Testament revealed two aspects about the Messiah. One aspect was His suffering. The other was His reign and rule. The overwhelming weight of the testimony of the prophets concerned God's kingdom on earth in which the Messiah would rule and reign over Israel and the nations. The Jews understood this and it occupied their hope. The prophets revealed almost nothing concerning His suffering.

In Genesis 49.8-12, Jacob blessed and foretold his sons' natures and futures. Regarding Judah, Jacob prophesied rule would be established in him. Through Judah, "Shiloh" (שִׁילֹה) "peace" and "rest" would come. Israel's great Sabbath will be the kingdom, under her Messiah. This was the great hope of believing Israel.

A cryptic allusion to the twofold role of the Messiah is in Genesis 35, the account of the birth of Benjamin and death of Rachel. The text reads:

> 16 And they journeyed from Bethel; and there was but a little
> way to come to Ephrath: and Rachel travailed, and she had
> hard labor. 17 And it came to pass, when she was in hard
> labor, that the midwife said unto her, Fear not; you will
> have this son also. 18 And it came to pass, as her soul was in
> departing, (for she died) that she called his name Benoni:
> but his father called him Benjamin. 19 And Rachel died, and
> was buried in the way to Ephrath, which is Bethlehem
> (Genesis 35.16-19).

Knowing she was dying, Rachel expressed her grief by stating her son would be named Benoni, "son of my sorrow." Jacob understood her anguish but overruled her. His faith saw past the tragedy and he named him Benjamin, "son of my right hand" or "son of my strength." These two names contained both roles of the Messiah: suffering and rule.

Psalm 22 spoke prophetically of Christ's suffering—"My God, my God, why have you forsaken me?"—but was not understood other than to record David's distress. Psalm 16.10—"For you will not leave my soul in the grave; neither will you permit your Holy One to see corruption"—was also Messianic but the meaning of this passage was not comprehended. In Isaiah 52, the prophet wrote about both the suffering and the glory of Israel's Messiah.

> [13] Behold, my servant shall deal prudently, he shall be exalted and extolled, and be very high. [14] As many were astonished at you; his visage was so marred more than any man, and his form more than the sons of men: [15] So shall he sprinkle many nations; the kings shall shut their mouths at him: for that which had not been told them shall they see; and that which they had not heard shall they consider (Isaiah 52.13-15).

Verse 13 revealed the Messiah in the kingdom. He would deal wisely and be exalted. Isaiah then shifted to His suffering and rejection. Verses 14 and 15 revealed His defacement—more than any man—and His denial. But verse 15 again spoke of the kingdom. He would heal the nations (Gentiles). The passage revealed the Messiah's suffering and glory, but it was all mixed together with His rule. The rabbis could not make sense of it.

Especially enigmatic was how the Messiah would deal with sin. Zechariah, the priest, in Luke's Gospel, addressed this aspect of His coming but how this would be accomplished was unknown. Luke recorded Zechariah's words concerning his son, John:

> [76] And you, child, shall be called the prophet of the Highest: for you shall go before the face of the Lord to prepare his ways; [77] To give knowledge of salvation unto his people by the remission of their sins (Luke 1.76-77).

Matthew recorded the angel's words to Mary:

> And she shall bring forth a son, and you shall call his name Jesus: for he shall save his people from their sins (Matthew 1.21).

Prior to this, only one passage dealt with the Messiah's dealing with sin in the prophets: Isaiah 53. Isaiah wrote:

> [1] Who has believed our report? and to whom is the arm of
> the LORD revealed? [2] For he shall grow up before him as a
> tender plant, and as a root out of a dry ground: he has no
> form nor comeliness; and when we shall see him, there is
> no beauty that we should desire him. [3] He is despised and
> rejected of men; a man of sorrows, and acquainted with
> grief: and we hid as it were our faces from him; he was
> despised, and we esteemed him not. [4] Surely, he has borne
> our griefs, and carried our sorrows: yet we did esteem him
> stricken, smitten of God, and afflicted. [5] But he was
> wounded for our transgressions, he was bruised for our
> iniquities: the chastisement of our peace was upon him; and
> with his stripes we are healed. [6] All we like sheep have gone
> astray; we have turned everyone to his own way; and
> the LORD hath laid on him the iniquity of us all (Isaiah
> 53.1-6).

This passage, in hindsight, revealed the Messiah, Jesus of Nazareth, and His work on the cross. But the Jews did not understand what it meant or how it would be fulfilled. The Ethiopian eunuch's question to Philip, which took place *after* Christ's crucifixion and resurrection, revealed this ignorance. The eunuch, an educated Jew, asked, "of whom speaks the prophet this? of himself, or of some other man" (Acts 8.34)?

Furthermore, Isaiah's prophecy *only* dealt with Israel. It said nothing about how the Messiah would deal with the sins of Gentiles. Isaiah's audience was Jews. The pronouns of the passage, "we shall see him," "we should desire him," "we hid our faces from him," "our griefs," "our sorrows," "we did not esteem him," "wounded for our transgressions," "bruised for our iniquities," "chastisement of our peace," "we are healed," "all we like sheep," "we have turned," "laid on him the iniquity of us all," referred to Jews, to Israel, not to Gentiles, and certainly not to the Church. The Old Testament revealed nothing about Christ suffering or dying for the whole world. That truth was not understood until Paul.

How little the Jewish religious professionals understood about the Messiah is evident from the questions Jesus asked them. Consider the following episode:

> [41] While the Pharisees were gathered together, Jesus asked them, [42] Saying, What think you of Christ? whose son is he? They say unto him, The son of David. [43] He said unto them, How then does David in spirit call him Lord, saying, [44] The LORD said unto my Lord, Sit on my right hand, till I make thine enemies thy footstool? [45] If David then called him Lord, how is he his son? [46] And no man was able to answer him a word, neither dared any man from that day forth ask him any more questions (Matthew 22.41-46).

Salvation in the Old Testament

How were men and women saved in the Old Testament? Unlike Paul's epistles, the Old Testament has no clear statement about how men and women were saved under Judaism. One thing *is* certain: salvation required faith *and* works. Works completely meshed with faith. Faith *and* works constituted the warp and woof of salvation. Paul's letter to the Hebrews emphasized the faith of Old Testament saints (Hebrews 11). But the Scriptures clearly revealed works were also required. Animal sacrifices had to be brought to the priest to cover one's sin. Salvation by faith alone was unknown before Paul.

Salvation and the Levitical Sacrifices

The book of Hebrews reveals the Levitical sacrifices were typical and temporary. They were a temporary propitiation (כָּפַר) for sin. The animal sacrifices were pictures or shadows of Christ's future, permanently effective sacrifice for sin (Hebrews 10.4). Looking back, they reveal how God laid the groundwork of a greater reality, i.e., the shed blood of the Messiah which satisfied the justice of God.

But the Jews of the Old Testament and the Jews of Christ's day had no idea of a greater reality beyond the animal sacrifices. They only knew God had commanded them. Leviticus outlined several types of animal sacrifices, i.e., burnt, meat, peace, sin, trespass offerings. Each had specific instructions for offerer and priest about how they were to be performed. The following instructions pertained to the individual sin offering:

> [27] Now if anyone of the common people sins unintentionally in doing any of the things which the Lord has commanded not to be done, and becomes guilty, [28] if his sin which he has committed is made known to him, then he shall bring for his offering a goat, a female without defect, for his sin which he has committed. [29] He shall lay his hand on the head of the sin offering and slay the sin offering at the place of the burnt offering. [30] The priest shall take some of its blood with his finger and put it on the horns of the altar of burnt offering; and all the rest of its blood he shall pour out at the base of the altar. [31] Then he shall remove all its fat, just as the fat was removed from the sacrifice of peace offerings; and the priest shall offer it up in smoke on the altar for a soothing aroma to the Lord. Thus the priest shall make atonement for him, and he will be forgiven. (Leviticus 4.27-31).[41]

Bringing an animal to a priest was a *work*. From the divine perspective, the sacrifice was effective for it fulfilled the Law and God's justice. For the individual, it was effective if he obeyed and believed the sacrifice dealt with his sin. Forgiveness required work

---

[41] Individuals had an option of offering a goat or a lamb as a sin offering (Leviticus 4.32-35). Notice this sacrifice pertained to unintentional sin. No individual sacrifice existed for deliberate sin. Only on the Day of Atonement was this category of sin addressed.

(bringing an animal to the priest) and faith (believing the sacrifice propitiated his sin): faith and works.

The Gospels: Nearness of the Kingdom

The ministry of John the Baptist and the ministry of Jesus revealed the prophesied time of the kingdom of God on earth had come.[42] After 400 years of prophetic silence, John the Baptist appeared and declared the kingdom of God was at hand. *Everything* in the Gospels concerns this earthly kingdom of God. This point cannot be stressed too strongly. Appropriately, this is the how the Gospels begin. Consider the following passages:

> [1] In those days came John the Baptist, preaching in the wilderness of Judaea, [2] And saying, Repent: for the kingdom of heaven is at hand. [3] For this is he that was spoken of by the prophet Isaiah, saying, The voice of one crying in the wilderness, Prepare the way of the Lord, make his paths straight (Matthew 3.1-3).
>
> From that time Jesus began to preach, and to say, Repent: for the kingdom of heaven is at hand (Matthew 4.17).
>
> [2] As it is written in the prophets, Behold, I send my messenger before your face, which shall prepare thy way before you. [3] The voice of one crying in the wilderness, Prepare the way of the Lord, make his paths straight. [4] John did baptize in the wilderness, and preach the baptism of repentance for the remission of sins (Mark 1.2-4).
>
> [14] Now after that John was put in prison, Jesus came into Galilee, preaching the gospel of the kingdom of God, [15] And saying, The time is fulfilled, and the kingdom of God is at hand: repent, and believe the gospel (Mark 1.14-15).

---

[42] By convention, the Gospels of Matthew, Mark, Luke, and John exist within the "New Testament." Despite this nomenclature, the Gospels are Old Testament books just as much as Exodus, Isaiah, or Jeremiah. They deal with God's prophetic plan with Israel under the Law.

> [32] He shall be great, and shall be called the Son of the Highest: and the Lord God shall give unto him the throne of his father David: [33] And he shall reign over the house of Jacob forever; and of his kingdom there shall be no end (Luke 1.32-33).

> [42] And when it was day, he departed and went into a desert place: and the people sought him, and came unto him, and stayed him, that he should not depart from them. [43] And he said unto them, I must preach the kingdom of God to other cities also: for therefore am I sent. [44] And he preached in the synagogues of Galilee (Luke 4.42-44).

> [45] Philip found Nathanael, and said unto him, We have found him, of whom Moses in the law, and the prophets, did write, Jesus of Nazareth, the son of Joseph. [46] And Nathanael said unto him, Can any good thing come out of Nazareth? Philip said unto him, Come and see. [47] Jesus saw Nathanael coming to him, and said of him, Behold an Israelite indeed, in whom is no guile! [48] Nathanael said unto him, How do you know me? Jesus answered and said unto him, Before Philip called you, when you were under the fig tree, I saw you. [49] Nathanael answered and said unto him, Rabbi, you are the Son of God; you are the King of Israel. [50] Jesus answered and said unto him, Because I said unto you, I saw you under the fig tree, you believe? You shalt see greater things than these. [51] And he said unto him, Verily, verily, I say unto you, Hereafter you shall see heaven open, and the angels of God ascending and descending upon the Son of man (John 1.45-51).

The Apostle Paul wrote the following concerning Jesus' earthly ministry:[43]

---

[43] Jesus' contact with Gentiles was extremely limited and He had no ministry to them. He interacted with the Canaanite woman (Matthew 15.21-28), the Roman centurion (Matthew 8.5-13; Luke 7.1-10), and healed some Gentiles (Matthew 12.14-21). These were rare exceptions.

> [8] Now I say that Jesus Christ was a minister of the circumcision for the truth of God, to confirm the promises made unto the fathers: [9] And that the Gentiles might glorify God for his mercy; as it is written, For this cause I will confess to you among the Gentiles, and sing unto thy name (Romans 15.8-9).

Paul's statement affirmed that Jesus' earthly ministry was to Jews to confirm the covenant promises. The kingdom was the great prophetic promise. Once it was established, the Jews could fulfill their destiny as a kingdom of priests to bless Gentiles (Zechariah 8.20-23). This is what the Gospels are all about.

John the Baptist and Jesus' ministry conformed to the Old Testament promises. The Jewish Scriptures, the Tanakh,[44] are organized so that they end with 2 Chronicles. The last chapter of 2 Chronicles recounts the ascension of Cyrus the Persian over Babylon and the promise of the Jews to return and rebuild the Temple. In Christian Bibles, the Old Testament ends with the book of Malachi and God's declaration that Elijah will come to restore the hearts of the fathers to the children and the children to the fathers before the Day of the Lord (Malachi 4.5-6). Both endings reveal the key Jewish hope: Jewish repentance, restoration to the land, and the establishment of the kingdom on earth. The Gospels snap onto 2 Chronicles or Malachi like vise grips. They are as Old Testament as Exodus or Isaiah.

The Gospel Message

The Gospels introduce John the Baptist as the herald of the King who harkened back to 2 Chronicles and Malachi, proclaiming, "repent for the kingdom of God is near" (Matthew 3.1-3; Mark 1.2-5; Luke 3.2-4). The prophecy of John's birth was that he would operate in the spirit and power of Elijah (Luke 1.17). Jesus stated John *was* Elijah *if* the people had listened to him. The text reads,

---

[44] "Tanakh" or "Tanach" is an acronym for the Torah (five books of Moses), Nevi'im (prophets), and Ketuvim (writings).

> [10] And His disciples asked Him, Why then do the scribes say that Elijah must come first? [11] And He answered and said, Elijah is coming and will restore all things; [12] but I say to you that Elijah already came, and they did not recognize him, but did to him whatever they wished. So also the Son of Man is going to suffer at their hands. [13] Then the disciples understood that He had spoken to them about John the Baptist (Matthew 17.10-13; Mark 9.11-13).

John could have fulfilled the prophecy of Malachi 4.4-6 at the time of Christ's earthly appearance had Israel repented.[45] But the nation refused, just as that generation of Jews whom God delivered from slavery in Egypt refused to enter the promised land at Kadesh-Barnea (Numbers 13-14).[46] Instead of repenting and believing the gospel of the kingdom, that Jesus was the Messiah, they conspired with the Romans to execute Him.

The theology of the Gospels is simple. The Gospels are about the King, the kingdom, and the fulfillment of God's covenant promises to Israel. Everything Jesus taught in the Gospels concerned God's kingdom on earth. The Sermon on the Mount and Beatitudes are about the nature of life in the earthly kingdom. The parables He began to use in His later ministry all concern the kingdom.

Christians have somehow gotten the idea the kingdom of God is only in heaven, not on earth. Such thinking is so alien to everything the prophets and Jesus taught that it is mind-boggling how anyone could be so misinformed. Perhaps some of the explanation is due to Matthew's phrase "kingdom of heaven" or because Paul wrote of believer's heavenly citizenship (Philippians 3.20). But not to see the Gospels concern God's promise of His earthly kingdom to the Jews is to miss their whole point.

With regard to Matthew's phrase, "kingdom of heaven" it is a genitive of source, not a genitive of location. The phrase meant that the source of the kingdom was heaven. Jesus told Pilate, "My

---

[45] This is an example of how human and divine wills cooperate.

[46] Paul noted this great failure in warning the Jews (Hebrews 3,7-4.6).

kingdom is not of this world" (John 18.36) and meant His kingdom will be established by divine power, not by earthly, human power. Jesus' admonition to the Jews to "lay up treasures in heaven" meant heaven was the place where rewards are kept safe. Once the Lord returns to rule, they will be enjoyed on earth (Matthew 6.19-20; Psalm 37.9).

God's abode is presently in heaven. The kingdom of God proclaimed by the prophets and taught in the Gospels is earthly. Jesus told His disciples to pray:

> Thy kingdom come. Thy will be done in earth, as it is in heaven (Matthew 6.10).

Could words be clearer? The kingdom of God will be upon the earth. Jews had no idea of dying and going to heaven. Not one verse in the Old Testament and Gospels offered such a hope. Jewish hope lay in resurrection and life upon the earth. Jesus told Martha her brother Lazarus would rise again and she knew it. The text reads:

> [23] Jesus said to her, Your brother will rise again. [24] Martha said to Him, I know that he will rise again in the resurrection on the last day (John 11.23-24).

Martha's response revealed the hope of believing Jews: resurrection to enjoy life in the earthly kingdom. They looked forward to God fulfilling His covenant promises of a land, a king, and being the premier nation of the world. Jewish hopes would be realized on earth.[47]

The Audience of the Gospels

As noted before, the Gospels are Old Testament. They concern the prophecies and promises God made to His covenant people which were the focus of Jesus' earthly ministry (Romans 15.8). Jesus

---

[47] Job revealed the hope of resurrection and life upon the earth (Job 19.25-26). The hope of heaven, of a heavenly citizenship and destiny, was a Pauline revelation. No one knew or taught this before Paul.

came to fulfill these promises, not to found the Church. This fact is seen clearly from the opening chapters of Luke's gospel. For 400 years, no prophet had ministered to Israel. Out of nowhere, after 400 years, an angel visited an elderly, barren couple, Zachariah and Elizabeth, to announce that Elizabeth would conceive. The couple would have an extraordinary son who would be great in the sight of the Lord and filled with the Holy Spirit from the womb (Luke 1.15). Luke wrote:

> [16] And he will turn many of the sons of Israel back to the Lord their God. [17] It is he who will go before Him in the spirit and power of Elijah, to turn the hearts of the fathers back to the children, and the disobedient to the attitude of the righteous, so as to make ready a people prepared for the Lord (Luke 1.16-17)

The angel told the couple their son would operate with the spirit and power of Elijah to turn the hearts of the fathers to the children and the hearts of the children to the fathers (Malachi 4.5-6). This began a revival of the Jewish hope foretold by the prophets.

Mary, the virgin espoused to Joseph, also experienced an encounter with an angel. The angel told her:

> [31] And behold, you will conceive in your womb and bear a son, and you shall name Him Jesus. [32] He will be great and will be called the Son of the Most High; and the Lord God will give Him the throne of His father David; [33] and He will reign over the house of Jacob forever, and His kingdom will have no end (Luke 1.31-33).

The angel's declaration to Mary concerned God's fulfillment of the Davidic Covenant. Her Son, from the line of David, would occupy David's throne and reign forever over the house of Jacob.

When Elizabeth, Mary's cousin, came to visit, Mary declared:[48]

---

[48] These words are from what has come to be known as "The Magnificat" (Luke 1.46-56).

> [54] He has given help to Israel His servant, in remembrance of His mercy, [55] as He spoke to our fathers, to Abraham and his descendants forever (Luke 1.54-55).

Could words be more Jewish? They confirmed Israel's place in God's plan based on the Abrahamic Covenant.

Zachariah the priest, the father of John the Baptist, prophesied and conveyed these same hopes:

> [67] And his father Zacharias was filled with the Holy Ghost, and prophesied, saying, [68] Blessed *be* the Lord God of Israel, for He has visited us and accomplished redemption for His people, [69] and has raised up a horn of salvation for us in the house of David His servant—[70] as He spoke by the mouth of His holy prophets from of old—[71] salvation from our enemies, and from the hand of all who hate us; [72] To show mercy toward our fathers, and to remember His holy covenant, [73] the oath which He swore to Abraham our father, [74] to grant us that we, being rescued from the hand of our enemies, might serve Him without fear, [75] in holiness and righteousness before Him all our days (Luke 1.68-74).

Zachariah's praise of God confirmed God's covenants and the promise to be freed from Gentile powers. Notice the nature of salvation of which Zachariah spoke: "salvation from our enemies and from all who hate us," "to be rescued from the hand of our enemies." This was the hope of godly Jews—freedom from the oppression of Gentile powers. His speech was no misguided Jewish hope. The text takes pains to note that Zechariah spoke under the power of the Holy Spirit (Luke 1.67).

God had promised Simeon he would live to see the Messiah (Luke 2.25-26). When Joseph and Mary brought their baby to the Temple, Simeon took the child in his arms and blessed Him saying:

> [29] Now Lord, You are releasing Your bond-servant to depart in peace, according to Your word; [30] For my eyes have seen Your salvation, [31] which You have prepared in

> the presence of all peoples, [32] A Light of revelation to the Gentiles and the glory of Your people Israel (Luke 2.29-32).

This declaration expressed the prophetic hope of the Abrahamic Covenant. God promised He would bless Gentiles through Israel (Isaiah 42.5-7, 49.6-7, 60.1-3).

While Simeon was speaking, Anna the prophetess also prophesied:

> At that very moment, she came up and began giving thanks to God, and continued to speak of Him to all those who were looking for the redemption of Jerusalem (Luke 2.38).

The key point to understand from all these prophecies is that they confirmed God's covenants and the words of the prophets. Israel was the favored nation. God had promised He would exalt them and when this occurred they would become a channel of blessing to Gentiles.

As noted above, the Gospels are Jewish. John the Baptist only addressed Jews and Jesus and the Twelve only ministered to Jews (apart from a few exceptions). Jesus explicitly stated His ministry was to Jews. Matthew wrote:

> [5] These twelve Jesus sent out after instructing them: Do not go in *the* way of *the* Gentiles, and do not enter any city of the Samaritans; [6] but rather go to the lost sheep of the house of Israel (Matthew 10.5-6).

These commands were clear. The disciples were not to go to Gentiles or Samaritans. When Jesus went to Tyre and Sidon, He did not go to minister to Gentiles, but to minister to Jews lived there.[49] Matthew's account of the Lord's encounter with the Canaanite

---

[49] The Gospels record Jesus went to areas of Israel inhabited by Gentiles. God had given this land to the twelve tribes but due to the invasions of the Babylonians, Medes, Persians, Greeks, and Romans, Gentiles resided in them along with Jews. For example, Decapolis (Ten Cities), was the land occupied by Manasseh and Gad.

woman reveals this fact clearly (Matthew 15.21-28). The Canaanite woman kept following and calling to Jesus. He refused to acknowledge her. Why? She was a Gentile. Annoyed by her persistence, His disciples begged Him to send her away. Why? They understood the Lord's words that their ministry was to Jews. Finally, the Lord spoke to her and said:

> I am not sent but unto the lost sheep of the house of Israel (Matthew 15.24).

In today's vernacular, Jesus said, "Look lady, you are a Gentile. My ministry is to Jews. Understand?" Undaunted by His slight, she bowed before Him and continued her appeal. Again, the Lord rebuffed her:

> It is not meet to take the children's bread, and to cast it to dogs (Matthew 15.26).

Despite the Lord's blunt, discouraging reply, she persisted. What a woman! Finally, the Lord commended her faith and granted her request. If He was in the habit of ministering to Gentiles, why was He resistant? The obvious explanation is He meant exactly what He said—His ministry was to Jews, not Gentiles. According to prophecy, Gentiles would be blessed *through* Israel, but national Israel had the priority of God's blessings based on the Abrahamic Covenant. Paul confirmed this truth in his letter to the Romans and wrote:

> [8] Now I say that Jesus Christ was a minister of the circumcision for the truth of God, to confirm the promises made unto the fathers: [9] And that the Gentiles might glorify God for his mercy; as it is written, For this cause I will confess to you among the Gentiles, and sing unto thy name (Romans 15.8-9).

Jesus knew the Scriptures. He ministered to Jews according to the Abrahamic Covenant and the prophecies. He healed the Canaanite woman's daughter, the Roman centurion's servant (Matthew 8.5-3; Luke 7.1-10), and some Gentiles after the Pharisees met to determine how to kill Him (Matthew 12.14-21). But these were *exceptions* which prefigured Jewish blessings of Gentiles and God's promise to the Son to inherit the nations in the kingdom (Psalm 2.8).

Salvation in the Gospels

Like salvation in the Old Testament, determining exactly how men and women were saved in the Gospels is difficult. But one thing is beyond doubt: salvation required faith *and* works. Several passages reveal this fact. The Gospel of Mark recorded this account of a Jew who approached Jesus regarding salvation (cf. Matthew 19.16-26; Luke 10.25-36, 18.18-30):[50]

> As He was setting out on a journey, a man ran up to Him and knelt before Him, and asked Him, Good Teacher, what shall I do to inherit eternal life (Mark 10.17)?

The man's question was straightforward: "How do I obtain eternal life?" What did the Lord tell him?

> 18 And Jesus said to him, Why do you call Me good? No one is good except God alone. 19 You know the commandments, Do not murder, Do not commit adultery, Do not steal, Do not bear false witness, Do not defraud, Honor your father and mother (Mark 10.18-19).

The man responded:

> And he said to Him, Teacher, I have kept all these things from my youth up (Mark 10.20).

To this, Jesus replied:

> Looking at him, Jesus felt a love for him and said to him, One thing you lack: go and sell all you possess and

---

[50] It is significant these accounts are given in Matthew, Mark, and Luke and that Luke included two separate accounts. God has made it abundantly clear salvation required works.

> give to the poor, and you will have treasure in heaven; and come, follow Me (Mark 10.21).

Jesus told the man that to obtain eternal life required keeping the commandments (cf. Matthew 19.17). After the man answered he had kept them, Jesus told him to do another work: sell his possessions, give them to the poor, and follow Him. Jesus taught salvation by works.

Did Jesus teach salvation by faith? Consider the following passage:

> 17 One day He was teaching; and there were Pharisees and
> teachers of the law sitting, who had come from every
> village of Galilee and Judea and Jerusalem; and the power
> of the Lord was present for Him to perform healing. 18 And
> some men were carrying on a bed a man who was
> paralyzed; and they were trying to bring him in and to set
> him down in front of Him. 19 But not finding any way to
> bring him in because of the crowd, they went up on the roof
> and let him down through the tiles with his stretcher, into
> the middle of the crowd, in front of Jesus. 20 Seeing their
> faith, He said, Friend, your sins are forgiven you (Luke
> 5.17-20).

Jesus saw the faith of the men and forgave the man's sins. Like the accounts examined above, this account is also repeated in the Gospels of Matthew Mark, and Luke.[51] Did Jesus teach salvation by faith? Yes, He did.

What are we to make of these passages? Did Jesus teach contradictory things? The unequivocal answer is that in the Jewish economy of the Mosaic Law and specifically, under the gospel of the kingdom, salvation required faith *and* works. They were inextricably joined.

Other passages demonstrate that in addition to faith and keeping the Mosaic Law, water baptism and forgiving another person's sins

---

[51] See Matthew 9.2-7; Mark 2.1-12, and Luke 5.17-26.

were required for salvation. With regard to water baptism, consider the following passages:

> John did baptize in the wilderness, and preach the baptism of repentance for the remission of sins (Mark 1.4).
>
> He who has believed and has been baptized shall be saved; but he who has disbelieved shall be condemned (Mark 16.16).
>
> [4] Nicodemus said to Him, How can a man be born when he is old? He cannot enter a second time into his mother's womb and be born, can he? [5] Jesus answered, Truly, truly, I say to you, unless one is born of water and the Spirit he cannot enter into the kingdom of God (John 3.4-5).
>
> [37] Now when they heard *this*, they were pierced to the heart, and said to Peter and the rest of the apostles, Brethren, what shall we do? [38] Peter *said* to them, Repent, and each of you be baptized in the name of Jesus Christ for the forgiveness of your sins; and you will receive the gift of the Holy Spirit (Acts 2.37-38).
>
> Now why do you delay? Get up and be baptized, and wash away your sins, calling on His name (Acts 22.16).

If words mean anything, these passages declare that water baptism was *required* for salvation under the gospel of the kingdom. Notice also that water baptism was not said to be a sign or a testimony of belief as some teach. The plain words of Scripture are that water baptism was required as a condition of salvation.[52]

As for forgiving sins as a condition of salvation, consider the Lord's words in the familiar passage known as the Lord's Prayer:

> [9] Pray, then, in this way: Our Father who is in heaven, hallowed be Your name. [10] Your kingdom come. Your will

---

[52] God can make exceptions. The thief on the cross believed Jesus was the Messiah but obviously could not be baptized (Luke 23.40-43).

> be done, on earth as it is in heaven. [11] Give us this day our daily bread. [12] And forgive us our debts, as we also have forgiven our debtors. [13] And do not lead us into temptation, but deliver us from evil. For Yours is the kingdom and the power and the glory forever. Amen. [14] For if you forgive others for their transgressions, your heavenly Father will also forgive you. [15] But if you do not forgive others, then your Father will not forgive your transgressions (Matthew 6.9-15).

Could words be clearer? The Lord taught one could not receive God's forgiveness unless one forgave others.[53] These passages should convince anyone that the gospel of the kingdom *required* both faith and works for salvation.

Faith in the Gospel of the Kingdom

Faith and works were necessary for salvation under the gospel of the kingdom. Works included keeping the Law, water baptism, and forgiving others. What was the content of faith? What was one to believe for salvation? The Scriptures provide a clear answer to this question. Faith under the gospel of the kingdom was to believe who Jesus was—that He was the Messiah, the Son of God. Consider the following passages:

> [13] Now when Jesus came into the district of Caesarea Philippi, He was asking His disciples, Who do people say that the Son of Man is? [14] And they said, Some say John the Baptist; and others, Elijah; but still others, Jeremiah, or one of the prophets. [15] He said to them, But who do you say that I am? [16] Simon Peter answered, You are the Christ, the Son of the living God. [17] And Jesus said to him, Blessed are you, Simon Barjona, because flesh and blood did not

---

[53] Paul wrote we should forgive one another because Christ *has forgiven* us (Ephesians 4.32). This is *vastly* different from what the Lord declared in Matthew 6.

> reveal this to you, but My Father who is in heaven (Matthew 16.13-17).

Peter believed in the *identity* of Christ: He was the Messiah, the Son of God. That was the content of faith for salvation under the gospel of the kingdom. Expressed another way, believing in the identity of Christ meant believing in His *name*. Thus, John wrote:

> [16] For God so loved the world, that he gave his only begotten Son, that whosoever believes in him should not perish, but have everlasting life. [17] For God sent not his Son into the world to condemn the world; but that the world through him might be saved. [18] He that believes on him is not condemned: but he that believes not is condemned already, because he has not believed in the name of the only begotten Son of God (John 3.16-18).

John's words "believes in him," "believed in the name" meant believing who Jesus was—He was the Messiah, the Son of God. This was the nature of faith of the gospel of the kingdom found throughout the Gospels and Acts. Luke made this point throughout Acts (Acts 2.21, 38, 3.6, 16, 4.7, 10, 12, 17, 18, 30, 5.28, 40, 41, 8.12, 16, 9.14, 15, 21, 27, 10.43, 48).

Other passages reveal this fact also. When Jesus met Nathaniel, what did Nathaniel declare? John wrote:

> [45] Philip found Nathanael, and said unto him, We have found him, of whom Moses in the law, and the prophets, did write, Jesus of Nazareth, the son of Joseph. [46] And Nathanael said unto him, Can any good thing come out of Nazareth? Philip said unto him, Come and see. [47] Jesus saw Nathanael coming to him, and said of him, Behold an Israelite indeed, in whom is no guile! [48] Nathanael said unto him, How do you know me? Jesus answered and said unto him, Before Philip called you, when you were under the fig tree, I saw you. [49] Nathanael answered and said unto him, Rabbi, you are the Son of God; you are the King of Israel. [50] Jesus answered and said unto him, Because I said unto

> you, I saw you under the fig tree, you believe? You shalt see greater things than these. [51] And he said unto him, Verily, verily, I say unto you, Hereafter you shall see heaven open, and the angels of God ascending and descending upon the Son of man (John 1.45-51).

Nathaniel believed in the *identity* of Christ: He was the Son of God, Israel's King.

John also wrote about the occasion of Jesus' friend Lazarus who died (John 11.5). Martha expressed her distress to Jesus when He arrived and told Him had He been there, her brother would not have died and that God would give Him whatever He asked (John 11.21-21). John recorded their conversation:

> [23] Jesus said to her, Your brother will rise again. [24] Martha said to Him, I know that he will rise again in the resurrection on the last day. [25] Jesus said to her, I am the resurrection and the life; he who believes in Me will live even if he dies, [26] and everyone who lives and believes in Me will never die. Do you believe this? [27] She said to Him, Yes, Lord; I have believed that You are the Christ, the Son of God, even He who comes into the world (John 11.23-27).

What did Martha believe? She believed in the *identity* of Christ: He was the Messiah, the Son of God. That was what constituted saving faith.

The book of Acts reveals the same thing regarding the salvation of Saul of Tarsus. Luke wrote:

> [3] As he was traveling, it happened that he was approaching Damascus, and suddenly a light from heaven flashed around him; [4] and he fell to the ground and heard a voice saying to him, Saul, Saul, why are you persecuting Me? [5] And he said, Who are You, Lord? And He said, I am Jesus whom you are persecuting, [6] but get up and enter the city, and it will be told you what you must do (Acts 9.3-6).

Saul asked who was speaking with him. The Lord told him He was Jesus. Saul believed in the *identity* of Christ: He was the Messiah, the Son of God. That was his salvation. This was the message Saul preached to the Jews following his salvation:

> [19] Now for several days he was with the disciples who were at Damascus, [20] and immediately he began to proclaim Jesus in the synagogues, saying, He is the Son of God (Acts 9.19-20).

In the gospel of the kingdom, believing in Jesus (John 3.16-18) meant believing in His *name*. His *name* conveyed His *identity*, that He was the Messiah, the Son of God.

John's first epistle reveals the same thing. John wrote to Jewish believers:

> Whosoever believes that Jesus is the Christ is born of God: and every one that loves him that begat loves him also that is begotten of him (1 John 5.1).

A few verses later, we read the following:

> [4] For whatsoever is born of God overcomes the world: and this is the victory that has overcome the world, even our faith. [5] Who is he that overcomes the world, but he that believes that Jesus is the Son of God (1 John 5.4-5)?
>
> The one who believes in the Son of God has the testimony in himself; the one who does not believe God has made Him a liar, because he has not believed in the testimony that God has given concerning His Son (1 John 5.10).
>
> These things I have written to you who believe in the name of the Son of God, so that you may know that you have eternal life (1 John 5.13).

These words agree with John's Gospel: faith under the gospel of the kingdom was to believe in the name of Christ, in His identity, that He was the Messiah, the Son of God. John never mentions the cross, Christ's shed blood, or His resurrection as part of belief for salvation.[54] Christ's death and resurrection for the forgiveness of sins were not part of the gospel of the kingdom.

A point should be noted regarding John's words in 1 John 5.4-5. John wrote one who is born of God and believes Jesus is the Son of God is one who "overcomes the world." This is not the language of the Church, the body of Christ. John's language of "overcoming" (νικάω) was the language of Jews who believed the gospel of the kingdom. The challenge to faith in the age of the Beast will be to believe the Antichrist is the Messiah and worship him (Revelation 13). Those who are faithful to Christ will "overcome" the Antichrist.[55] This was what Jesus spoke about in His warnings in Revelation 2-3. In John's Gospel, Jesus warned the Jews of this temptation:

> I am come in my Father's name, and you receive me not: if another shall come in his own name, him you will receive (John 5.43).

Peter told the Jews on the day of Pentecost to be baptized in the *name* of Jesus Christ for the forgiveness of sins:

> Peter *said* to them, Repent, and each of you be baptized in the name of Jesus Christ for the forgiveness of your sins; and you will receive the gift of the Holy Spirit (Acts 2.38).

Peter did not tell the Jews that Jesus died for their sins and had risen for their justification. He did not know this truth. Why should he? God had not revealed it. God had only revealed the gospel of the

---

[54] Almost all commentators maintain John's gospel, letters, and the book of Revelation were written after A.D. 90. John's message of salvation militates against a late date. It fits more favorably between A.D. 50-60.

[55] The attentive student will note the following verses: 1 John 2.13-14, 4.4, 5.4-5; Revelation 2.7, 11, 17, 26, 3.5, 12, 21, 5.5, 6.2, 11.7, 12.11, 13.7, 15.2, 17.14, 21.7. John expected the Beast, the Antichrist, to appear soon and challenge the faith of those who had believed in Jesus' name, that He was the Christ, the Son of God.

kingdom which required repentance, keeping the commandments, forgiving other's sins, water baptism, and believing Jesus was the Messiah, the Son of God. Many verses confirm this truth: John 3.18; Acts 3.6, 16, 4.7, 10, 12,17-18, 30, 5.28, 40-41, 8.12, 16, 9.14-15, 21, 27, 10.43, 48, 19.5, 22.16, 26.9.

What if Israel Had Repented?

If the Jews had repented, would Jesus have been crucified? Christ's death had to occur. God had revealed this fact (Genesis 3.15; Isaiah 53) and the animal sacrifices all pointed to this goal. Christ's death was the only way to solve mankind's problem of sin and death. The Scriptures revealed a collusion of Jews and Gentiles against the Messiah (Psalm 2.1-3) but what was not revealed was who would lead this opposition. The Jews chose to take the lead. Had they not, the Romans would have assumed that role. Jesus' kingship would have threatened Caesar and the power of Rome.

The Great Commission

Christendom has become obsessed with and confused by the idea the Church's "Great Commission" is in Matthew 28.18-20 and that the Church's main effort is to fulfill this commission. Several problems attend this view. One is that the Church did not exist when Jesus spoke these words to the Eleven. Another is the Lord commanded them to teach the things He had taught them. This meant keeping the Mosaic Law since He ministered under it and obeyed it. But Paul wrote that members of the Church, the body of Christ, are not under the governance of the Mosaic Law but under grace (Romans 6.14). Yet another problem is Christ's statement about baptism. Under the gospel of the kingdom, water baptism was required for salvation. But Paul wrote, "For Christ sent me not to baptize, but to preach the gospel: not with wisdom of words, lest the cross of Christ should be made of none effect (1 Corinthians 1.17). The Church's gospel is that Christ died for our sins and rose from the dead and that by believing this one is saved. Baptism is not part of this gospel.

The "Great Commission" of Matthew 28 has nothing to do with the Church, the body of Christ. It was part of Israel's prophetic program and anticipated Jewish repentance and the fulfillment of God's covenant promises to Israel. Once Israel repented, Gentiles would be evangelized. This is why the Lord stated the order of ministry would be Jerusalem, Judaea, Samaria, and the uttermost part of the earth (Acts 1.8). When Israel refused to repent, the "Great Commission" could not be fulfilled because the nation could not fulfill its destiny as a kingdom of priests and a blessing to Gentiles.

In the next section, The Church, we will examine what God did in response to Israel's failure to repent and how God was able to bless Gentiles in spite of Israel's disobedience. We will also discover what the Church's "Great Commission" is and that it is greater and more glorious than what the Lord gave the Eleven.

Salvation of Gentiles

Few examples of the salvation of Gentiles are found during God's program with Israel. From the beginning of God's call of Abraham, God kept His covenant people detached from the Gentile world. This separation became formalized with the giving of the Mosaic Law. Israel's laws served to keep them distinct from the surrounding nations. For example, the Law forbade sowing vineyards with different seeds, plowing with an ox and donkey together, wearing clothing of mixed linens, or having clothing with fringes (Deuteronomy 22.9-12). The dietary laws forbade eating pork and any fish or sea creature without scales. God gave these odd laws to make the Jewish people different from the Gentiles and to remind them of this fact.

As part of this separation, God did not tell the Jews to evangelize the surrounding nations. Despite this, some Gentiles were saved. After Israel escaped Egypt, Rahab the prostitute hid the Jewish spies and became a believer in the God of Israel (Joshua 2.9-13). Ruth left her own people, went with Naomi, became a believer in the Lord, and married Boaz, the great-grandfather of King David. Naaman, the Syrian general, believed in the God of Israel after he was cured of his leprosy by washing in the Jordan River.

Nebuchadnezzar believed in the Most High after God removed and restored his sanity and his kingdom. And the greatest evangelism event in history occurred with the reluctant Jonah, whom God sent to the Assyrian city of Nineveh. In spite of Jonah's resistance, everyone from the king to the street-sweeper was saved. All these were examples of God's grace. Yet they were exceptions. Few Gentiles came to know the Lord.

Usually, when Israel intermixed with Gentiles, it was to their detriment. They began to worship the gods of the Gentiles and abandoned the Lord for idols. To bring them back to Himself, God brought Gentile powers against them militarily. The reason why the Lord or His disciples had no ministry to Gentiles was because that had been the program for 2,000 years. As few Gentiles were saved in those 2,000 years, few were saved in the Lord's ministry. They were *exceptions*. And, as we saw in Chapter 1, the nations, except Israel, are under the operational control of Satan. God had declared:

> For you are a holy people unto the LORD your God, and the LORD has chosen you to be a peculiar people unto himself, above all the nations that are upon the earth (Deuteronomy 14.2).

Summary of God's Program for Israel

God's program for Israel began with the Abrahamic Covenant and was built upon His covenant promises and the revelations He had given through His prophets. The main subjects of His revelation were that He would judge Israel and the nations in His wrath, the Day of the Lord, and establish His kingdom on the earth. When Jesus arrived, these two events were near to being accomplished. Had the Jews repented, God would have initiated the Day of the Lord and returned to establish His kingdom on earth. God would have fulfilled His covenant promises to Israel and they would have served as a kingdom of priests to bless the nations.

Chapter 3

The Church: Program Three

Let a man so account of us, as of the ministers of Christ, and stewards of the secrets of God (1 Corinthians 4.1).

Wherefore henceforth know we no man after the flesh: yea, though we have known Christ after the flesh, yet now henceforth know we him no more (2 Corinthians 5.16).

God's third program is the Church, the body of Christ. The key to this program is to understand Paul's "secrets" (μυστήριον).[1] Like Poe's letter,[2] for most of Christendom, Paul's secrets reside in plain sight unperceived. They constitute revelations the risen Lord gave Paul that He had not revealed in the Old Testament and Gospels. They were new revelations. Most of Christendom is ignorant of this great fact. As a result, it has an unsound understanding of Church theology. The reader may think I am overstating the case. I am not.

By the time Paul came onto the stage, God had dealt with the human race for 4,000 years. Throughout this time, He had revealed nothing about the Church. Israel's covenants contained no revelation about the Church nor had God disclosed anything through His prophets concerning the Church. And Jesus had revealed nothing of the Church in His earthly ministry. God had revealed Gentiles would be blessed through Israel. But that He would create a new body

---

[1] The word μυστήριον means a secret, a truth previously unknown and unrevealed. For 2,000 years, God had kept secret that He would cease dealing with all mankind and choose a man, make a covenant with Him, and create a new race through whom He would bless the world. God reserves the right to keep secrets and reveals them when He wishes.

[2] Poe, Edgar A., "The Purloined Letter" 1844.

composed of Jew and Gentile equal in Christ was unknown. It was a divine secret.

God's secret of the Church remained hidden until He revealed it to Paul. Paul wrote the Corinthians that the risen Christ gave him several revelations (2 Corinthians 12.1, 7). Undoubtedly, Paul received much of what the Lord would reveal to him in the three years following his salvation while he was in Arabia and Damascus (Galatians 1.15-18). Concerning these revelations, Paul wrote the Corinthians:

> [6] For though I would desire to glory, I shall not be a fool; for I will say the truth: but now I forbear, lest any man should think of me above that which he sees me to be, or that he hears of me.[7] And lest I should be exalted above measure through the abundance of the revelations, there was given to me a thorn in the flesh, the messenger of Satan to buffet me, lest I should be exalted above measure (2 Corinthians 2.6-7).

Later in the letter, Paul declared:

> It is not expedient for me doubtless to glory. I will come to visions and revelations of the Lord (2 Corinthians 12.1).

These new revelations, these secrets, were the vehicles through which God revealed the Church, the body of Christ, salvation by faith alone, the believer's identification with Christ, how believers are to live the Christian life, and what Israel's future was in light of the nation's rejection of their Messiah. These secrets are to the Church what God's covenants were to Israel. Unless one understands these secrets, one cannot understand Church theology.[3]

---

[3] Most of Christendom is unaware of Paul's secrets and misunderstands his apostleship. Paul is viewed merely as an addition and extension of the Twelve rather than God's apostle who began a new theological program. As long as this view exists, the Church will remain confused.

In the Preface, I noted that failure to recognize, understand, and differentiate God's programs has resulted in vast confusion in Christendom. The heart of this error has been the failure to understand Paul's ministry and his theology—Paul's secrets. This problem began in Paul's lifetime and has continued for over 1,900 years. Paul wrote Timothy shortly before his execution: "This you know, that all they which are in Asia be turned away from me; of whom are Phygellus and Hermogenes" (2 Timothy 1.15). The churches of Asia Minor—Ephesus, Colossae, Galatia, Iconium, Derbe, Lystra, Antioch Pisidia, Laodicea—all these churches abandoned Paul's teachings.

How did they abandon Paul? Early Church history provides numerous examples. For example, the first line of the *Didache* is telling.[4] It reads, "The teaching of the Lord to the Gentiles (or Nations) by the twelve apostles." This statement is stunning to anyone who has read the New Testament. The Twelve *had no ministry to Gentiles*. Not one word in Scripture supports the idea the Twelve ministered to Gentiles—ever. But here we find, at about 100 A.D., this glaring falshood. The *Didache* is proof how the apostasy that began in Paul's lifetime continued in the early church and continues today.

The *Didache* does not mention Christ's death on the cross for our sins, His resurrection, or salvation by faith alone. It contains nothing of Paul's great teachings about the Church, the body of Christ, the truths Paul taught about the believer's relationship to Christ and his identification with Christ. It contains no mention of Paul's watchwords—faith, hope, love. It says nothing about the Holy Spirit or Paul's "secrets." In short, the *Didache* contains *nothing* of Paul. It focuses on Christ's earthly ministry to Israel under the Mosaic Law and the teaching of the Twelve to Jewish believers. It is an example of the teaching of those whom Paul

---

[4] The *Didache,* "Teaching" was one of the earliest writings (c. 100 A.D.) of the Apostolic Fathers. Its language is wholly Jewish and devoid of Pauline teaching and Church theology. The *Didache* reflects the teaching of those Paul described as "fallen from grace" (Galatians 5.4) and is the earliest extra-Biblical example of Church heresy.

battled throughout his ministry and demonstrates how Church doctrine became corrupted in its earliest years and why Christendom remains confused to this day.

Paul's letters reveal the nature of his fight with false teachers and false doctrine. His letter to the Galatians gives a detailed account of the conflict. False teachers were telling the Galatians believers (mostly Gentiles but with some Jews) that the Christian life was to be governed by the Mosaic Law. But Paul had taught them they were not under the administration of the Mosaic Law but under the administration of grace (Romans 6.14; Galatians 5.1). Paul taught the Christian life was to be lived by faith through love in the power of the Holy Spirit, not by the Mosaic Law. Despite Paul's great effort, he failed. The Galatians and all of Asia abandoned their freedom in Christ and placed themselves under the bondage of the Law. The Church has never freed itself from this error.

Preface to Program Three: The Book of Acts

The book of Acts is a transitional book, a bridge between the Gospels and Paul's letters.[5] Luke had two primary purposes in writing Acts. One was to reveal to Jews why the kingdom of God did not come on earth. The other was to reveal how and why God saved Saul of Tarsus to establish His new program: the Church, the body of Christ.

The way Luke structured Acts and repeated key events revealed these purposes. The first part of Acts deals with Peter and the Twelve and the seven chosen deacons (Acts 6.3), particularly Philip and Stephen. After Acts 9, the first account of Paul's salvation, the emphasis begins to shift to Paul. After Acts 15, Peter, the Twelve, and the deacons disappear.[6]

---

[5] Luke, the physician, was Paul's constant companion. He traveled with Paul on his missionary journeys and was with him right before his death (2 Timothy 4.11). Paul needed a personal physician present with him due to his great sufferings (2 Corinthians 11-12).

[6] Peter, James, John, and Jude's letters provide little information about their ministry. In Acts 21, Paul met with James when he came to

Key events in Acts are found in repetitions of threes. When God states something, we should take notice. If He repeats it three times, it should concentrate our minds.

Repetition of Threes	Passage	Result
Rejections of the King by the Jews Under the Twelve's Ministry	Acts 4.5-31	Threat
	Acts 5.12-42	Imprisonment
	Acts 7.1-60	Execution
Rejections of the King by the Jews Under Paul's Ministry	Acts 13.44-52	Expelled, turns to Gentiles
	Acts 18.1-7	Opposed, turns to Gentiles
	Acts 28.17-29	Opposed, turns to Gentiles
Accounts of Paul's Salvation	Acts 9.1-16	Initial account
	Acts 22.1-21	To Jews in Jerusalem
	Acts 26.1-32	To Agrippa, in Caesarea
Paul's Defense Before Gentile Rulers	Acts 24.1-27	To Felix, in Caesarea
	Acts 25.1-12	To Festus, in Caesarea
	Acts 25.13-32	To Agrippa and Bernice, in Caesarea

Luke's record in Acts documented Jewish rejection of Christ and the offer of the kingdom of God. The first three rejections dealt with the ministry of Peter and the Jerusalem assembly. The Jews rejected their appeal to repent and accept Jesus as the Messiah so He could return and establish His kingdom. After the Sanhedrin had stoned Stephen (Acts 7), God saved Saul and commissioned him to be "the apostle of the Gentiles" (Romans 11.13; 2 Timothy 1.11). The

---

Jerusalem. James was not a member of the Twelve but the Lord's half-brother who believed in Christ after His resurrection. Acts 15 reveals he had supplanted Peter as the leader of the Jerusalem believers and that his focus was upon the Mosaic Law (Acts 21.17-20).

remaining record deals with Paul's ministry and shows how Paul's appeals to the Jews also failed. Luke's account of Paul's ministry ends in about 60 A.D. with his imprisonment in Rome. There, Paul made his last appeal to the Jews. The pattern is clear: Paul first went to Jews. When they rejected his message, he turned to Gentiles (cf. Romans 1.16-17).

The threefold record of Paul's conversion draws attention to God's commission of Paul to become the apostle of a new divine program. Paul was *not* a 13th apostle, an extension of the Twelve. He was the apostle of a *whole new order*: He was God's apostle of the grace of God—the Apostle of the Gentiles. Unless one understands this truth, Church theology is impossible to comprehend.

Paul's Conversion

The gospel of the kingdom, the good news the kingdom of God was near, began with John the Baptist's preaching (Matthew 3.1-2). Instead of responding to the gospel of the kingdom, the Jews rejected John and crucified the Messiah. Peter's messages on the day of Pentecost (Acts 2) and at the Temple after the Lord's resurrection (Acts 3) gave the Jewish nation more opportunities to repent. Peter told them if they would, God would send His Son and establish His kingdom on earth (Acts 3.19-20). They refused.

A few chapters later in Acts, Luke recorded how Stephen, one of the deacons of the believers in Jerusalem (Acts 6.1-6), defended himself before the Sanhedrin against the charge of teaching against the Temple and the Law (Acts 6.8-15). Stephen brilliantly summarized Jewish history, turned the tables on them, and placed the Council on trial, accusing them of unbelief. He told them that as their fathers had rejected and killed the prophets, they had rejected and killed the Messiah (Acts 7.51-53). At the end of his address, he declared he saw Jesus standing at the right hand of God (Acts 7.56).[7] Stephen's trial was the crisis point for the Jewish

---

[7] Psalm 110.1 states the Messiah will sit at the Father's right hand until His enemies became His footstool (cf. Matthew 22.44; Mark 12.36; Luke 20.42). Several passages declare Christ is now *seated* at God's right hand (Acts 2.34; Colossians 3.1; Hebrews 1.3, 12, 8.1, 10.12,

nation. The Council represented the nation and when they stoned Stephen, they sealed the nation's fate.[8] No national repentance would take place. Even with indisputable evidence the Messiah had risen from the dead, they refused to believe.[9]

Acts 7 ends with an introduction of Saul of Tarsus (Acts 7.58). Saul was so inflamed against those who were believing Jesus of Nazareth was the promised Messiah that he exercised all his religious zeal to destroy followers of "the way."[10] Traveling to Damascus to extend his persecution beyond the borders of Israel, he met the ascended, glorified Lord on the road near the city. He was never the same. The risen Lord transformed Saul of Tarsus from being His greatest enemy to the Apostle Paul, His most devoted servant and advocate.

The most logical thing for Paul to have done after his conversion would have been to meet with the Twelve and learn about the Lord from them. That did not happen. God kept Saul separated from them throughout his ministry.[11] Paul gave this account to the Galatians:

12.2). But Stephen said he saw Him *standing*. When the Council heard this, they became enraged. They understood Stephen was saying the Messiah had arisen (קוּם) and was about to return and judge His enemies—them (cf. Psalm 3.7, 7.6, 10.12, 17.13, 68.1, 82.8).

[8] God the Father commissioned John the Baptist. The Jew's rejection of his message was a sin against the Father. They sinned against the Son, crucifying Him. The third rejection, represented by Stephen, constituted the sin against the Holy Spirit (Matthew 12.31). The only unforgivable sin today is to reject Paul's gospel: faith alone in the work of Christ: He died for our sins and rose from the dead (1 Corinthians 15.1-4).

[9] Jesus predicted this in Luke 16.31.

[10] Believers in the Messiah were not called Christians at this stage. They were known as followers of "the way" (Acts 9.2, 19.9, 23, 22.4, 24.14, 22). The term "Christian" began as a term describing mainly Gentiles who believed Paul's gospel. It was first used in Antioch, Syria, outside the borders of Israel (Acts 11.26).

[11] Paul's contact with any of the Twelve was rare and limited.

> [15] But when God, who had set me apart even from my mother's womb and called me through His grace, was pleased [16] to reveal His Son in me so that I might preach Him among the Gentiles, I did not immediately consult with flesh and blood, [17] nor did I go up to Jerusalem to those who were apostles before me; but I went away to Arabia, and returned once more to Damascus. [18] Then three years later I went up to Jerusalem to become acquainted with Cephas, and stayed with him fifteen days. [19] But I did not see any other of the apostles except James, the Lord's brother.

Paul stayed with Peter a couple weeks and saw only James, the half-brother of Jesus. That was the extent of his early association with the Twelve.

Why Paul?

The question, "Why Paul?" is the *most critical question* in New Testament studies. Answer it correctly and the entire Bible aligns properly. Answer it incorrectly and error and confusion are the result—the existing state of Christendom.

Why did God save Paul? The nature of this question is not one of personal salvation—God wishes all to be saved (1 Timothy 2.4)—but a question of ministry. God had twelve apostles to proclaim the gospel. Why did He need a thirteenth? He didn't. God did not need another apostle to proclaim the gospel of the kingdom. The Twelve were adequate to this task. The Lord had taught and trained them for three years, given them the Holy Spirit, and told them they would rule the twelve tribes of Israel (Matthew 19.28). He did not need Paul to help them.

What God did need was an apostle to begin a new program in light of Israel's rejection of the Messiah. Instead of initiating the Day of the Lord, the next event of the prophetic program, God chose to deal with Gentiles in mercy and grace. Israel had refused to accept its Messiah and could not fulfill its role as God's channel of blessings to Gentiles. But God, being rich in mercy, determined to save Gentiles in spite of Israel's failure.[12] That was the significance of Paul's conversion. Paul wrote the Lord had set him apart from his mother's womb (ὁ ἀφορίσας με ἐκ κοιλίας μητρός μου). Truly, God's ways are past finding out. He is the Master of the unexpected.

In Program One, Mankind, Adam was the key figure. He represented all mankind and during this program, God dealt with the entire human race. In Program Two, Israel, Abraham was the key figure. Through Abraham, God created a new, covenant people to bless all mankind. In Program Three, the Church, God saved Paul to become the key figure and revelator of the Church, the body of Christ.

Paul wrote in 1 Corinthians 10.32, "Give no offense, either to the Jews or to the Greeks or to the church of God." Before Paul, the human race was composed of Jew and Gentile. After Paul's commission, God created the Church, the body of Christ. The human race is now composed of Jew, Gentile, and Church. When one believes Paul's gospel (1 Corinthians 15.1-4), he is no longer Jew or Gentile. He is "Church"—a member of the body of Christ—a new creation. Paul expressed this truth in his letter to the Galatians:

> [27] For as many of you as have been baptized into Christ have put on Christ. [28] There is neither Jew nor Greek, there is neither bond nor free, there is neither male nor female: for you are all one in Christ Jesus (Galatians 3.27-28).

Thus, God laid the foundation for a whole new program with Paul. It was not based upon *promise* like God's program with Israel, but upon *grace*. As the program God began with Abraham operated under different rules from those He gave mankind beginning with Adam, the Church operates under different rules from those God gave Israel.

---

[12] God knew they would fail but they had a choice (Matthew 23.37-39).

Key Figures	God's Programs
Adam	Mankind
Abraham	Israel
Paul	Church
Jesus the Messiah-King	Kingdom
God the Father	Eternity

A New Program

Paul wrote the Corinthians in his second letter:

> [16] So then, we now know no one according to the flesh: if we have known Christ after the flesh, but now we know him no longer. [17] Therefore if anyone is in Christ, a new creation: old things are passed away; behold, new things have come into existence (2 Corinthians 5.16-17).

In verse 16, Paul stated, "we now know no one according to the flesh." Many have supposed Paul meant we now no longer know one another in a carnal, unspiritual way. While that may be true, that was not what Paul had in mind. Paul's point was that believers now know one another as members of the Church, the body of Christ. In this new relationship, one is no longer Jew or Gentile but "Church"— members of His body. This is made clear in verse 17, in which Paul stated: "if anyone is in Christ: a new creation." Unfortunately, translators have added "he is" to the text. But the text simply reads, "new creation" (εἴ τις ἐν Χριστῷ καινὴ κτίσις). This "new creation" was the Church, the body of Christ. The "new things have come into existence" are the things concerning our relationship with and identity in Christ and the truths Paul called "secrets." Paul wrote similarly to the Galatians: "For in Christ Jesus neither circumcision avails anything, nor uncircumcision, but a new creation (καινὴ κτίσις, Galatians 6.15). The "new creation" is the Church, the body of Christ.

What are we to make of Paul's statement in verse 16, "if we have known Christ after the flesh, but now we know him no longer" (εἰ καὶ ἐγνώκαμεν κατὰ σάρκα Χριστόν, ἀλλὰ νῦν οὐκέτι γινώσκομεν)? The first verb, ἐγνώκαμεν, is a perfect active indicative of γινώσκω, "we have known" and the second, γινώσκομεν, is a present active indicative, "we now know." The meaning is that Christ may have been known in the flesh, but He is now no longer to be known this way. What did he mean by "after the flesh?" The most reasonable meaning of "after the flesh" is Christ's earthly ministry.

Jesus set aside His power and glory in His earthly ministry (Philippians 2.6-8). He allowed Himself to be mocked, beaten, and crucified. In His earthly ministry, He became weak. This was necessary to accomplish His work of man's salvation. His resurrection changed all that. His resurrection revealed the power of God (Romans 1.4). The Church came into existence not in Christ's earthly ministry but in His heavenly ministry. The glorified, heavenly, resurrected Christ appeared to Paul and commissioned him as the Apostle of the Gentiles and revealed the Church with its attendant secrets.

Thus, Paul wrote:

> 19 And what is the exceeding greatness of his power toward us who believe, according to the working of his mighty power, 20 Which he wrought in Christ, when he raised him from the dead, and set him at his own right hand in the heavenly places, 21 Far above all principality, and power, and might, and dominion, and every name that is named, not only in this world, but also in that which is to come: 22 And hath put all things under his feet, and gave him to be the head over all things to the church, 23 Which is his body, the fulness of him that fills all in all (Ephesians 1.19-23).

> 9 For in him dwells all the fulness of the Godhead bodily. 10 And you are complete in him, who is the head of all principality and power (Colossians 2.9-10).

Unlike the Twelve, Paul received his revelations from the risen, glorified Christ. Paul knew only the *resurrected* Christ, not the

Christ who ministered on earth in humility. The resurrected Christ was conqueror of sin and death.

What Paul meant by not knowing Christ "after the flesh" was that all Church doctrine comes from the risen, glorified Christ, not Christ in His earthly ministry.[13]

Paul: "Unto Me"

Paul wrote in his letters that God had revealed the Church, the body of Christ, and other secrets with the words "unto me." Paul's point was to emphasize Christ had revealed these secrets to him, not to the Twelve, not to others. God gave them *exclusively* to Paul, just as He had given the Abrahamic Covenant exclusively to Abraham and the Mosaic Law exclusively to Moses. Peter acknowledged this great truth in his last letter (2 Peter 3.15). The chart notes Paul's statements.

"Unto Me"	
Romans 12.3	For I say, through the grace given **unto me**, to every man that is among you, not to think of himself more highly than he ought to think; but to think soberly, according as God has dealt to every man the measure of faith.
Romans 15.15-16	15 Nevertheless, brethren, I have written the more boldly unto you in some sort, as putting you in mind, because of the grace that is given **to me** of God, 16 that I should be the minister of Jesus Christ to the Gentiles, ministering the gospel of God, that the offering up of the Gentiles might be acceptable, being sanctified by the Holy Ghost.
1 Corinthians 3.10	According to the grace of God which is given **unto me**, as a wise masterbuilder, I have laid the foundation, and another builds thereon. But let every man take heed how he builds thereupon.

[13] One of the great tragedies in Christendom is that most churches spend most of the time in the Gospels, i.e., Christ's earthly ministry. Their primary focus is upon Christ "after the flesh." In so doing, they reject Paul's words of 2 Corinthians 5.16 and Galatians 6.15.

1 Corinthians 9.16-17	[16] For though I preach the gospel, I have nothing to glory of: for necessity is laid upon me; yea, woe is unto me, if I preach not the gospel! [17] For if I do this thing willingly, I have a reward: but if against my will, a dispensation of the gospel is committed **unto me**.
Galatians 2.7, 9	[7] But contrariwise, when they saw that the gospel of the uncircumcision was committed **unto me**, as the gospel of the circumcision was unto Peter; [9] And when James, Cephas, and John, who seemed to be pillars, perceived the grace that was given **unto me**, they gave to me and Barnabas the right hands of fellowship; that we should go unto the heathen, and they unto the circumcision.
Ephesians 3.1-3, 7-9	[1] For this cause I Paul, the prisoner of Jesus Christ for you Gentiles, [2] If you have heard of the dispensation of the grace of God which is given **me to you-ward**: [3] How that by revelation he made known **unto me** the secret; (as I wrote afore in few words, [7] Whereof I was made a minister, according to the gift of the grace of God given **unto me** by the effectual working of his power. [8] **Unto me**, who am less than the least of all saints, is this grace given, that I should preach among the Gentiles the unsearchable riches of Christ; [9] And to make all men see what is the fellowship of the secret, which from the beginning of the world hath been hid in God, who created all things by Jesus Christ:
Ephesians 6.19	[19] And for me, that utterance may be given **unto me**, that I may open my mouth boldly, to make known the secret of the gospel,
Colossians 1.25	Whereof I am made a minister, according to the dispensation of God which is given **to me** for you, to fulfill the word of God;

Titus 1.3	But has in due times manifested his word through preaching, which is committed **unto me** according to the commandment of God our Savior;
2 Peter 3.15	And account that the longsuffering of our Lord is salvation; even as our beloved brother Paul also according to the wisdom given **unto him** has written unto you; [14]

Imitate Paul

In light of Paul's "unto me" statements, which attested to God's revelations to him, Paul encouraged believers to imitate him. No other person in Scripture wrote such things. This fact alone should arrest our attention. Paul used the nouns μιμητής, συμμιμητής and the verb μιμέομαι.[15] Words such as "mimeograph" come from them. The nouns mean "imitator" and the verb "imitate." Paul used the same term (μιμητής) in Ephesians 5.1 to exhort believers to be imitators of God. In addition, Paul coupled with the "μιμ*" words the noun τύπος, an "example" or "pattern" (Philippians 3.17, 2 Thessalonians 3.9).

Passage	The Imitation Texts
1 Corinthians 4.16	παρακαλῶ οὖν ὑμᾶς, μιμηταί μου γίνεσθε.
	I beseech you therefore, become [present middle imperative] imitators of me.
	μιμηταί μου γίνεσθε, καθὼς κἀγὼ Χριστοῦ.

---

[14] The last statement is from Peter, who at the end of his life, counseled believing Jews to look to Paul for instruction.

[15] These words mean "imitate" or "copy." One of the problems of translations is inconsistency of language. The KJV translators used the word "follow" for Paul's statements. But Paul used different language than Jesus. The word Jesus used most frequently for following Him was ἀκολουθέω (cf. Matthew 8.22, 9.9, 19.21, 28; Mark 1.17, 2.14, 8.34, 10.21; Luke 5.27, 9.23, 59; 18.22; John 1.43; 8.12; 10.27, 12.26, 21.19, 22. This word means "to follow one who precedes and accompany him." Another word Jesus used was δεῦτε (Matthew 4.19, 11.28; Mark 1.17).

1 Corinthians 11.1	Become [present middle imperative] imitators of me, as I am of Christ.
Galatians 4.12	Γίνεσθε ὡς ἐγώ, ὅτι κἀγὼ ὡς ὑμεῖς, ἀδελφοί, δέομαι ὑμῶν. οὐδέν με ἠδικήσατε:
	Become [present middle imperative] as I, because I became as you, brethren, I beg of you. You have done me no wrong;
Philippians 3.17	Συμμιμηταί μου γίνεσθε, ἀδελφοί, καὶ σκοπεῖτε τοὺς οὕτω περιπατοῦντας καθὼς ἔχετε τύπον ἡμᾶς.
	Become [present middle imperative] fellow imitators of me, brothers, and fix your attention on [present active imperative] those who walk according to our pattern.
1 Thessalonians 1.6	καὶ ὑμεῖς μιμηταὶ ἡμῶν ἐγενήθητε καὶ τοῦ κυρίου, δεξάμενοιτὸν λόγον ἐν θλίψει πολλῇ μετὰ χαρᾶς πνεύματος ἁγίου,
	And you have become [aorist passive indicative] imitators of us and of the Lord, having received the word in much affliction with joy of the Holy Spirit.
2 Thessalonians 3.7	αὐτοὶ γὰρ οἴδατε πῶς δεῖ μιμεῖσθαι ἡμᾶς, ὅτι οὐκ ἠτακτήσαμεν ἐν ὑμῖν
	For you yourselves know how it is necessary to be imitators [present middle infinitive] of us, because we were not disorderly (quit ranks) among you.
2 Thessalonians 3.9	οὐχ ὅτι οὐκ ἔχομεν ἐξουσίαν, ἀλλ' ἵνα ἑαυτοὺς τύπον δῶμεν ὑμῖν εἰς τὸ μιμεῖσθαι ἡμᾶς.
	Not that we do not have the power (or right), but in order that we might give ourselves as an example to you to imitate [present middle infinitive] us.

Paul's statements are imperatives: *commands*. As Christ's chosen representative of His new program, the Church, the body of Christ, believers are commanded to imitate or copy Paul. To be an obedient and godly Christian requires imitating Paul and obeying his teaching. Paul is the Church's example. He is to the Church what Abraham, Moses, and the prophets were to Israel. The following chart outlines Paul's role in God's new program of the Church compared to God's revelation of His new program of Israel.

ABRAHAM	New Program (Israel)	P	New Program (Church)
MOSES	Under Law	A U	Under Grace
PROPHETS	Covenants	L	Secrets

Abraham was the father of God's covenant people, Israel. Moses gave Israel the Law which governed their moral, civil, and ceremonial life. The prophets gave the people the covenants, God's promises of how He would bless them. Paul combined all these positions with reference to the Church. God chose him as the founder of the Church, revealed to him that members of the Church are to live by grace, and disclosed to him the secrets of the Church.

Paul: Proxy Israel

The Abrahamic Covenant stated God would bless Gentiles through Israel, the covenant people. How could God bless Gentiles apart from Israel? The answer is He couldn't. God had no revealed way to bless Gentiles apart from Israel.

The Old Testament anticipated an obedient Israel. According to prophecy, Israel was to accept its Messiah and become the channel of blessing to Gentiles. But the nation chose to *reject* its Messiah, the source of blessing. God in His foreknowledge knew this would happen but the nation had a choice (Matthew 23.37-39). God had *not* revealed what would happen if Israel rejected its Messiah. Put another way, God had revealed nothing about the creation of the Church, the body of Christ. Had Israel accepted the Messiah, the Church would not have come into existence. There would have been no need.

Even though the Jewish leadership initiated Jesus' crucifixion in concert with Rome, Peter anticipated the nation would respond and accept Jesus as the Messiah after His resurrection. That was his appeal on the day of Pentecost. According to God's prophetic program, the next event on the timeline was the Day of the Lord. Peter anticipated this event to occur soon and quoted Joel 2. Along with the coming of the Holy Spirit, Peter expected the "sun to be turned to darkness and the moon to blood" (Acts 2.19-20). The prophets seemed to indicate that "last days" events would occur in a short timeframe. Jesus, in His dissertation in Matthew 24 on end-time events seemed to imply the Tribulation would soon occur followed by His victorious return to set up His kingdom. The Lord's addresses to the seven Jewish assemblies in Revelation 2-3 counseled the Jews to overcome and endure until the end. These events seemed to be at hand. Nothing in the prophetic literature or Jesus' declarations in His earthly ministry indicated a large gap of time in fulfilling prophetic events or in the formation of the Church.

The crisis of Israel's national rejection occurred when the Jewish leadership, the Sanhedrin, stoned Stephen (Acts 7). In light of this continued rejection, God did the unexpected and unpredicted. He belayed His prophetic program to bless Gentiles in spite of Israel's unbelief. How could He do this?

God saved Saul of Tarsus and commissioned him to be the Apostle of the Gentiles. Through Paul, God chose to bless Gentiles. God could do this and adhere to the Abrahamic Covenant because Paul was a Jew. Paul became proxy Israel. As believing Israel, he became the channel of blessing to Gentiles outside of God's prophetic, revealed program. In his illustration of the olive tree, Paul declared God had broken off the natural branches (Israel) from the place of blessing because of unbelief (Romans 11.20) and grafted into the tree wild branches (Gentiles). The olive tree represented God's place of favor (the Abrahamic Covenant). In this illustration, Paul declared he was the apostle of the Gentiles (Romans 11.13; 2 Timothy 1.11) and celebrated this role (εἰμι ἐγὼ ἐθνῶν ἀπόστολος τὴν διακονίαν μου δοξάζω). God's grafting

Gentiles (wild branches) into the olive tree became His blessings to Abraham's heavenly seed—which are based upon faith (Genesis 15.4-6).

Paul wrote the Corinthians:

> [3] For I delivered unto you first of all that which I also received, how that Christ died for our sins according to the scriptures; [4] And that he was buried, and that he rose again the third day according to the scriptures: [5] And that he was seen of Cephas, then of the twelve: [6] After that, he was seen of above five hundred brethren at once; of whom the greater part remain unto this present, but some are fallen asleep. [7] After that, he was seen of James; then of all the apostles. [8] And last of all he was seen of me also, as of one born out of due time (1 Corinthians 15.3-8).

Verses 3-4 are Paul's gospel: Christ died for our sins, was buried, and rose from the dead. Believing this is how one is saved from sin and death and gains eternal life. Paul recounted the order by which Lord had revealed Himself after His resurrection: Peter, the Twelve, 500 Jews, James, all the apostles, and lastly, Paul. Paul declared he was "born out of due time" (τῷ ἐκτρώματι) and likened his salvation to an untimely birth. What did he mean?

Peter had told the Jews at Pentecost that every Jew must repent (Acts 2.36-38). The Lord told the nation He would not return until they said, "Blessed is He who comes in the name of the Lord" (Matthew 23.37-39). Isaiah asked if a nation could be born in a day (Isaiah 66.8) It will be. At the end of the Tribulation, national Israel will repent and the Lord will return. This is what Paul meant when he wrote in Romans 11.26, "all Israel will be saved." But until then Paul represented believing Israel, "born prematurely" in light of Israel's national rejection.

Could God have not used the Twelve? The Lord told them they were to be His witnesses, "in Jerusalem, and in all Judaea, and in Samaria, and unto the uttermost part of the earth" (Acts 1.8). They were to go to all the world. But their commission was based upon God's *prophetic* program which expected Israel's repentance and acceptance of Jesus as the Messiah. Acts 8.1 reveals Acts 1.8:

> And Saul was consenting unto his death. And at that time there was a great persecution against the church which was at Jerusalem; and they were all scattered abroad throughout the regions of Judaea and Samaria, except the apostles (Acts 8.1).

Due to Saul's persecution, all believing Jews fled Jerusalem, *except the apostles*. Why did they stay in Jerusalem? They stayed because they were obedient. They could not leave Jerusalem until it repented and believed Jesus was the Messiah. The Twelve's ministry was to Israel *first*. The Lord had promised they would rule over the twelve tribes on twelve thrones (Matthew 19.28). Their focus was upon the kingdom of God on earth.

Unlike the Twelve, the risen Lord commissioned Paul as the Apostle of the Gentiles, not as an apostle of Israel. Paul was not part of God's *prophetic* program. He was God's choice to found the Church, a new, unrevealed program. In the above discussion, we saw how Paul could serve as proxy Israel in concert with the Abrahamic Covenant to bless Gentiles. Specifically, he served as proxy Israel as a priest and as a minister of the New Covenant.

Paul: Priest of the Church

Paul wrote concerning Church offices, gifts, and ministries. He noted apostles, prophets, bishops/elders, deacons, pastors, teachers, evangelists, and mentioned several gifts—administration, mercy, teaching, giving, faith, healing, tongues, etc. The one office, so prominent to Israel, unmentioned in the Church, was "priest."[16]

---

[16] The Church has *no* priests. Some have taught that every believer is a priest. No Biblical support exists for this teaching. Every believer is a saint (Romans 1.7) and every believer is an ambassador (2 Corinthians 5.20) but no member of the Church is a priest. Such an idea comes from 1 Peter 2.9. But Peter wrote to Jews (1 Peter 1.1) who had believed the gospel of the kingdom in fulfillment of Exodus 19.6, not to members of the Church, the body of Christ.

Except once. Paul wrote *he* served as a priest. Romans 15.15-16 reads:

> [15] Nevertheless, brethren, I have written the more boldly unto you in some sort, as putting you in mind, because of the grace that is given to me of God. [16] That I should be the minister of Jesus Christ to the Gentiles, ministering [as a priest] the gospel of God, that the offering up of the Gentiles might be acceptable, being sanctified by the Holy Ghost (Romans 15.15-16).

Paul used the noun λειτουργὸν in verse 16, "minister of Jesus Christ to the Gentiles." The word λειτουργός was used of public servants (Romans 13.6), those rendering general service (Philippians 2.25), angelic service (Hebrews 1.7), and for Christ ministering as High Priest (Hebrews 8.2). In the second part of the verse, "ministering the gospel of God," Paul used the present active participle ἱερουργοῦντα of the verb ἱερουργέω. This word means to minister as a priest.

Paul was of the tribe of Benjamin, not Levi. Not being a descendant of Aaron, he could not serve as a priest under the Mosaic Law.[17] Paul knew the Mosaic Law. What then did Paul mean by his statement?

God's destiny for Israel was to be a holy nation, a kingdom of priests (Exodus 19.6). This destiny went beyond the service of the Levitical priesthood. In the kingdom, every Jew will serve as a priest. Zechariah wrote:

> [22] Many people and strong nations shall come to seek the Lord of hosts in Jerusalem, and to pray before the Lord. [23] Thus says the Lord of hosts; In those days it shall come to pass, that ten men shall take hold out of all languages of the nations, even shall take hold of the skirt of him that is a

---

[17] Eligibility to serve as a priest depended on being a descendant of Aaron (Exodus 28.1; Numbers 3.10; Hebrews 5.1-4).

> Jew, saying, We will go with you: for we have heard that God is with you (Zechariah 8.22-23).

Repentant, believing Israel will fulfill its Exodus 19.6 destiny. Every Jew will be a priest. But until then, Paul, as proxy Israel, served this role to Gentiles. This role complied with God's promise to bless Gentiles *through Israel*, according to the Abrahamic Covenant.

Paul: Minister of the New Covenant

God established the New Covenant with Israel.[18] Jeremiah 31 and Ezekiel 36 state this clearly. As "new," it was to replace the "old" covenant, the Mosaic Covenant, the Mosaic Law. Unlike the other covenants God gave Israel, which included land, kingdom, and other physical blessings, the New Covenant was entirely spiritual.

The New Covenant is mentioned infrequently in the New Testament.[19] Jesus, at the Last Supper, initiated it with His words, "this is My blood of the covenant, which is poured out for many for forgiveness of sins" (Matthew 26.28; cf. Mark 14.24; Luke 22.20).

Paul wrote the Corinthians:

> [23] For I have received of the Lord that which also I delivered unto you, that the Lord Jesus the same night in which he

---

[18] The New Covenant has been a difficult subject for those who believe God established His covenants with Israel alone and that He will literally fulfill His promises to them despite their unbelief in rejecting the Messiah. Those who believe God will literally fulfill His promises to the nation of Israel are known as Dispensationalists. Reformed theologians teach the Church has assumed God's promises to Israel. For them, the matter of the Church fulfilling the New Covenant is not a problem since they teach all Israel's covenants are fulfilled figuratively by the Church. This handy solution comes at an exorbitant price: God's sovereignty and integrity.

[19] Outside of the gospel writers, Paul is the only New Testament writer who mentions the New Covenant (1 Corinthians 11.23-36; 2 Corinthians 3.5-6; Hebrews 7.22, 8.6-13, 9.15-20, 10.16, 29, 12.24). Peter, James, John, and Jude never mention it.

> was betrayed took bread: [24] And when he had given thanks, he broke it, and said, Take, eat: this is my body, which is broken for you: this do in remembrance of me. [25] After the same manner also he took the cup, when he had supped, saying, this cup is the new testament in my blood: this do, as often as you drink it, in remembrance of me. [26] For as often as you eat this bread, and drink this cup, you show the Lord's death till he come (1 Corinthians 11.23-26).

The Lord communicated directly with Paul about the Lord's Supper and validated it as a celebration for the Church. In addition to what the Lord told the Twelve, He revealed to Paul that this celebration is a memorial that "shows the Lord's death until He comes."

The other passage Paul wrote concerning the New Covenant was in his second letter to the Corinthians:

> [4] And such trust have we through Christ toward God: [5] Not that we are sufficient of ourselves to think anything as of ourselves; but our sufficiency is of God; [6] Who also has made us able ministers of a new covenant; not of the letter, but of the spirit: for the letter kills, but the spirit gives life (2 Corinthians 3.4-6).

In the phrase, "ministers of a new covenant," Paul identified himself (and those who were part of his ministry) as ministers of a new covenant[20] and noted its spiritual nature.

God had established the Old Covenant, the Mosaic Law, with Israel, not with Gentiles. But Paul wrote in Romans 3.19:

> Now we know that whatever things the Law says, it says to them who are under the law: that every mouth may be stopped, and all the world may become guilty before God.

Israel was in view in the first part of the verse for God established the Mosaic Law with Israel. But Paul also made the point that when

---

[20] The word here for "minister" is the general word διάκονος.

Gentiles encountered the Law, it had the same effect upon them as upon the Jews—it pronounced them guilty.

The "blood of the New Covenant" (Matthew 26.28) was shed not only to redeem Israel but to replace the Mosaic Law with a "better covenant" (Hebrews 8.6). Paul also wrote that Christ's death (His shed blood) blotted out and took away the ordinances (the Mosaic Law) against us, nailing them to His cross (Colossians 2.14). The Old Covenant has been replaced by the New Covenant.

New Covenant Established by the Blood of Christ Matthew 26.28; 1 Corinthians 11.25; Ephesians 2.13	
Provisions	Application to the Church
Forgiveness of sins (Jeremiah 31.34; Ezekiel 36.25, 29)	Ephesians 1.7, 4.33; Colossians 1.14, 2.13
God's people (Jeremiah 31.33)	Titus 2.14
Indwelling Holy Spirit (Ezekiel 36.26-27)	1 Corinthians 2.12, 6.19; 2 Corinthians 1.22, 5.5; Ephesians 1.14

God had *promised* these blessings to Israel. Gentiles had no such promise (Ephesians 2.11-12). Gentiles were separated from Israel's covenants. We, the Church, members of the body of Christ, have received these blessings, *not by promise* but *by grace*. God has given the spiritual blessing of the New Covenant, the indwelling Holy Spirit and the forgiveness of sins by grace. Christ's death on the cross and His resurrection reconciled the world (2 Corinthians 5.18-19) to Himself. Jews or Gentiles who believe Paul's gospel receive this blessing. Paul wrote the Romans:

> It has pleased them truly; and their debtors they are. For if the Gentiles have been made partakers of their spiritual things, their duty is also to minister unto them in carnal things (Romans 15.27).

Gentiles share in Israel's *spiritual* blessings, the forgiveness of sins, the indwelling Holy Spirit, by grace, as "the seed of Abraham."[21] Paul became what disobedient, unrepentant Israel refused to be—the channel of blessing to the Gentiles.

Paul: Proxy Israel	Scripture
Apostle of the Gentiles	Romans 11.13; Galatians 2.7-9; Ephesians 3.1; 2 Timothy 1.11
Priest	Romans 15.16
Minister of New Covenant	2 Corinthians 3.6

We have examined how the risen, glorified Christ commissioned Paul to reveal His grace to Gentiles, to serve as proxy Israel, and to be our example for Christian living. In the next section, we will examine the things God revealed to Paul alone—His secrets.

Paul's Secrets: Key to His Theology

UNLESS ONE UNDERSTANDS PAUL'S SECRETS, ONE CANNOT UNDERSTAND CHURCH THEOLOGY

Every believer should fix his mind on the above statement. One must understand Paul's secrets to understand Church theology for Paul's "secrets" (μυστήριον) *are* Church theology.

Paul used the word "secret" (μυστήριον) 20 times in his letters.[22] Despite the witness he left, one rarely finds Paul's secrets discussed in books, commentaries, articles, or from pulpits or classrooms. Most Bible scholars, expositors, and teachers seem ignorant of them.

---

[21] More will said on this subject later.

[22] Romans 11.25, 16.25; 1 Corinthians 2.7, 4.1, 13.2, 14.2, 15.51; Ephesians 1.9, 3.3-4, 9, 5.32, 6.19; Colossians 1.26-27, 2.2, 4.3; 2 Thessalonians 2.7; 1 Timothy 3.9, 16. Paul used μυστήριον in 1 Corinthians 14.2 to an unknown or secret language, not a new revelation.

Paul wrote the Corinthians:

> Let a man regard us in this manner, as servants of Christ and stewards of the secrets [μυστήριον] of God (1 Corinthians 4.1).

The word rendered "mystery" (μυστήριον) is a transliteration, not a translation.[23] It does not mean "mystery." It means "secret," what was previously hidden and unknown. Paul was the steward of the secrets of God concerning the Church, the body of Christ.[24]

Paul's "secrets" were *new revelations* he received from the risen Lord. They were *new theology*. They constituted a new theological program of which Paul was God's spokesman.[25] The chart below shows the passages in which Paul used the word μυστήριον and the new truths he revealed.

Paul's Secrets	Scripture
The Body of Secrets	1 Corinthians 2.7, 4.1, 13.2; Colossians 4.3;1 Timothy 3.9
The Church, the Body of Christ	Ephesians 3.3, 4, 9, 5.32; Colossians 1.26
The Gospel of the Grace of God	Romans 16.25; Ephesians 6.19
The Blinding of Israel	Romans 11.15
The Rapture of the Church	1 Corinthians 15.51
Gathering All Things in Christ	Ephesians 1.9-10; Colossians 2.2
The Secret of Godliness	1 Timothy 3.16
The Secret of Iniquity	2 Thessalonians 2.7

---

23 Most Bible versions fail to translate the word correctly. This indicates the translators are unaware of Paul's secrets.

24 The word translated "steward" is οἰκονόμος and was used of one who managed a household or estate.

25 The greatest error of Christendom for the past 1,900 years has been its failure to recognize that Paul's doctrines were not known before him and that the ascended Christ revealed them to Paul alone.

All of Paul's theology was a new revelation whether he specifically identified it with the word μυστήριον or not. This is why it is essential to understand that Paul was *not* an addition or extension of the Twelve but God's founder of an entirely new program: the Church.

The Revelation of Paul's Secrets

Paul wrote about this body of secrets the risen Lord gave him in several passages. They include the following:

> Let a man so account of us, as of the ministers of Christ, and stewards of the secrets [μυστήριον] of God. (1 Corinthians 4.1).
>
> And though I have the gift of prophecy, and understand all secrets [μυστήριον], and all knowledge; and though I have all faith, so that I could remove mountains, and have not charity, I am nothing (1 Corinthians 13.2).
>
> Withal praying also for us, that God would open unto us a door of utterance, to speak the secret [μυστήριον] of Christ, for which I am also in bonds (Colossians 4.3):
>
> Holding the secret [μυστήριον] of the faith in a pure conscience (1 Timothy 3.9).

The word μυστήριον was used in only three passages (Matthew 13.11; Mark 4.11; Luke 8.10) before Paul wrote his letters. Each concerned the prophesied earthly kingdom. The Lord used the word μυστήριον to mean His hiding the truths of the earthly kingdom from the crowds and antagonistic religious authorities by the use of parables. Jesus told His disciples they were privy to these "secrets." The kingdom of God was not a secret. God had revealed it in hundreds of passages through the prophets. Rather, the parables were Christ's "secret language" to hide truths of the kingdom to those with closed hearts. Matthew wrote:

> [10] And the disciples came, and said unto him, Why do you speak unto them in parables? [11] He answered and said unto them, Because it is given unto you to know the secrets [μυστήριον] of the kingdom of heaven, but to them it is not given. [12] For whosoever has, to him shall be given, and he shall have more abundance: but whosoever has not, from him shall be taken away even that he has. [13] Therefore speak I to them in parables: because they seeing see not; and hearing they hear not, neither do they understand. [14] And in them is fulfilled the prophecy of Esaias, which says, By hearing you shall hear, and shall not understand; and seeing you shall see, and shall not perceive: [15] For this people's heart is waxed gross, and their ears are dull of hearing, and their eyes they have closed; lest at any time they should see with their eyes and hear with their ears, and should understand with their heart, and should be converted, and I should heal them (Matthew 13.10-15).

The secrets the risen Lord revealed to Paul were an entirely new and different set of revelations. None of them concerned the kingdom of God on earth. Paul's secrets concerned the Church, an unknown creation before Paul. What were these secrets?

Paul's Secrets:

1. The Church, the Body of Christ

To understand the subject of the Church requires a clear definition of it. The Church is defined by three elements:

1. The Church is the body of Christ (Ephesians 1.22-23; 1 Corinthians 12.12-13; Romans 12.3-5; Colossians 1.24).
2. One becomes part of the Church, the body of Christ through:
    a. Believing Paul's gospel (1 Corinthians 15.1-4) and by the

   b. Baptism of the Holy Spirit (1 Corinthians 12.13; Galatians 3.27).[26]
3. Jews and Gentiles who have believed Paul's gospel are equal in Christ (Romans 10.12; Galatians 3.28) and members of the Church, the body of Christ. They are no longer designated Jew or Gentile but "Church" (1 Corinthians 10.32).

The ascended Lord revealed this new truth to Paul. Peter and the Twelve knew nothing of it. Paul wrote the Ephesians:

> [1] For this reason I, Paul, the prisoner of Christ Jesus for the sake of you Gentiles— [2] if indeed you have heard of the stewardship of God's grace which was given to me for you; [3] that by revelation there was made known to me the secret [μυστήριον], as I wrote before in brief. [4] By referring to this, when you read you can understand my insight into the secret [μυστήριον] of Christ, [5] which in other generations was not made known to the sons of men, as it has now been revealed to His holy apostles and prophets in the Spirit; [6] to be specific, that the Gentiles are fellow heirs and fellow members of the body, and fellow partakers of the promise in Christ Jesus through the gospel, [7] of which I was made a minister, according to the gift of God's grace which was given to me according to the working of His power. [8] To me, the very least of all saints, this grace was given, to preach to the Gentiles the unfathomable riches of Christ, [9] and to bring to light what is the administration of the secret [μυστήριον] which for ages has been hidden in God who created all things (Ephesians 3.1-9).

The most striking characteristic of this passage is how often Paul referred to himself. The reader is encouraged to read the passage in light to see how often Paul used the personal and possessive pronouns "I," "me," and "my." It is almost as important to

---

[26] Man's part is believing Paul's gospel. God's part is the baptism of the Holy Spirit. This baptism is a real experience but not attended with signs. The believer takes it by faith because God has declared it.

understand what *is not* in the Scriptures as to understand what *is* in them. Note what Paul wrote concerning the Church from the above passage:

1. Paul (not Peter or the Twelve) was a prisoner of Christ for Gentiles (v. 1).
2. God gave stewardship of God's grace to Paul (not to Peter or the Twelve) for Gentiles (v. 2).
3. God gave Paul (not Peter or the Twelve) the secret [μυστήριον] (v. 3).
4. Paul (not Peter or the Twelve) had insight into the secret [μυστήριον] of Christ (v. 4-6)
5. Paul (not Peter or the Twelve) was made a minister of this secret by the gift of God's grace (v. 7).
6. Paul (not Peter or the Twelve), the least of saints, was given God's grace to preach to Gentiles (v. 8).
7. Paul (not Peter or the Twelve) was given the mission to reveal the secret [μυστήριον] of the Church which God had kept hidden from previous ages (v. 9).

Could words be clearer? The Church was *unknown* before Paul. Some have argued Paul's words, "now been revealed to His holy apostles and prophets in the Spirit" (Ephesians 3.5) referred to the Twelve and therefore the Church, the body of Christ, was not a secret revealed to Paul alone.

Such an assertion reveals ignorance of Paul's writings. Paul used the word "apostle" to refer to men in addition to the Twelve. Barnabas was named an apostle (Acts 14.14), as were Andronicus and Junia (Romans 16.7), Apollos (1 Corinthians 4.6, 9), Titus (2 Corinthians 8.23), and Epaphroditus (Philippians 2.25).

In addition, one must also distinguish between an "apostle of Christ" and an "apostle of the Church." The former referred to one who had seen the risen Lord and had been directly commissioned by Him (1 Corinthians 9.1). The latter referred to those chosen by Paul or local congregations. In addition to the above, Silas, Timothy, Luke, and possibly others were probably considered apostles. Whatever the Twelve came to understand about the

Church, the body of Christ, they learned from Paul. The whole idea of Jew and Gentile equal in Christ was alien to them. Indeed, Paul was the only one who wrote about the "body of Christ." It is not found in the writings of Peter, James, John, or Jude. And Peter, even at the end of his ministry, shortly before his death, wrote that Paul's doctrines were hard to understand (2 Peter 3.15-16). This was because they were all *new*.

Paul wrote similar words concerning the secret nature of the Church to the Colossians:

> [24] Now I rejoice in my sufferings for your sake, and in my flesh I do my share on behalf of His body, which is the church, in filling up what is lacking in Christ's afflictions. [25] Of this church I was made a minister according to the stewardship from God bestowed on me for your benefit, so that I might fully carry out the preaching of the word of God, [26] that is, the secret [μυστήριον] which has been hidden from the past ages and generations, but has now been manifested to His saints, [27] to whom God willed to make known what is the riches of the glory of this secret [μυστήριον] among the Gentiles, which is Christ in you, the hope of glory (Colossians 1.24-27).

Paul reminded the Gentile believers in Ephesus that prior to his revelation of the secret of the Church, they were excluded from Israel's covenants and were without hope:

> [11] Therefore remember that formerly you, the Gentiles in the flesh, who are called "Uncircumcision" by the so-called "Circumcision," which is performed in the flesh by human hands— [12] remember that you were at that time separate from Christ, excluded from the commonwealth of Israel, and strangers to the covenants of promise, having no hope and without God in the world (Ephesians 2.11-12).

As noted above, God had set Gentiles aside with His call of Abraham. But God began a new program with His commission of Paul. He established a relationship with both Jews and Gentiles based upon faith alone in the work of Christ's death and resurrection. Paul expressed this new reality with "but now," (νυνὶ δὲ), his favorite expression of contrast.[27]

> [13] But now in Christ Jesus you who formerly were far off have been brought near by the blood of Christ. [14] For He Himself is our peace, who made both groups into one and broke down the barrier of the dividing wall, [15] by abolishing in His flesh the enmity, which is the Law of commandments contained in ordinances, so that in Himself He might make the two into one new man, thus establishing peace, [16] and might reconcile them both in one body to God through the cross, by it having put to death the enmity. [17] And He came and preached peace to you who were far away, and peace to those who were near; [18] for through Him we both have our access in one Spirit to the Father. [19] So then you are no longer strangers and aliens, but you are fellow citizens with the saints, and are of God's household, [20] having been built on the foundation of the apostles and prophets, Christ Jesus Himself being the corner stone, [21] in whom the whole building, being fitted together, is growing into a holy temple in the Lord, [22] in whom you also are being built together into a dwelling of God in the Spirit. (Ephesians 2.13-22).

Paul wrote that the Church, the body of Christ, was a new creation composed of Jews and Gentiles and that one becomes a member by believing the gospel (1 Corinthians 15.1-4) and the baptism of the Holy Spirit. Paul wrote:

> [12] For even as the body is one and yet has many members, and all the members of the body, though they are many, are one body, so also is Christ. [13] For by one Spirit we were all baptized into one body, whether Jews or Greeks, whether

---

[27] Paul used the expression νῦν δὲ or νυνὶ δὲ in Romans 3.21, 6.22, 7.6, 11.30, 16.25-26; 1 Corinthians 7.14, 12.18, 20, 13.13, 15.20; Galatians 4.9; Ephesians 2.13, 5.8; Colossians 1.22, 26, 3.8; 2 Timothy 1.10 to reveal the "secrets" of believers new relationship to God as "Church."

> slaves or free, and we were all made to drink of one Spirit (1 Corinthians 12.12-13).

Each part of the body of the Body of Christ is vital to its function, even as each part of the human body is needed to function properly. Paul explained:

> [14] For the body is not one member, but many. [15] If the foot says, Because I am not a hand, I am not a part of the body, it is not for this reason any the less a part of the body. [16] And if the ear says, Because I am not an eye, I am not a part of the body, it is not for this reason any the less a part of the body. [17] If the whole body were an eye, where would the hearing be? If the whole were hearing, where would the sense of smell be? [18] But now God has placed the members, each one of them, in the body, just as He desired (1 Corinthians 12.14-29).

Paul also made several points about the function of the Church when he wrote the Ephesians concerning the subject of marriage (Ephesians 5.22-33). He stated: 1) Christ is Head of the Church (v. 23), 2) Christ loved the Church and gave Himself for it (v. 25), 3) Christ's goal is to sanctify the Church by the Word of God (v. 26-27), 4) Members of the Church are members of Christ's body, His flesh and bones (v. 30), 5) The relationship between Christ and the Church was a secret [μυστήριον] (v. 32).[28]

Paul's purpose in this passage was to teach about marriage. Husbands were to love their wives as Christ loved the Church and wives were to be subject to their husbands as the Church is subject to Christ. Paul did not to teach the Church is the bride of Christ but that the Church is the body of Christ with Christ as its Head

---

[28] This passage is often used to support the idea the Church is the "bride of Christ." The passage does not state this. The phrase "bride of Christ" never occurs in the Scriptures. Paul explicitly stated the Church is the body of Christ, not the bride of Christ. God has a bride/wife relationship with Israel, not with the Church.

(Ephesians 1.22; 4.15; 5.23; Colossians 1.18; 2.19). This was a new, organic relationship with God that Israel did not enjoy.

The Scriptures do not teach Christ is the "King of the Church." The titles of Christ with respect to the Church are "Lord" and "Head." Paul wrote that members of the Church, the body of Christ, are heirs of God and joint-heirs with Christ (Romans 8.17). A joint-heir enjoys a different relationship than a subject to a king. A joint-heir is one who shares all that belongs to the heir. Paul also wrote that members of the Church will govern angels (1 Corinthians 6.3). Promises such as joint-heirship and ruling angels were never given to Israel. These are promises exclusive to the Church. This is grace!

What Does the Word "Church" Mean?

The word translated "church" is ἐκκλησία. The simplest definition of ἐκκλησία is an assembly of people, a group. Its specific meaning depends on its context. Acts 19 is a good example of the meaning of ἐκκλησία where it occurs three times: verses 32, 39, and 41. Luke wrote that when Paul went to Ephesus, he aroused the anger of the silversmiths and other tradesmen whose manufactured and sold idols. A silversmith named Demetrius stirred up a riot against Paul since Paul's ministry was destroying the idol business. People were believing in Christ and abandoning their idols. The chart below shows how ἐκκλησία was used in these verses. In each case, it was translated "assembly." More precise translation would render it "mob" (v. 32), "court" (v. 39), and "crowd" (v. 41).

Ἐκκλησία in Acts 19	
Passage	Meaning
So then, some were shouting one thing and some another, for the ἐκκλησία [assembly] was in confusion, and the majority did not know for what cause they had come together (v. 32).	Mob
But if you want anything beyond this, it shall be settled in the lawful ἐκκλησία [assembly] (v. 39).	Court
And after saying this he dismissed the ἐκκλησία [assembly] (v. 41).	Crowd

The Septuagint (LXX) used ἐκκλησία most often for קָהָל, (e.g., Deuteronomy 4.10, 9.10, 23.1) and usually rendered it "assembly" or "congregation."

The word ἐκκλησία occurs only twice in the Gospels. The first is the Lord's well-known statement to Peter, "upon this Rock will I build My church" (Matthew 16.18). The second is Jesus' instruction in dealing with a sinning Jewish brother. Jesus said if the brother refused reproof, the "church" was to regard him as a Gentile. Such language could not possibly refer to the Church, the body of Christ, in which Jew and Gentile are equal.[29]

Ἐκκλησία in the New Testament	
Gospels	Matthew 16.18, 18.17
Acts	Acts 2.47, 5.11, 7.38, 8.1, 3, 11.22, 26, 12.1, 5, 13.1, 14.23, 27, 15.3-4, 22, 18.22, 20.17, 28
Paul	Romans 16.1, 5, 23 1 Corinthians 1.2, 4.17, 6.4, 10.32, 11.18, 22, 12.28, 14.4-5, 12, 19, 23, 28, 35, 15.9, 16.19 2 Corinthians 1.1 Galatians 1.13 Ephesians 1.22, 3.10, 21, 5.23-25, 27, 29, 32 Philippians 3.6, 4.15 Colossians 1.18, 24, 4.15-16 1 Thessalonians 1.1 2 Thessalonians 1.1 1 Timothy 3.5, 15, 5.16 Philemon 1.2
Hebrews	Hebrews 2.12, 12.23
James	James 5.14
Peter	1 Peter 5.13
John	3 Jo 1.6, 9-10
Revelation	Revelation 2.1, 8, 12, 18, 3.1, 7, 14

[29] Writing Jews (James 1.1), James used συναγωγή, "synagogue" (James 2.2) and ἐκκλησία (James 5.14) as synonyms for the assembly of believing Jews. The "churches" (ἐκκλησία) of Revelation 2-3 were Jewish assemblies or synagogues.

When Did the Church Begin?

Most of Christendom teaches the Church, the body of Christ, began at Pentecost. The logic for this traditional view is the following: 1) The Church is the body of Christ; 2) Membership into the body of Christ is through the baptism of the Holy Spirit; 3) The baptism of the Holy Spirit occurred at Pentecost; 4) Therefore, the Church began at Pentecost. This logic *appears* strong but breaks upon examination.

Three major problems exist for the traditional view. The first is that Paul stated the Church, the body of Christ, was a "secret" [μυστήριον]. If the Church began at Pentecost, Paul was wrong. What occurred at Pentecost, the coming of the Holy Spirit, was *not* a secret. Jesus told the Twelve the Holy Spirit would come (John 7.39, 14.16-17, 26; Acts 1.4-5) and Jeremiah, Ezekiel, and Joel had written about the coming of the indwelling Holy Spirit. Peter stated Pentecost was the "last days" (Acts 2.17) of God's prophetic program with Israel, *not* the first days of the Church.

The second problem is that Peter addressed only Jews at Pentecost. Luke gave a detailed record of the event:

1. And there were dwelling at Jerusalem <u>Jews</u>, devout men, out of every nation under heaven (Acts 2.5).
2. But Peter, standing up with the eleven, lifted up his voice, and said unto <u>them</u>, <u>You men of Judaea</u>, and all <u>that dwell at Jerusalem</u>, be this known <u>unto you</u>, and hearken to my words (Acts 2.14).
3. <u>You men of Israel</u>, hear these words; Jesus of Nazareth, a man approved of God <u>among you</u> by miracles and wonders and signs, which God did by him <u>in the midst of you</u>, as <u>you yourselves also know</u> (Acts 2.22).
4. <u>Men and brethren</u>, let me freely speak <u>unto you</u> of the patriarch David, that he is both dead and buried, and his sepulcher is <u>with us</u> unto this day (Acts 2.29).
5. Therefore let <u>all the house of Israel</u> know assuredly, that God hath made that same Jesus, <u>whom you have crucified</u>, both Lord and Christ (Acts 2.36).

6. Now when they heard this, they were pricked in their heart, and said unto Peter and to the rest of the apostles, Men and brethren, what shall we do (Acts 2.37)?
7. For the promise is unto you, and to your children, and to all that are afar off, even as many as the Lord our God shall call (Acts 2.39).

These verses make it abundantly clear that Peter addressed *only Jews*. He had no idea of Jews and Gentiles being equal in Christ, which is the definition of the Church, the body of Christ.

Peter told the Jews that while they had crucified the Messiah (Acts 2.23, 36), He had risen from the dead (Acts 2.24-36) and could return and establish the long-awaited kingdom of God on earth. This fact was uppermost in his mind and explains the urgency of the Eleven to fill the spot vacated by Judas (Acts 1.21-26). For the kingdom to come, twelve apostles had to be present. Jesus had answered Peter's question about their future with these words:

> And Jesus said to them, Truly I say to you, that you who have followed Me, in the regeneration when the Son of Man will sit on His glorious throne, you also shall sit upon twelve thrones, judging the twelve tribes of Israel (Matthew 19.28).

One does not forget such a promise. The Twelve anticipated they would soon be occupying thrones ruling Israel's twelve tribes. Is there any doubt why their last question to Him before He ascended concerned when He would establish His kingdom on earth (Acts 1.6)?

Their expectation that God would soon establish His earthly kingdom was confirmed further by Peter's second sermon to Israel. After he healed the lame man at the Temple (Acts 3.1-10), he said to the Jews:

> [12] Men of Israel, why are you amazed at this, or why do you
> gaze at us, as if by our own power or piety we had made
> him walk? [13] The God of Abraham, Isaac and Jacob, the
> God of our fathers, has glorified His servant Jesus, whom

> you delivered and disowned in the presence of Pilate, when he had decided to release Him. [14] But you disowned the Holy and Righteous One and asked for a murderer to be granted to you, [15] but put to death the Prince of life, whom God raised from the dead, to which we are witnesses (Acts 3.12-15).

Is any language here to Gentiles? Peter addressed Jews. He blamed them for Christ's death but declared that despite this sin, God had raised Him from the dead. He continued, stating they had acted in ignorance but had fulfilled the words of the prophets:

> [17] And now, brethren, I know that you acted in ignorance, just as your rulers did also. [18] But the things which God announced beforehand by the mouth of all the prophets, that His Christ would suffer, He has thus fulfilled. [19] Therefore repent and return, so that your sins may be wiped away, in order that times of refreshing may come from the presence of the Lord; [20] and that He may send Jesus, the Christ appointed for you, [21] whom heaven must receive until *the* period of restoration of all things about which God spoke by the mouth of His holy prophets from ancient time (Acts 3.17-21).

The "times of refreshing" (verse 19) was the earthly kingdom and the "restoration of all things" (verse 21) was God's restoration of the earth to its Edenic state at creation (Isaiah 51.3). Peter told the Jews if they repented, Christ would return and establish His kingdom on the earth. God gave this promise to Israel (Matthew 23.37-39), not to the Church.

Even years later, when Peter received his vision to go to the Cornelius' house, he resisted obeying it (Acts 10). Why? Cornelius was a Gentile. If Peter and the Twelve had been evangelizing and ministering to Gentiles since Pentecost why would he hesitate? If the Church began at Pentecost, why did Peter question it? Indeed, why did God need to give him a vision? And after Peter obeyed and returned to Jerusalem, why did the believers there upbraid him for visiting a Gentile (Acts 11.1-18)? Furthermore, Acts 11.19 states:

> Now they which were scattered abroad upon the persecution that arose about Stephen traveled as far as Phenice, and Cyprus, and Antioch, preaching the word to none but unto the Jews only (Acts 11.19).

The last point which proves the Church did not begin at Pentecost is that Peter mentioned nothing on Pentecost or in his message at the Temple about Christ having died for sins. For Peter, Jesus' crucifixion was a heinous crime for which Israel had to repent, not a message of salvation. He declared:

> Therefore let all the house of Israel know assuredly, that God hath made that same Jesus, whom you have crucified, both Lord and Christ (Acts 2.36).

How did the Jews respond? Luke recorded:

> Now when they heard this, they were pricked in their heart, and said unto Peter and to the rest of the apostles, Men and brethren, what shall we do (Acts 2.37)?

And how did Peter answer them? Did he tell them to believe Christ had died for them and risen from the dead? Luke wrote:

> Then Peter said unto them, Repent, and be baptized every one of you in the name of Jesus Christ for the remission of sins, and you shall receive the gift of the Holy Ghost (Acts 2.38).

Peter made no mention of Christ's death for their sins or resurrection for salvation. Peter told the nation that *every one* of them must repent and be baptized for the forgiveness of sins (cf. Acts 3.26). When that happened, they would receive the gift of the Holy Spirit. This was the gospel of the kingdom which required national repentance (Matthew 3.2, 4.17). Does this sound like Church language? Is this the gospel of salvation proclaimed by the Church? Is it through repentance and water baptism that one becomes a Christian? Is it through repentance and water baptism that members of the Church, the body of Christ, receive the Holy Spirit?

The traditional view, that the Church begin at Pentecost, is just that—tradition. It has *no* Scriptural support. It is Scripturally *impossible* for the Church to have begun at Pentecost.

Paul: Founder of the Church

If the Church did not begin at Pentecost, when did it begin? The Scriptures provide a clear answer. Paul wrote the Church, the body of Christ, God's new program to bless Gentiles apart from national Israel, began with him. Two passages provide direct evidence of this fact. Addressing the problem of divisions within the Corinthian church, Paul wrote:

> [9] For we are God's fellow workers; you are God's field, God's building.[10] According to the grace of God which was given to me, like a wise master builder I laid the foundation, and another is building on it. But each man must be careful how he builds on it. [11] For no man can lay a foundation other than the one which is laid, which is Jesus Christ (1 Corinthians 3.9-11).

Paul wrote that according to the grace of God given to him, "like a wise master builder I laid the foundation." What foundation did Paul lay? He laid the foundation of the Church. Paul declared he was σοφὸς ἀρχιτέκτων, the "wise master builder" or "wise architect" of the Church.[30] An architect *begins* a building project. He doesn't come on the scene *after* construction has begun. Paul wrote that *he* laid the foundation of the Church and that foundation was Christ. If Paul laid the foundation, the Church did not begin at Pentecost, it began with Paul.

A second passage that confirms Paul began the Church is 1 Timothy 1.15-16. It reads:

> [15] This is a faithful saying, and worthy of all acceptation, that Christ Jesus came into the world to save sinners; of whom I am first [πρῶτος]. [16] Howbeit for this cause I

---

[30] An ἀρχιτέκτων oversaw the design and construction of a building.

> obtained mercy, that in me first [πρῶτος] Jesus Christ might demonstrate all longsuffering, for a pattern [ὑποτύπωσις] to them who should hereafter believe on him to life everlasting.

Most translations read, "of whom I am chief" (KJV) or "foremost" (NASB) or "worst" (NIV, NET). These renderings are *interpretations*, not translations. They interpret the verse to mean Paul thought he was the chief or greatest sinner. The word rendered "chief," "foremost," "worst" is πρῶτος. It *means* "first."[31]

Why have translators interpreted πρῶτος as "chief," "foremost," or "worst" when Paul always used the word in its primary sense, "first?" They extend Paul's statement of verse 13, in which he wrote that he was once a blasphemer, etc. into this verse.[32] They do this because they have no idea what to make of the sense that Paul was the "first sinner."

Translators do their best work when they translate. This is a case in which they have tried to do exegetical work and failed. Like Alexander, let us cut the knot.

Paul elaborated on his meaning in the next verse. He wrote he obtained mercy "that in me first" [πρῶτος] Jesus Christ might demonstrate all longsuffering, for a pattern to them who should hereafter believe on him to life everlasting." Paul was the "first sinner" in the sense that he was the pattern of God's grace to those who would be saved *afterward*. The word ὑποτύπωσις means an "example" or "pattern" and provides additional exegetical help. Expressed another way, Paul was the model, the prototype of

---

[31] Paul used this word 29 times: Romans 1.8, 16, 2.9-10, 3.2, 10.19, 15.24; 1 Corinthians 11.18, 12.28, 14.30, 15.3, 15.45-47; 2 Corinthians 8.5; Ephesians 6.2; Philippians 1.5; 1 Thessalonians 4.16; 2 Thessalonians 2.3; 1 Timothy 1.15-16, 2.1, 2.13, 3.10, 5.4, 5.12; 2 Timothy 1.5, 2.6, 4.16. In each case, he used the word in its primary sense, i.e., "first in time, place, etc."

[32] Paul was a great sinner. But that is not the point of the passage.

salvation in God's new program, the Church. Paul expressed this thought to the Galatians:

> [15] But when it pleased God, who separated me from my mother's womb, and called me by his grace, [16] To reveal his Son in me, that I might preach him among the Gentiles; immediately I conferred not with flesh and blood (Galatians 1.15-16).

God began a new age of grace with Paul. No one was more undeserving of God's grace than he. But God saved Paul to demonstrate His love for Gentiles. National Israel had failed to fulfill its opportunity to be a light to Gentiles. Rather than initiate the prophesied Day of the Lord, God interrupted His prophetic program and saved Paul as the "first" and the "pattern" of His grace towards Gentiles.

Identification With Christ

Closely related to the revelation of the Church, the body of Christ, is the relationship the believer has with Christ in being identified in His death and in His resurrection. The one who believes Paul's gospel (1 Corinthians 15.1-4) becomes a member of the Church, the body of Christ and God baptizes the believer into His Body. Paul alone taught this baptism. He wrote the Corinthians:

> [12] For as the body is one, and has many members, and all the members of that one body, being many, are one body: so also is Christ. [13] For by one Spirit are we all baptized into one body, whether we be Jews or Gentiles, whether we be bond or free; and have been all made to drink into one Spirit (1 Corinthians 12.12-13).

Romans 6 is the great passage which reveals our identification with Christ in His death and resurrection. Paul wrote the Romans:

> [3] Know you not, that so many of us as were baptized into Jesus Christ were baptized into his death? [4] Therefore we are buried with him by baptism into death: that like as

> Christ was raised up from the dead by the glory of the Father, even so we also should walk in newness of life. [5] For if we have been planted together in the likeness of his death, we shall be also in the likeness of his resurrection: [6] Knowing this, that our old man is crucified with him, that the body of sin might be destroyed, that henceforth we should not serve sin (Romans 6.3-6).

When one believes Paul's gospel the Holy Spirit baptizes (identifies) him with Christ in His death and resurrection.[33] The identification in Christ's death means the believer's old nature is crucified with Christ. God views the believer's Adamic nature as dead. The believer is also identified in Christ's resurrection. God sees the believer positionally resurrected in Christ.[34] This was a secret Paul alone taught.

Paul wrote similarly to the Colossians:

> [11] In whom also you are circumcised with the circumcision made without hands, in putting off the body of the sins of the flesh by the circumcision of Christ: [12] Buried with him in baptism, wherein also you are risen with him through the faith of the operation of God, who has raised him from the dead (Colossians 2.11-12).

The baptism of the Holy Spirit is dry.[35] It is the "one baptism" of the Church (Ephesians 4.5). Since only "*one* baptism" exists, it is

---

[33] The primary sense of baptism is identification. The baptism of the Holy Spirit is not seen or felt. The Scriptures declare it and we accept it by *faith*. Christians live by faith, not sight (2 Corinthians 5.7).

[34] Paul's great dissertation on resurrection is in 1 Corinthians 15. Paul explained more about resurrection in this chapter than is found in all the other Scriptures. One of the great mysteries is how life comes out of death. Nature reveals this truth (John 12.14) as does supernature at a higher level. Every human being will experience resurrection: some to eternal life and others to eternal condemnation (John 5.29).

[35] Some have taught Paul's phrase, "buried with Him in baptism" involves water. Paul's statement, "buried with Him in baptism" is a *spiritual identification with Christ*, not an aquatic experience.

the only *valid* baptism of the Church. While many arguments have raged concerning water baptism, Paul declared *no* water baptism exists in the Church. Any church that practices water baptism today is a disobedient church. How different and how unified the Church would be if it only believed and obeyed Paul!

Identification Truths	Scripture
Baptized into Christ's death and resurrection	Romans 6.3-5, 8; 1 Corinthians 12.13; Colossians 2.12; 3.3; Philippians 3.10; Titus 3.5-7
Crucified with Christ	Romans 6.6; Galatians 2.20
No longer a slave to sin	Romans 6.6-7, 18, 22
Possessor of eternal life	Romans 6.22-23
Dead to and released from the Law	Romans 7.4, 6
Under Grace, not Law	Romans 6.14, 7.4, 6; Galatians 5.18
No condemnation or separation from God	Romans 8.1, 37-39
Received Spirit of adoption	Romans 8.15
Complete in Christ	Colossians 2.10
Seated with Christ in heaven	Ephesians 2.6; Philippians 3.20
Sons of God and Joint-Heirs with Christ	Romans 8.17

In addition to these identification truths, Paul taught that the believer is justified, reconciled, redeemed, regenerated, and forgiven. Experientially, the believer is being sanctified to become conformed into the image of Christ (Romans 8.28-29; 2 Corinthians 3.18). What a package!

The Magic Mirror

The fairy tale, *Snow White*, tells of a magic mirror which identified beauty. God has His own magical mirror. Paul wrote the Corinthians:

> But we all, with open face beholding as in a mirror the glory of the Lord, are changed into the same image from glory to glory, even as by the Spirit of the Lord (2 Corinthians 3.18).

The Word of God reveals God's glory. It is God's mirror. Paul used the figure of a mirror to illustrate that occupation with the Word, through the work of the Holy Spirit, transforms the believer into the image of Christ, from glory to glory.[36] Paul wrote that Christ is the image of God:[37]

> 3 But if our gospel be hid, it is hid to them that are lost: 4 In whom the god of this world hath blinded the minds of them which believe not, lest the light of the glorious gospel of Christ, who is the image of God, should shine unto them (2 Corinthians 4.4-5).

> 14 In whom we have redemption through his blood, even the forgiveness of sins: 15 Who is the image of the invisible God, the firstborn of every creature: 16 For by him were all things created, that are in heaven, and that are in earth, visible and invisible, whether they be thrones, or dominions, or principalities, or powers: all things were created by him, and for him: 17 And he is before all things, and by him all things consist (Colossians 1.14-17).

Once one believes the gospel, God begins His work of sanctification, transforming believers into the likeness of Christ. Paul wrote the Romans and the Colossians:

> 28 And we know that all things work together for good to them that love God, to them who are the called according to his purpose. 29 For whom he did foreknow, he also did predestinate[38] to be conformed to the image of his Son, that

---

36 Paul discussed "glory to glory" in 1 Corinthians 15.39-49 anticipating the glory of the believer's resurrection body.

37 "Image" is the word εἰκών. It means a visible representation. Christ is the visible representative of the invisible God (John 1.18, 14.9).

38 Some have taught that predestination concerns heaven and hell for believers and unbelievers. Such teaching is not Scriptural. Paul wrote

> he might be the firstborn among many brethren (Romans 8.28-29).
>
> [10] And have put on the new man, which is renewed in knowledge after the image of him that created him: [11] Where there is neither Greek nor Jew, circumcision nor uncircumcision, Barbarian, Scythian, bond nor free: but Christ is all, and in all (Colossians 3.10-11).

In the 2 Corinthians 3.18 passage, Paul used the word μεταμορφούμεθα (present passive indicative), "is being transformed."[39] The passive voice indicates God is the one doing the work. What a remarkable truth! And like Paul's other secrets, this is a truth Paul alone revealed.

This transformation ends with the believer's glorification, his resurrection.[40] Paul discussed "glory" in his first letter to the Corinthians.

> [39] All flesh is not the same flesh: but there is one kind of flesh of men, another flesh of beasts, another of fishes, and another of birds. [40] There are also celestial bodies, and bodies terrestrial: but the glory of the celestial is one, and the glory of the terrestrial is another. [41] There is one glory of the sun, and another glory of the moon, and another glory of the stars: for one star differs from another star in glory. [42] So also is the resurrection of the dead. It is sown in corruption; it is raised in incorruption: [43] It is sown in dishonor; it is raised in glory: it is sown in weakness; it is raised in power: [44] It is sown a natural body; it is raised a spiritual body. There is a natural body, and there is a spiritual body. [45] And so it is written, The first man Adam was made a living soul; the last Adam was made a

---

that predestination (προορίζω) only concerns believers, not unbelievers. Believers are predestinated to a purpose and a position (Romans 8.29-30; Ephesians 1.5, 11).

[39] Our word "metamorphosis" comes from this word.

[40] This transformation is known as "sanctification" and ends with "glorification," i.e., resurrection.

> quickening spirit. [46] Howbeit that was not first which is spiritual, but that which is natural; and afterward that which is spiritual. [47] The first man is of the earth, earthy; the second man is the Lord from heaven. [48] As is the earthy, such are they also that are earthy: and as is the heavenly, such are they also that are heavenly. [49] And as we have borne the image of the earthy, we shall also bear the image of the heavenly (1 Corinthians 15.39-49).

Paul revealed that every part of God's creation has an innate glory. Man's natural body has a glory since he was made in the image of God (Genesis 1.27). But God is in the process of transforming believers into a greater glory. This is a cooperative work between the believer and God. As the believer is occupied with God's Word, the Holy Spirit transforms the believer into the image of Christ. The believer *lives* by faith. The transformation culminates in the believer's glorification which Paul explained takes place at the Rapture. This is the resurrection of the Church, the body of Christ (1 Corinthians 15.51-54).

Abraham's Seed

Scripturally, Abraham's "seed" (σπέρμα Ἀβραάμ) has three senses and its meaning is determined by context:

1. Ethnic Israel (all Jews), the descendants of Jacob (John 8.37; Acts 3.25; Romans 11.1; 2 Corinthians 11.22)
2. Believing Israel, Jews who have believed God (Romans 2.28-29, 9.6-7)
3. Gentiles saved like Abraham (Romans 4.16; Galatians 3.7-8, 29)

The phrase "seed or children of Abraham" is *not* synonymous with "Israel."[41] Just as heaven and earth are separate entities throughout

[41] "Israel" is a *technical* term. It *always* refers to the descendants of Jacob, the Jews. Sometimes it referred to the ten tribes and other times to the whole nation. Gentiles or the Church are *never* called "Israel." Paul's phrase, "Israel of God" (Galatians 6.16) were Jews who had

eternity, Israel and the Church are separate identities throughout eternity. The teaching that the Church is Israel or part of Israel is one of the greatest theological errors in Christendom. It has compounded error upon error and led to great doctrinal confusion in the Church. To mix and mingle Israel and the Church reveals a failure to understand Paul and ecclesiology at the most basic level.

Paul separated "true" or "believing" Israel from ethnic Israel in his statement, "for they are not all Israel, who are of Israel" and "neither are they all children of the seed of Abraham" (Romans 9.6-7).[42] In this context, "Israel" meant believing Israel. Believing Israel is who Paul had in mind when he wrote in Romans 11.26, "all Israel will be saved." He meant Jews who believe the gospel of the kingdom—that Jesus was the Christ (Matthew 24.14)—not all Jews.

Paul expressed this thought earlier in his introduction to the Romans of the pervasion of sin throughout both the Gentile and Jewish world:

> [28] For he is not a Jew, which is one outwardly; neither is that circumcision, which is outward in the flesh: [29] But he is a Jew, which is one inwardly; and circumcision is that of the heart, in the spirit, and not in the letter; whose praise is not of men, but of God (Roman 2.28-29).

A "true Jew" was not simply a Jew who had been circumcised in the flesh but one who had been circumcised in heart: a Jew who knew God, one who had believed God.

Romans 9-11 is Paul's great discussion of Israel in light of its rejection of the Messiah. Paul disclosed God's mercy and that His mercy was a sovereign choice (Romans 9.15). But Paul did not limit

---

believed the gospel of the kingdom, not members of the Church, the body of Christ.

[42] Jesus told the Jews who opposed Him that Satan was their father, not God (John 8.39-44). He distinguished "true" believing Israel from the mere physical offspring of Abraham.

his discussion of mercy to Israel alone. It extended also to Gentiles. Paul wrote:

> [23] And that he might make known the riches of his glory on the vessels of mercy, which he had afore prepared unto glory, [24] Even us, whom he has called, not of the Jews only, but also of the Gentiles? [25] As he says also in Hosea, I will call them my people, which were not my people; and her beloved, which was not beloved. [26] And it shall come to pass, that in the place where it was said unto them, You are not my people; there shall they be called the children of the living God (Romans 9.23-26).

God's promise of calling "not my people," Loammi (לֹא עַמִּי), to "my people," Ammi, עַמִּי, referred to Jews. But Paul applied this passage to Gentiles, specifically, to believers, based upon faith.

Paul wrote similarly to the Corinthians:

> [13] Now for a recompense in the same, (I speak as unto my children,) be also enlarged. [14] Be not unequally yoked together with unbelievers: for what fellowship has righteousness with unrighteousness? and what communion has light with darkness? [15] And what concord has Christ with Belial? or what part has he that believeth with an infidel? [16] And what agreement has the temple of God with idols? for you are the temple of the living God; as God has said, I will dwell in them, and walk in them; and I will be their God, and they shall be my people. [17] Wherefore come out from among them, and be separate, says the Lord, and touch not the unclean thing; and I will receive you. [18] And will be a Father unto you, and you shall be my sons and daughters, says the Lord Almighty (2 Corinthians 6.13-18).

Paul again took a promise God gave Israel and applied it to Gentile believers. Did he mean Israel included Gentiles? Not at all. Believers of Paul's gospel are "children of Abraham" *by faith*. Paul explained this in his letter to the Galatians:

> [7] Know therefore that they which are of faith, the same are the children of Abraham. [8] And the scripture, foreseeing that God would justify the Gentiles through faith, preached before the gospel unto Abraham, saying, In you shall all nations be blessed. [9] So then they which be of faith are blessed with faithful Abraham (Galatians 3.7-9).

The Abrahamic covenant anticipated God blessing Gentiles. Paul's point in applying the Hosea and other prophetic passages to Gentiles was to show that the Abrahamic Covenant was being fulfilled through him in revealing God's grace of salvation by faith alone. Abraham was the prototype of such salvation (Romans 4.1-5) and all who are saved by faith alone are Abraham's children. Believing Israel occupied God's favor by *promise* but believing Gentiles occupy it by *grace*.

2. The Gospel of the Grace of God

Immediately after Paul was saved he proclaimed the gospel of the kingdom, the gospel proclaimed by John, Jesus, and the Twelve. Luke wrote in Acts 9.20, "And straightway he preached Christ in the synagogues, that he is the Son of God." Paul did not preach Christ's death and resurrection for salvation because he, like the Twelve, did not know this truth. All he knew was that Jesus was the Christ, which was the faith component of the gospel of the kingdom. Paul believed in the *identity* of Christ.

The gospel Paul came to preach was a secret. It was the gospel of the grace of God (Acts 20.24), the "glorious gospel" (2 Corinthians 4.4; 1 Timothy 1.11). Paul most likely received this gospel during his three years in Arabia and Damascus (Galatians 1.15-18) and he wrote that he received it directly from the risen Lord (Galatians 1.11-12).

Writing the Ephesians, Paul asked them to pray for him, that he might proclaim the "secret of the gospel." This passage should settle any doubt that Paul's gospel was different from the gospel proclaimed by the Twelve. The passage reads:

> [18] With all prayer and petition pray at all times in the Spirit, and with this in view, be on the alert with all perseverance and petition for all the saints, [19] and *pray* on my behalf, that utterance may be given to me in the opening of my mouth, to make known with boldness the secret [μυστήριον] of the gospel, [20] for which I am an ambassador in chains; that in *proclaiming* it I may speak boldly, as I ought to speak (Ephesians 6.18-20).

Paul wrote a similar message to the Romans:

> [25] Now to Him who is able to establish you according to my gospel and the preaching of Jesus Christ, according to the revelation of the secret [μυστήριον] which has been kept secret [μυστήριον] for long ages past, [26] but now is manifested, and by the Scriptures of the prophets, according to the commandment of the eternal God, has been made known to all the nations, leading to obedience of faith (Romans 16.25-26).

The expression "secret of the gospel" is a genitive of apposition, "the secret which is the gospel" or "the secret, namely, the gospel." In other passages, Paul used the phrase "my gospel" to show that his gospel was different from and not known by those who were before him (Romans 2.16; 2 Timothy 2.8; 1 Corinthians 15.1; Galatians 1.1, 11-12, 2.2).

Believing Paul's gospel is how one is saved from sin and death in our present age. It is how one obtains eternal life. The word "gospel" (εὐαγγέλιον) means "good news." Paul's gospel was the good news that Christ's death and resurrection had solved the problem of sin and death and removed the barrier between God and man. It was the heart of his ministry.

The clearest definition of Paul's gospel is in his first letter to the Corinthians. He wrote:

> [1] Now, brethren, I keep making known to you the gospel which I proclaimed to you, which also you received, and in

> which you stand; [2] Through which you are being saved,[43] if you possess[44] what I preached unto you, unless you believed in vain. [3] For I delivered to you first what I also received, that Christ died for our sins according to the scriptures; [4] And that he was buried, and that he rose again the third day according to the scriptures (1 Corinthians 15.1-4).

Paul's gospel is that Christ died for us, was buried, and rose from the dead.[45] By placing one's trust in the work of Christ (His death and resurrection) one is saved from sin and death. God gives the one who trusts in Christ's work eternal life.

Paul's Gospel	
"My Gospel"	Romans 2.16; 2 Timothy 2.8; 1 Corinthians 15.1; Galatians 1.1, 11-12, 2.2; 1 Timothy 1.11
Paul's Gospel: Content and Response	
Content	Christ died for our sins and rose from the dead (1 Corinthians 15.3-4).
Response	Salvation is by faith *alone*—believing Christ died for one's sins and rose from the dead (1 Corinthians 15.2).[46]

---

[43] The word σῴζεσθε is a present passive indicative, "are being saved." Paul wrote that believing his gospel had saved them and this action continued as sanctification (Philippians 1.6). In numerous passages Paul stated salvation was a present possession (Ephesians 1.3, 7, 11; Colossians 1.13) and an ongoing process.

[44] The word κατέχετε is a present active indicative and is best rendered "possess" or "are possessing." Such a translation agrees with the latter part of the verse, "unless you believed in vain" or "unless you didn't believe."

[45] Presentations of the gospel often mention Christ's death for our sins with no mention of His resurrection. But Christ's resurrection is essential to the salvation message. If Christ did not rise, we are still in our sins and our faith is in vain (1 Corinthians 15.17). One cannot be saved apart from believing in Christ's resurrection.

[46] Paul wrote many verses that establish the fact salvation is by faith alone. A few are the following: Romans 1.16-17, 3.21-22, 26, 28, 30, 4.5, 5.1).

Christ finished the work of salvation by His death on the cross (John 19.30). His resurrection proved His work had satisfied God's justice and that He had defeated sin and death. One only need trust Him. Salvation is a gift received by faith *alone*.

Paul wrote the Corinthians:

> [17] For Christ sent me not to baptize, but to preach the gospel: not with wisdom of words, lest the cross of Christ should be made of none effect. [18] For the preaching of the cross is to them that perish foolishness; but unto us which are saved it is the power of God (1 Corinthians 1.17-18).

Water baptism was the centerpiece of the gospel of the kingdom. God sent John the Baptist to baptize (Matthew 3.1-6; Mark 1.4) and Jesus sent the Twelve to baptize (Matthew 28.19). But the risen Lord did *not* send Paul to baptize. He sent him to proclaim the gospel, the preaching of the cross. This one fact shows how different Paul's ministry was from the Twelve (Matthew 28.19; Acts 2.38). Paul declared his gospel was the power of God for salvation to anyone who *believes* (Romans 1.16-17, 3.22, 26, 4.1-5, 5.1).[47] The gospel is the power of Christianity.[48] He wrote:

> [1] And I, brethren, when I came to you, came not with excellency of speech or of wisdom, declaring unto you the testimony of God. [2] For I determined not to know anything among you, save Jesus Christ, and him crucified (1 Corinthians 2.1-2).

To the Romans he wrote:

---

[47] Paul practiced water baptism early in his ministry but ceased by the time he wrote the Corinthians. Paul's wrote in Ephesians 4.5 (c. 60-62 A.D.) that there was "one baptism." That was the baptism of the Holy Spirit (1 Corinthians 12.13). It is the only valid baptism for the Church, the body of Christ. Water baptism has ceased for Christians.

[48] Too many in Christendom look for signs and experiences. The true power of God is the gospel. It is the power of God unto salvation to everyone who *believes* (Romans 1.16).

> 16 For I am not ashamed of the gospel of Christ: for it is the power of God unto salvation to everyone that believes; to the Jew first, and also to the Greek. 17 For therein is the righteousness of God revealed from faith to faith: as it is written, The just shall live by faith (Romans 1.16-17).

The Council of Jerusalem: The Great Hinge

Luke's account of the Council of Jerusalem (Acts 15), held in 51 A.D., reveals how different Paul's gospel was from the gospel proclaimed by the believing Jews at Jerusalem. Luke recorded the human reason for the meeting and Paul recorded the divine reason. Luke wrote that the church at Antioch decided Paul should go to Jerusalem to meet with its leaders (Acts 14.25-15.2). But Paul wrote that he went by revelation (κατὰ ἀποκάλυψιν). He went by order of the risen Christ (Galatians 2.2).

> 1 Then fourteen years after I went up again to Jerusalem with Barnabas, and took Titus with me also. 2 And I went up by revelation, and communicated to them that gospel which I preach among the Gentiles, but privately to them which were of reputation, lest by any means I should run, or had run, in vain.

Luke gave the reason for the need of the meeting:

> 1 Some men came down from Judea and began teaching the brethren, Unless you are circumcised according to the custom of Moses, you cannot be saved. 2 And when Paul and Barnabas had great dissension and debate with them, the brethren determined that Paul and Barnabas and some others of them should go up to Jerusalem to the apostles and elders concerning this issue. 3 Therefore, being sent on their way by the church, they were passing through both Phoenicia and Samaria, describing in detail the conversion of the Gentiles, and were bringing great joy to all the brethren. 4 When they arrived at Jerusalem, they were received by the church and the apostles and the elders, and they reported all that God had done with them. 5 But some

> of the sect of the Pharisees who had believed stood up, saying, It is necessary to circumcise them and to direct them to observe the Law of Moses (Acts 15.1-5).

The Jerusalem leaders maintained (rightly, according to the gospel of the kingdom) that salvation required faith and works. Because of this, some of them were going to Paul's converts and telling them that to be saved required circumcision and keeping the Mosaic Law (Acts 15.1, 5).

Paul wrote he "communicated" (ἀνεθέμην, aorist middle indicative) his gospel to the believers at Jerusalem (Galatians 2.2). The word ἀνατίθημι means "set forth" or "communicate."[49] Why would Paul need to explain his gospel if they were proclaiming the same gospel? The answer is obvious. They were *not* proclaiming the same gospel. Had they been, there would have been no need for a council.

The meeting was contentious (Acts 15.7; Galatians 2.5). Neither side would give an inch. Why should they? Both the gospel of the kingdom and Paul's gospel were valid! Both had come from God. The gospel of the kingdom required repentance, belief that Jesus was the Messiah, the Son of God, and works. Paul's gospel required only faith—trusting in the work of Christ, His death on the cross for our sins and His resurrection. These gospels were entirely different. The reason Paul had to communicate his gospel to the leaders at the Council was because *they did not know it.*

After much argument, Peter, who had remained quiet during the debate made a remarkable statement.[50] Luke wrote:

> 7 After there had been much debate, Peter stood up and said to them, Brethren, you know that in the early days God made a choice among you, that by my mouth the Gentiles

---

[49] This word is used one other time in the New Testament: Festus explained (ἀνέθετο) Paul's legal case to King Agrippa (Acts 25.14).

[50] It is significant that Peter was not in charge of the Council. Peter's authority had been supplanted by James, the Lord's half-brother. In the years since Pentecost, Peter had lost his position of leadership.

> would hear the word of the gospel and believe. [8] And God, who knows the heart, testified to them giving them the Holy Spirit, just as He also did to us; [9] and He made no distinction between us and them, cleansing their hearts by faith. [10] Now therefore why do you put God to the test by placing upon the neck of the disciples a yoke which neither our fathers nor we have been able to bear? [11] But we believe that we are saved through the grace of the Lord Jesus, in the same way as they also are. (Acts 15.7-11).

At the critical moment, God the Holy Spirit moved Peter to recall his visit, many years before, to the house of Cornelius, a Gentile, a Roman centurion (Acts 10.1-48).[51] After he remembered this experience, Peter rose to Paul's defense. He recalled that in that remarkable visit, Cornelius and his family had been saved without circumcision or keeping the Mosaic Law. Peter recognized and reminded the Jewish believers in Jerusalem that Gentiles, by his mouth, had been saved by faith alone. Then, Peter made a transformational statement:

> But we believe that we are saved through the grace of the Lord Jesus, in the same way as they also are (Acts 15.11).

Peter's statement was stunning. Jews were to be saved like Gentiles? This statement overturned two millennia of Jewish theology. For 2,000 years, Jews had occupied God's favored position. Gentiles had come to God through Israel's rule book for salvation. But *now*, Peter recognized God was doing something entirely new and different through Paul. From now on *Jews* had to be saved by faith *alone* believing *Paul's gospel*—just like Gentiles.[52] The gospel of the kingdom ended the instant Peter

---

[51] Peter went to Cornelius' house under duress (Acts 10.9-16). When he arrived, he told Cornelius it was prohibited (ἀθέμιτος) for a Jew to associate with a Gentile (Acts 10.28) but that God had permitted his visit. When Peter returned to Jerusalem, the Jewish believers rebuked him for going, proving they were not evangelizing Gentiles (cf. Acts 11.19).

[52] Did Peter have the authority to do this? Indeed he did. The Lord Himself had given him the keys of the kingdom and told him that

pronounced those words.[53] From that moment forward, only one gospel existed: Paul's gospel.

The Gospel of Grace: By Faith Alone

The Scriptures reveal faith has always been required for salvation (Hebrews 11). They also reveal men and women were *not* saved by faith *alone*.[54] Salvation by faith *alone* began with Paul.

From the time of Paul's return from Arabia until the Council of Jerusalem, two gospels, the gospel of the kingdom and the gospel of grace were valid salvation messages. The gospel of the kingdom began with John the Baptist and continued until the Council of Jerusalem. Paul's gospel began after he returned from Arabia.[55] The Jerusalem Council (51 A.D.) formally recognized that only Paul's gospel was valid for salvation. Paul wrote the Galatians concerning this about 55 A.D., four years after the Council:[56]

> 6 I marvel that you are so soon removed from him that
> called you into the grace of Christ unto another gospel:
> 7 Which is not another; but there be some that trouble you,

---

whatever he bound on earth would be bound in heaven (Matthew 16.19, 18.18). Peter exercised his God-given authority.

53 Paul's gospel will continue until the completion of the Church, the body of Christ. After this, the gospel of the kingdom returns and will be the gospel which saves until Christ's 2nd Advent (Matthew 24.14). In Revelation 2-3, Jesus revealed the conditions for salvation during the Tribulation.

54 One of God's absolutes is the requirement of faith for salvation. Paul wrote the Jews that apart from faith, it was impossible to please God (Hebrews 11.6).

55 Acts 9.20 states Paul preached the gospel of the kingdom immediately after his salvation. However, during the three years he spent in Arabia and Damascus, the Lord revealed the gospel of the grace of God, that Christ died for our sins and rose from the dead and that by believing this one is saved.

56 Paul wrote all his letters *after* the Council of Jerusalem. His first letter was to the Thessalonians and was probably written in 51 or 52 A.D. Thus, God settled the matter of the gospel before Paul began to write doctrine for the Church.

> and would pervert the gospel of Christ. [8] But though we, or an angel from heaven, preach any other gospel unto you than that which we have preached unto you, let him be accursed. [9] As we said before, so say I now again, if any man preach any other gospel unto you than that you have received, let him be accursed (Galatians 1.6-9).

Paul's warning was extremely strong. He could not have used such language until after the Council of Jerusalem's decision regarding the gospel. During God's program of the Church, the body of Christ, Paul declared anyone—man or angel—who proclaims a gospel different from his, "let him be accursed" (ἀνάθεμα ἔστω).[57] The Greek phrase is a present active imperative. Anyone who teaches one is saved by anything but by believing Christ died for his sins and rose from the dead is cursed. This should strike fear into any who add water baptism, taking Communion, tithing, joining a church, being good, etc. to Paul's gospel. Doing so places oneself under God's condemnation.[58]

Before "The Faith" Came

Paul's teaching in Galatians 3 is extremely important to understand. One cannot live the Christian life apart from it. Throughout his letter, Paul wrote to instruct the Galatians that God sanctifies believers the same way He justified them: by faith. God sanctifies believers by faith, through the power of the Holy Spirit, not through the administration of the Mosaic Law. Paul wrote:

> [23] But before the faith came, we were kept in custody under the law, being shut up to the faith which was later to be revealed. [24] Therefore the Law has become our tutor to Christ, so that we may be justified by faith. [25] But now the

---

[57] The word "another," in verse 6, is ἕτερος. In verse 7, the word "another" is ἄλλος. The word ἕτερος means "another of a different kind" while ἄλλος means "another of the same kind." The Galatians were abandoning Paul's gospel and embracing a different gospel (verse 7).

[58] This is such a serious matter Paul repeated it twice (vv. 8-9).

> faith has come, we are no longer under a tutor. For you are all the children of God through the faith in Christ Jesus (Galatians 3.23-26).

What did Paul mean? Was faith not always required for salvation? The Scriptures clearly reveal faith, believing God, has *always* been required for salvation. Hebrews 11.6 states it is impossible to please God apart from faith and Hebrews 11 is Paul's great summary of Old Testament saints saved by faith. But this was not Paul's point.

Galatians 3.23-26 requires careful attention since almost all translations render the verses incorrectly.[59] Verse 23 does not read, "before faith came" but "before **the** faith came" (πρὸ τοῦ δὲ ἐλθεῖν τὴν πίστιν). The text includes the definite article τὴν. When a definite article is present in Greek it calls attention to the identity of the noun, i.e., "the faith." The definite article is also found in the latter part of the verse, "to **the** faith about to be revealed" (εἰς τὴν μέλλουσαν πίστιν ἀποκαλυφθῆναι). Verse 25 has the same construction, "but since **the** faith came" (ἐλθούσης δὲ τῆς πίστεως). And in verse 26, Paul wraps up the thought, "for you are all the children of God through **the** faith in Christ Jesus" (διὰ τῆς πίστεως ἐν Χριστῷ Ἰησοῦ). These four instances of the definite article with the noun, "the faith," emphasize the identity of faith.[60]

What did Paul mean by "the faith" in these verses? "The faith" was *Paul's gospel*—the gospel of the grace of God (Acts 20.24; 1 Corinthians 15.1-4). It also included the other revelations Paul had received from Christ—*the secrets*. Put another way, "the faith" was that *body of truth Paul had received from the risen Lord.*

---

[59] Young's Literal Translation (YLT) is a happy exception.

[60] Greek has no indefinite article. A noun can be definite without the definite article but with the article it is always definite and calls attention to the identity of the noun.

The well-known verse, Ephesians 2.8 reveals the same truth. And, like the Galatians passage, translators have erred in its translation.[61] The KJV reads:

> For by grace are you saved through faith; and that not of yourselves: it is the gift of God (Ephesians 2.8).

But the Greek text reads: τῇ γὰρ χάριτί ἐστε σεσῳσμένοι διὰ τῆς πίστεως καὶ τοῦτο οὐκ ἐξ ὑμῶν θεοῦ τὸ δῶρον. A more accurate translation is the following:

> For by **the grace** you have been saved through **the faith** and this not from yourselves, the gift of God.

The grammatical construction of ἐστε σεσῳσμένοι is a perfect passive periphrastic participle. This construction uses the present tense of εἰμί with a perfect passive participle. Literally, it reads, "you are having been saved." Such construction gives the sense, "you have been saved and continue in this status."[62] Paul's point was to emphatically declare one is saved through "the faith"—his gospel.

Before Paul, no one understood the significance of Christ's death and resurrection with respect to salvation. No one proclaimed Christ died for our sins and rose from the dead and that by believing this one is saved.[63] And, in addition to Paul's gospel, no one knew

---

[61] A textual variant exists without the article τῆς. Its presence is supported by A, D^2, Ψ, 1881 and the great majority of the manuscripts. Its absence is supported by א, B, D, F, G, P. 6, 33, 104, 1175, 1739, 2464, 2495, and a few Coptic versions. Internally, Ephesians 3.17 includes the article with faith and supports the article's inclusion. Thus, external and internal evidence support the reading with the article. The inclusion of the definite article with χάρις also lends weight to this reading. Paul is speaking specifically of the grace he received from the risen Lord (1 Corinthians 3.10, 15.10; 2 Corinthians 6.1, etc.).

[62] Moule, C F. D. *Idiom Book of New Testament Greek*. Cambridge: Cambridge University Press, 1979, p. 18-19.

[63] This may be shocking. If it is, it is because so few know the Biblical record because tradition has replaced the Biblical text. Christendom

the body of truth he revealed. It was all new—previously hidden by God.

Lastly, Paul wrote Timothy concerning deacons:

> 8 Likewise must the deacons be grave, not double-tongued, not given to much wine, not greedy of filthy lucre; 9 Holding the secret [μυστήριον] of the faith in a pure conscience (1 Timothy 3.8-9).

Paul included the definite article with "faith" and with "secret" (τὸ μυστήριον τῆς πίστεως), "**the** secret of **the** faith."[64] Faith was no secret. But Paul's gospel was a secret. "The faith" was Paul's gospel and in this passage most likely included Paul's other secrets.

The Assurance of Salvation

God's salvation is a gift—the greatest imaginable gift. Paul wrote the Ephesians:

> 8 For by the grace you have been saved through the faith; and that not of yourselves, it is the gift of God; 9 not as a result of works, so that no one may boast (Ephesians 2.8-9).

Some have argued that faith (or grace) in this passage is the gift. But since a pronoun normally agrees with its antecedent in gender and number there is a grammatical problem with "grace" or "faith" being the "gift." If Paul had meant "grace" or "faith" to be the antecedent, he would have used the feminine form of "this" (αὕτη) rather than the neuter form (τοῦτο). A neuter pronoun can refer to a phrase or summarize a thought. And this is just the case. The sense of the passage is that the "gift of God" is salvation--the entire salvation experience of being saved by the grace (of God) through

---

has become like the Judaism of Jesus' day. Jesus had two main problems with the religious professionals: self-righteousness and tradition. Christianity, like Judaism, has become poisoned by tradition.

[64] This phrase is a genitive of apposition and literally reads "the secret which is (or namely) "the faith," i.e., Paul's gospel.

the faith (Paul's gospel). Such a reading agrees with other statements of Paul regarding salvation as God's gift (Romans 5.15-18, 6.23; 2 Corinthians 9.15; Ephesians 3.7, 4.7).

Nowhere is the assurance of salvation more pronounced than in Paul's writings. Time and again he declared salvation was a present possession of the one who believed his gospel (Romans 3.21-28, 4.1-5; Galatians 2.16, 21; 1 Corinthians 15.1-4. Consider the following:

> [8] But God commends his love toward us, in that, while we were yet sinners, Christ died for us. [9] Much more then, having been justified by his blood, we shall be saved from wrath through him (Romans 5.8-9).[65]
>
> In whom we have redemption through his blood, the forgiveness of sins, according to the riches of his grace (Ephesians 1.7).
>
> [12] Giving thanks unto the Father, who made us meet to be partakers of the inheritance of the saints in light: [13] Who delivered us from the power of darkness, and translated us into the kingdom of his dear Son: [14] In whom we have redemption through his blood, even the forgiveness of sins (Colossians 1.12-14).
>
> [5] Not by works of righteousness which we have done, but according to his mercy he saved us, by the washing of regeneration, and renewing of the Holy Ghost; [6] Which he shed on us abundantly through Jesus Christ our Savior; [7] That having been justified by his grace, we have become heirs according to the hope of eternal life (Titus 3.5-7).

All these passages speak of the believer's salvation in the past tense. Salvation is a past event and present possession. Eternal life does not begin after a believer dies but the instant he believes the

---

[65] The salvation from wrath is the Lord's deliverance of believers from the Tribulation, not from hell (1 Thessalonians 1.10, 5.9). This is a Rapture passage.

gospel. Thanks be to God for His indescribable gift! (χάρις δὲ τῷ θεῷ ἐπὶ τῇ ἀνεκδιηγήτῳ αὐτοῦ δωρεᾷ, 2 Corinthians 9.15).

The Extent of Christ's Work

The extent of Christ's atoning work has been debated throughout Christendom for generations. As examined above, God revealed little concerning His atoning work in the Old Testament but had revealed two things: *only* Jews were included and *all* Jews were included. Isaiah 53 reads,

> [5] But he was wounded for our transgressions, he was bruised for our iniquities: the chastisement of our peace was upon him; and with his stripes we are healed. [6] All we like sheep have gone astray; we have turned every one to his own way; and the Lord has laid on him the iniquity of us all.

The pronoun "our" referred only to Jews but included *all* Jews "we have turned everyone to his own way and the Lord has laid on him the iniquity of us all." Isaiah wrote the Messiah would suffer for *all Jews*. Gentiles were *not* in view.

As noted above, the great day of sacrifice for Israel was the Day of Atonement (יוֹם כִּיפּוּר). All Israel was in view and all sins were in view. On the Day of Atonement, the High Priest went into the Holy of Holies and sprinkled the blood on the mercy seat for all the sins of all the people (Leviticus 16.15-17). The scape goat was taken to the desert, symbolically carrying the sins of all the people (Leviticus 16.20-22, 30, 33-34).

When it became known the Virgin Mary would have a child, the angel of the Lord appeared to Joseph to reassure him. Matthew wrote:

> [20] But while he thought on these things, behold, the angel of the LORD appeared unto him in a dream, saying, Joseph, son of David, fear not to take unto you Mary your wife: for that which is conceived in her is of the Holy Ghost. [21] And

> she shall bring forth a son, and you shall call his name Jesus: for he shall save his people from their sins (Matthew 1.20-21).

The "his people" in verse 21 were Jews. As in the prophetic literature, Gentiles were not included.

Jesus told the Jews: "I am the good shepherd: the good shepherd gives his life for the sheep" (John 10.11, 15). The sheep were Jews. "Sheep" are God's designation for Israel, not Gentiles.

God did not reveal the full extent of Christ's atoning blood until Paul. God knew He would redeem the entire human race but kept this truth secret.[66] Paul wrote:

> [4] But when the fullness of the time came, God sent forth His Son, born of a woman, born under the Law, [5] so that He might redeem those who were under the Law, that we might receive the adoption as sons (Galatians 4.4-5).

Paul wrote God had redeemed Israel so Gentiles could be saved. Such a statement is consistent with the Abrahamic Covenant, in which Gentiles would be blessed through Israel.[67]

---

[66] Some may object, noting that John the Baptist said, "Behold the Lamb of God who takes away the sin of the world" (John 1.29) and John the Apostle declared God so loved the world that whoever believed in Christ would have eternal life (John 3.15-17). These are difficult passages but one thing is clear: no one proclaimed Christ's atoning death and resurrection for the whole world before Paul. The Twelve likely learned Christ died for all—Jew and Gentile—from Paul and John probably wrote his Gospel after this. The prophets often prophesied things they did not understand and John the Baptist could have spoken this prophecy without understanding it. Also, God may have hidden the understanding of this truth as He had hidden His death and resurrection from the Twelve (Luke 18.31-34).

[67] The "we" of verse 5 does not mean Paul thought of himself as a Gentile. He spoke in his office as "the apostle of the Gentiles" and specifically of God's program of favor for Gentiles (Romans 11).

Paul's letters have many texts which state Christ died for all. Some of these include Romans 5.6-10; 2 Corinthians 5.14-17, 20-21; 1 Timothy 1.15-16. Those who argue against Christ's dying for all mankind argue that if Christ died for all, all are saved. This logic not only has no Scriptural support but reveals a gross misunderstanding of God's saving work. The Scriptures reveal salvation is a work in which both God and man participate. God has done everything to secure man's salvation but man must appropriate it for it to become effective.

Going back to the case of Israel, the sacrifices on the Day of Atonement were for every Jew but every Jew was not saved. To be saved, one had to exercise faith and obey the Law. The sacrifices were shadows of Christ's work. He died for all but not everyone is saved. He satisfied the justice of God but God's salvation is effective only for those who believe.

Those who argue Christ died only for "the elect" state that since Paul and the other writers wrote to believers their statements about Christ's death applies to believers, not to all. This is a valid point, however, several texts explicitly state Christ died for *everyone*. Paul wrote:

> [3] For this is good and acceptable in the sight of God our
> Savior; [4] Who will have all men to be saved, and to come
> unto the knowledge of the truth. [5] For there is one God, and
> one mediator between God and men, the man Christ Jesus;
> [6] Who gave himself a ransom for all, to be testified in due
> time (1 Timothy 2.3-6).

This passage states God desires all be saved.[68] How would it be possible for all to be saved if Christ died only for some? The remainder of the verse states that Christ was a ransom for all. The only way to limit Christ's work to "the elect" is by abusing the text.

---

[68] The verb θέλω here is a present active indicative, "keeps wishing," "desires." God's will is that everyone be saved. The reason people are not saved is because they repulse God's will, not because God has not made salvation available for them.

Paul wrote Timothy:

> For it is for this we labor and strive, because we have fixed our hope on the living God, who is the Savior of all men, especially of believers (1 Timothy 4.10).

Paul stated God is the Savior of all, and in particular, believers. Believers are "the elect." But the passage also states God is the Savior of *all.* To read "all" to mean the "elect" renders the passage unintelligible. The sense would be, "who is the Savior of the elect, especially of the elect." Almost as bad is the attempt to make "all men" read "all kinds of men." Such desperate twisting of the text is at odds with the testimony of both Old and New Testaments.

This dichotomy is also seen in 2 Corinthians 5.15. Paul wrote:

> And that he died for all, that they which live should not henceforth live unto themselves, but unto him which died for them, and rose again.

His statement, "he died for all" refers to every human being and "they who live" refers to those who have appropriated God's salvation. This theological pattern is repeated many times in the Scriptures. Paul wrote similarly in his first letter to the Corinthians. He stated, "For after that in the wisdom of God the world by wisdom knew not God, it pleased God by the foolishness of preaching to save them that believe" (1 Corinthians 1.21). Christ died for all but only those who believe are saved.

In what should be regarded by Christendom as the Church's "Great Commission," Paul wrote:

> [18] And all things are of God, who hath reconciled us to himself by Jesus Christ, and hath given to us the ministry of reconciliation; [19] To wit, that God was in Christ, reconciling the world unto himself, not imputing their trespasses unto them; and hath committed unto us the word of reconciliation (2 Corinthians 5.18-19).

Paul declared God's salvation of believers (verse 18). He then stated God had reconciled the world to Himself. Reconciliation means God has removed the barrier between Himself and mankind. Nothing exists between God and man except Jesus Christ (1 Timothy 2.5-6) for He paid for the sins of every person and satisfied God's justice. One only needs to trust in Christ's death and resurrection for salvation. This is grace! Paul declared God has given this wonderful "word of reconciliation" to the Church, the body of Christ.

Paul's letter to the Jews revealed the same truth:

> [9] But we do see Him who was made for a little while lower than the angels, namely, Jesus, because of the suffering of death crowned with glory and honor, so that by the grace of God He might taste death for everyone. [10] For it was fitting for Him, for whom are all things, and through whom are all things, in bringing many sons to glory, to perfect the author of their salvation through sufferings (Hebrews 2.9-10).

This text states Christ tasted death for every person (verse 9) but that only some benefitted, i.e., "many sons of glory." Again, one cannot obtain that which is refused.

Peter's testimony agreed:

> [18] For Christ also died for sins once for all, the just for the unjust, so that He might bring us to God, having been put to death in the flesh, but made alive in the spirit; [19] in which also He went and made proclamation to the spirits now in prison, [20] who once were disobedient, when the patience of God kept waiting in the days of Noah, during the construction of the ark, in which a few, that is, eight persons, were brought safely through the water (1 Peter 3.18-20).

> [1] But false prophets also arose among the people, just as there will also be false teachers among you, who will secretly introduce destructive heresies, even denying the

> Master who bought them, bringing swift destruction upon themselves. [2] Many will follow their sensuality, and because of them the way of the truth will be maligned; [3] and in their greed they will exploit you with false words; their judgment from long ago is not idle, and their destruction is not asleep (2 Peter 2.1-3).

Both texts state Christ died for everyone: "the just for the unjust" and "even denying the Master who bought them."

John's testimony also agreed with Paul and Peter:

> [1] My little children, I am writing these things to you so that you may not sin. And if anyone sins, we have an Advocate with the Father, Jesus Christ the righteous; [2] and He Himself is the propitiation for our sins; and not for ours only, but also for those of the whole world (1 John 2.1-2).

> We have seen and testify that the Father has sent the Son to be the Savior of the world (1 John 4.14).

John declared Christ died not only for the sins of believers "our sins" but for the sins of the "whole world." Could words be clearer?

The Gospel of the Kingdom Redux

As noted above, Paul's gospel replaced the gospel of the kingdom at the Council of Jerusalem (Acts 15.11). But the gospel of the kingdom will return after God has completed the Church, the body of Christ.[69] Jesus declared the gospel of the kingdom will be proclaimed during the Tribulation until His 2nd Advent:

---

[69] Paul's phrase, the "fullness of the Gentiles" (Romans 11.25) means God's completion of His program of favor with Gentiles. The chief beneficiary in this program is the Church, the body of Christ. Once completed, God removes it.

> And this gospel of the kingdom shall be preached in all the world for a witness unto all nations; and then shall the end come (Matthew 24.14).

After God has completed and removed His Church, men and women will be saved once again by believing the gospel of the kingdom—that Jesus is the Messiah, the Son of God. The reason for this is twofold. During Jesus' earthly ministry, God had revealed only the gospel of the kingdom. Had Israel accepted Christ, the gospel of the kingdom would have been the only gospel since the Church would not have come into existence. God would have continued His revealed, prophetic plan with Israel and the nation would have fulfilled its role under the covenants.

The second reason is that sometime after God completes and removes His Church, the Antichrist will emerge. During that time, the temptation will be to believe the Beast is God. Jesus warned of this deceit: "I am come in my Father's name, and you receive me not: if another shall come in his own name, him you will receive" (John 5.43). Salvation will be based again upon believing in the *identity* of Christ, that Jesus is the Christ, not the Beast. This explains the Lord's warning, "he that shall endure unto the end, the same shall be saved" (Matthew 24.13) and His warnings in Revelation 2-3 to the seven Jewish assemblies. He instructed the Jews to overcome (νικάω) which will mean rejecting the Antichrist as God—not worshipping him and taking his mark (Revelation 13.8, 15-16, 14.9-11). These will inherit eternal life.[70]

Timetable of the Gospels					
Valid Gospels	John the Baptist	Paul	Council of Jerusalem	Rapture	Tribulation
Kingdom Gospel	X	X	X		X
Grace Gospel		X	X	X	

[70] The Antichrist will demand worship of himself and his image (Revelation 13.8, 14, 15, 14.9). Those who "overcome" keep the first and second commandments of the Decalogue (Exodus 20.2-6).

Timetable of the Gospels	
Gospel of the Kingdom	John the Baptist until the Council of Jerusalem (Matthew 3.1-2; Acts 15.11)
Gospel of Grace	Paul until Rapture (Galatians 1.15-18)
Gospel of the Kingdom	Rapture until 2nd Advent (Matthew 24.14)

Only One Gospel?

One of Christendom's great errors is the teaching that "there has always only been one gospel." Such teaching is so egregiously wrong one wonders if those who proclaim this have ever opened their Bibles! Paul's gospel, the gospel by which one is saved today, is to believe Christ died for one's sins and rose from the dead (1 Corinthians 15.1-4). Did Abraham believe this? Did Moses? Did David? Did the Twelve? Not according to the Scriptures. Luke wrote:

> 31 Then he took unto him the twelve, and said unto them, Behold, we go up to Jerusalem, and all things that are written by the prophets concerning the Son of man shall be accomplished. 32 For he shall be delivered unto the Gentiles, and shall be mocked, and spitefully entreated, and spit on: 33 And they shall scourge him, and put him to death: and the third day he shall rise again. 34 And they understood none of these things: and this saying was hid from them, neither knew they the things which were spoken (Luke 18.31-34).

The text states, "they understood none of these things." They had no idea Christ was going to die and rise from the dead. If they did not know the Lord was going to die and rise how could they be saved by believing this? The answer is obvious. They couldn't and they weren't. If they knew Jesus was going to rise from the dead, why weren't they at His tomb? John wrote that when he and Peter came to Jesus' tomb, "For as yet they knew not the scripture, that he must rise again from the dead" (John 20.9). Could words be clearer?

And as we have noted above, the leaders in Jerusalem had no understanding of Paul's gospel. They taught salvation required circumcision and keeping the Mosaic Law. Had they been proclaiming the same gospel as Paul, there would have been no argument and no need for a council.

Men and women are saved by believing what God has revealed at a particular time. Abraham was saved by believing what God told him (Genesis 15.1-6; Romans 4.1-3). The Jews were saved by believing and obeying what God had told them—by the Levitical sacrifices and keeping the Mosaic Law. Salvation during Christ's earthly ministry was by believing in the identity of Christ—He was the Messiah, the Son of God, water baptism, and keeping the Law.

Today there is but one gospel—Paul's gospel. That became a reality at the Council of Jerusalem. But Paul's gospel was not known until God revealed it to Paul (Galatians 1.11-12). It was a *secret.*

3. The Blinding of Israel

Paul wrote in Romans 11.25-27:

> [25] For I do not want you, brethren, to be uninformed of this secret [μυστήριον]—so that you will not be wise in your own estimation—that a partial hardening has happened to Israel until the fullness of the Gentiles has come in; [26] and so all Israel will be saved; just as it is written, the Deliverer will come from Zion, he will remove ungodliness from Jacob. This is My covenant with them, when I take away their sins.

God told the Jews that if they obeyed Him He would bless them and if they disobeyed He would discipline them (Deuteronomy 28-30). This truth was confirmed throughout Jewish history. Beginning with the Babylonian Captivity, Israel became subject to Gentile powers: the Babylonians, Medes and Persians, Greeks, and Romans. This remains Israel's current status. This was known. But God revealed to Paul something He had kept secret. He revealed a period of partial hardening (πώρωσις) for national Israel (Romans 11.25).[71]

This partial hardening of Israel—not total and not forever—would last *until* the fullness of the Gentiles (Romans 11.25). The fullness of the Gentiles is the completion of the Church, the body of Christ. Once the Church is complete God will revisit His program with Israel and begin removing this hardening.

The gospel of the kingdom required the whole nation to repent. Peter understood this. In his Pentecost address, he commanded all Israel to repent (Acts 2.36, 38).[72] Israel's repentance had been taught by the prophets (Isaiah 66.7-9, 25.9; Zechariah 12.10, 13.6), proclaimed in the Gospels, and Paul quoted Isaiah 59.20, "remove ungodliness from Jacob" in the above passage. Jesus told the Jews He would return when they repented (Matthew 23.37-39). This change of mind will remove Jacob's ungodliness.[73]

At the end of the Tribulation, national Israel will believe Jesus is the Messiah, the Son of God. "All Israel" will be saved ((Isaiah 66.8; Jeremiah 30.7; Zechariah 12.10, 13.6; Acts 2.36, 38; Romans 11.25-26) and enter the promised kingdom (Acts 1.6; Romans 11.16, cf. Matthew 6.10). Unlike the generation of Jesus' day, who failed to repent, the Tribulation generation will respond and believe Jesus is Messiah. This generation will be the "other sheep" of whom Jesus spoke in John 10.16: "And other sheep I have, which are not of this fold: them also I must bring, and they shall hear my voice; and there shall be one fold, and one shepherd." God

---

[71] A πώρωσις was a callus. Figuratively, it means a hardening or dullness of perception. It is used three times in the New Testament (Mark 3.5; Romans 11.25; Ephesians 4.18).

[72] Μετανοήσατε "repent" in Acts 2.38 is an aorist active imperative—a command. It means a change of mind.

[73] Interestingly, Paul used the name "Jacob," not "Israel." Jacob was Isaac's son's name before the Lord named him "Israel" at Peniel (Genesis 32.27-30). Peniel (פְּנוּאֵל) means "face of God" for Jacob declared he saw God face to face and lived. The Jews will live when they see God face to face at His 2nd Coming. Jacob will become Israel.

promised Israel will enjoy the kingdom (Romans 9.29 cf. Deuteronomy 28.1-14). He will keep His word.

4. The Rapture: Resurrection of the Church

No Christian doctrine is under greater assault at the present time than the Rapture. This opposition indicates the end of the Church is growing near (Ephesians 6.12).[74] Opponents state the Rapture is not found in the Old Testament, Gospels, the letters of James, Peter, John, or Jude.[75] They are right. The fact the Rapture is *not* in the Old Testament, Gospels, the letters of James, Peter, John, or Jude *proves* the opponents wrong. If the Rapture *were* in these Scriptures, Paul would be wrong and the doctrine of the Rapture would be error.

Paul wrote the Corinthians that the Rapture was a *secret*. Paul alone wrote of the Rapture. It is found only in his letters because it was a secret the risen Lord revealed to him alone. This is why it is not in any other portion of the Scriptures. Paul's opening words in 1 Corinthians 15.51 were ἰδοὺ, μυστήριον ὑμῖν λέγω, "Pay attention! I am telling you a secret!" Such words are so clear no one should misunderstand them. Christ's 2nd Advent was *not* a secret. What Paul wrote was a *new revelation*. Since it was new, it cannot be

---

[74] The word "rapture" does not occur in our English Bibles. We get the word from St. Jerome's (c. 347-420 A.D.) translation of the Greek New Testament into Latin (the Vulgate). He translated the word ἁρπάζω into the Latin "rapiemur." The Latin verb means to be "caught up" or "taken away." Our English word, "rapture" is a transliteration of the Latin. Paul used the word ἁρπάζω only once (1 Thessalonians 4.17) but taught the doctrine of the Rapture in other places with other expressions. The word ἁρπάζω means to "seize" or "snatch away" and is found 13 times in the following verses: Matthew 11.12, 13.19; John 6.15, 10.12, 28-29; Acts 8.39, 23.10; 2 Corinthians 12.2, 12.4; 1 Thessalonians 4.17; Jude 1.23; Revelation 12.5.

[75] Matthew 24.40-41, "Then shall two be in the field; the one shall be taken, and the other left. Two women shall be grinding at the mill; the one shall be taken, and the other left" has sometimes been cited as a Rapture passage. This is to misread the passage. The one "taken" is taken to judgment. The one "left" enters the kingdom.

found in the Old Testament, Gospels, or the letters of James, Peter, John, or Jude.

Concerning the Rapture, Paul wrote the Corinthians:

> [51] Behold, I tell you a secret [μυστήριον]; we will not all sleep, but we will all be changed, [52] in a moment, in the twinkling of an eye, at the last trumpet; for the trumpet will sound, and the dead will be raised imperishable, and we will be changed. [53] For this perishable must put on the imperishable, and this mortal must put on immortality (1 Corinthians 15.51-53).

The Rapture is the Church's resurrection. It is that event in which Christ returns in the atmosphere and transforms the mortal bodies of members of the Church, the body of Christ, into eternal, resurrection bodies. It occurs "in a moment, in the twinkling of an eye" according to the words of the KJV translators.[76] It will occur once the body of Christ is complete, what Paul described as the "fullness of the Gentiles" (Romans 11.25).

Paul detailed the order of the Rapture in his letter to the Thessalonians and used the word was ἁρπάζω, "seize" or "snatch away" to describe the event.

> [13] But we do not want you to be uninformed, brethren, about those who are asleep, so that you will not grieve as do the rest who have no hope. [14] For if we believe that Jesus died and rose again, even so God will bring with Him those who have fallen asleep in Jesus. [15] For this we say to you by the word of the Lord, that we who are alive and remain until the coming of the Lord, will not precede those who have fallen asleep. [16] For the Lord Himself will descend from heaven with a shout, with the voice of the archangel

---

[76] The word ἄτομος "moment" is the word from which we get the word "atom" and meant the smallest indivisible unit. It was created by the α privative (not) and τόμος (what has been cut off). Thus, ἄτομος was that which could not be cut or divided. The word ῥιπή "twinkling" means a throw, stroke, or beat.

> and with the trumpet of God, and the dead in Christ will rise first. [17] Then we who are alive and remain will be caught up [ἁρπάζω] together with them in the clouds to meet the Lord in the air, and so we shall always be with the Lord. [18] Therefore comfort one another with these words. (1 Thessalonians 4.13-18).

Paul's grand message was the gospel—Christ died for our sins and rose from the dead. He could not stop talking about it. And here we find it included in verse 14. Paul revealed the resurrection sequence of the body of Christ: First, believers who have died will be raised and transformed; Second, immediately following believers who have died, God will transform believers who are alive. Both will meet the Lord in the air. This wonderful doctrine reveals one generation of believers will escape physical death.

This return of the Lord is an entirely different event from His return at the end of the Tribulation. At the Rapture, the Lord will meet the Church, the body of Christ, in the clouds. It is a heavenly return for a heavenly people (Ephesians 1.3; Philippians 3.20-21). In the 2nd Advent, the Lord will return to earth. It is an earthly return for an earthly people (Zechariah 14.4).

Passages Teaching the Rapture	
Romans 5.9-10, 13.11-12	2 Thessalonians 2.1-4
1 Corinthians 1.4-8, 3.13, 5.1-5, 15.50-51	Philippians 1.3-6, 8-10, 2.14-16, 3.10-11, 20-21
2 Corinthians 1.12-14	Titus 2.13
1 Thessalonians 1.10, 4.13-18, 5.9	2 Timothy 1.16-18, 4.6-8

The Rapture is the "blessed hope" (Titus 2.13) of believers in the body of Christ. Paul wrote his first letter to the Thessalonians to remind them that members of the Church will not experience the Tribulation:

> [9] For they themselves report about us what kind of a reception we had with you, and how you turned to God from idols to serve a living and true God, [10] and

> to wait for His Son from heaven, whom He raised from the dead, Jesus, who rescues us from the wrath to come (1 Thessalonians 1.10).

This verse explicitly states members of the Church will *not* experience the Tribulation. Christ will "rescue us from the wrath to come," the Tribulation. The doctrine of the Pre-Tribulational Rapture is as clear a doctrine as Paul's gospel. Paul repeated this teaching later in his letter:

> 8 But since we are of *the* day, let us be sober, having put on the breastplate of faith and love, and as a helmet, the hope of salvation. 9 For God has not destined us for wrath, but for obtaining salvation through our Lord Jesus Christ, 10 who died for us, so that whether we are awake or asleep, we will live together with Him. 11 Therefore comfort one another and build up one another, just as you also are doing (1 Thessalonians 5.8-11).

In verse 9, Paul stated God has not destined the body of Christ for wrath (the Tribulation) but for salvation (the Rapture).[77] Paul again commanded believers to "encourage one another" with the doctrine of the Rapture.[78]

Paul wrote the Romans:

> 9 Much more then, having now been justified by His blood, we shall be saved from the wrath of God through Him. 10 For if while we were enemies we were reconciled to God

---

77 The wrath is not hell but the Tribulation, the Day of the Lord. Whenever Paul wrote about the Rapture he meant the Pre-Tribulation Rapture. Paul unequivocally taught that believers will not experience the 7-year period of Tribulation.

78 Twice Paul commanded believers to "comfort one another" (παρακαλεῖτε ἀλλήλους) with the doctrine of the Rapture (1 Thessalonians 4.18, 5.11). The word "comfort" in its original sense meant "with fortification." The word παρακαλεῖτε means "strengthen" or "encourage." To deny the Pre-Tribulational Rapture and not teach it as an encouragement to believers is to disobey God.

> through the death of His Son, much more, having been reconciled, we shall be saved by His life. [11] And not only this, but we also exult in God through our Lord Jesus Christ, through whom we have now received the reconciliation. (Romans 5.9-11).

The passage above is rarely taught as a Rapture passage. This is a major error for it is one of the *great* Rapture passages. Paul began his dissertation with the words, "Therefore having been justified by faith, we have peace with God through our Lord Jesus Christ (Romans 5.1).[79] Throughout this passage, Paul declared a believer's salvation has been made certain by God's justification of believers. No threat of separation from God remains (Romans 8.31-39). What did remain was the prophesied Day of the Lord. Paul understood God's prophetic plan of judgment. To give believers the assurance they would be spared this judgment Paul wrote, "we shall be saved from the wrath of God through Him" and "we shall be saved through His life." These two verses explicitly declare the Pre-Tribulational Rapture and that Christ's rescuing return was our "blessed hope" (Titus 2.13).

One of the surest ways to detect a false teacher is a denial of the Rapture. This theological error began early in the Church and has continued in Christendom for over 1,900 years. Paul addressed this heresy in his second letter to the Thessalonians. Someone, apparently posing as Paul, wrote the Thessalonians that the persecution they were experiencing was the Day of the Lord, the Tribulation.[80] Paul wrote to address this error:

> [1] Now we request you, brethren, with regard to the coming of our Lord Jesus Christ and our gathering together to Him, [2] that you not be quickly shaken from your composure or be disturbed either by a spirit or a message or a letter as if from us, to the effect that the day of the Lord

---

[79] A variant reading is in this verse: ἔχομεν, "we have" vs. ἔχωμεν "let us have." Strong external witnesses exist for both readings but ἔχομεν is preferred based on internal evidence. It fits Paul's declarative case of the believer's sure salvation.

[80] This was the beginning of the error of Post-Tribulationalism.

> has come. [3] Let no one in any way deceive you, for it will not come unless the departure [ἀποστασία] comes first, and the man of lawlessness is revealed, the son of destruction, [4] who opposes and exalts himself above every so-called god or object of worship, so that he takes his seat in the temple of God, displaying himself as being God. [5] Do you not remember that while I was still with you, I was telling you these things (2 Thessalonians 2.1-5)?

Paul had warned the Thessalonians they would experience testing and tribulations (1 Thessalonians 3.4) but that this was not the Day of the Lord.[81] Paul's enemies were using the Thessalonians' suffering to attack Paul's doctrine of the Rapture.

An Examination of Ἀποστασία

The word ἀποστασία occurs twice in the Scriptures–here, translated "departure" in 2 Thessalonians 2.3 and in Acts 21.21. In Luke's record, James and company questioned Paul about what they had heard—that he was teaching Jews to depart from or forsake Moses. The verb associated with ἀποστασία is ἀφίστημι and occurs 15x in the New Testament. Paul used this word 5x if we include Hebrews.[82]

---

[81] The KJV text of 2 Thessalonians 2.2 reads "day of Christ" and is based solely upon the second corrector of D (D^2, 9th century). Earlier evidence in all forms (manuscripts, versions, fathers) supports the reading "day of the Lord." Also in support of "day of the Lord" is Paul's usage of ἐνίστημι in 2 Thessalonians 2.2. Paul used this term in Romans 8.38; 1 Corinthians 3.22, 7.26; Galatians 1.4; 2 Thessalonians 2.2, 2 Timothy 3.1; Hebrews 9.9. In every case, he used it to mean that which was present or had come. If the text was "day of Christ" it would read, "That you be not soon shaken in mind, or be troubled, neither by spirit, nor by word, nor by letter as from us, as that the day of Christ is present." Such a reading would mean the Rapture had already occurred since the "day of Christ" is the Rapture.

[82]The only other writer to use the verb ἀφίστημι (as is the case of the noun) was Luke, Paul's constant companion Luke 2.37, 4:13, 8.13, 13.27; Acts 5.37-38, 12.10, 15.38, 19.9, 22.29.

Pauline Passage		Qualifier
ἀποστασία		
2 Thessalonians 2.3	Let no one in any way deceive you, for it will not come unless the ἀποστασία comes first, and the man of lawlessness is revealed, the son of destruction,	Physical withdrawal
Acts 21.21	and they have been told about you, that you are teaching all the Jews who are among the Gentiles to forsake Moses, telling them not to circumcise their children nor to walk according to the customs.	"depart from Moses"
ἀφίστημι		
2 Corinthians 12.8	Concerning this I implored the Lord three times that it might leave me.	Physical withdrawal
1 Timothy 4.1	But the Spirit explicitly says that in later times some will fall away from the faith, paying attention to deceitful spirits and doctrines of demons,	"depart from the faith"
1 Timothy 6.5	Perverse disputings of men of corrupt minds, and destitute of the truth, supposing that gain is godliness: from such withdraw thyself. (KJV)	Physical withdrawal
2 Timothy 2.19	Nevertheless, the firm foundation of God stands, having this seal, The Lord knows those who are His, and, Everyone who names the name of the Lord is to abstain from wickedness.	"depart from wickedness"
Hebrews 3.12	Take care, brethren, that there not be in any one of you an evil, unbelieving heart that falls away from the living God.	"depart from the living God"

1. Only Luke and Paul used the noun and verb ἀποστασία and ἀφίστημι. Paul used ἀποστασία with the definite article "ἡ"—"ἡ ἀποστασία." The inclusion of the definite article emphasizes the identity of the noun, "THE departure." This was a specific event, synonymous with the ἁρπάζω of 1 Thessalonians 4.17.
2. Paul's use of the noun ἀποστασία and verb ἀφίστημι always defined a physical departure *except when accompanied by a qualifying prepositional phrase*, e.g., "departure from *x*."
3. Paul taught the Rapture, not apostasy. He taught the Thessalonians they were not experiencing the Day of the Lord and that God would remove believers from earth before the Tribulation (1 Thessalonians 4.13-18; 1 Thessalonians 1.10; 5.9).
4. Early English Bibles translated ἀποστασία as "departure" or "departing" e.g., Wycliffe (1384), Tyndale (1525), Coverdale (1535), Cranmer (1539), Breeches (1576), Beza (1583), Geneva (1587). Jerome's Latin Vulgate (circa 400 A.D.) translated ἀποστασία with "discessio," "departure." What these men believed about the Rapture is unknown but what *can* be said is that they translated the word accurately.
5. Paul wrote to refute the claim that the suffering of the Thessalonians was the Day of the Lord. To prove it, he provided a clear indicator: ἡ ἀποστασία, "the departure," the Rapture. "Apostasy" is not a helpful indicator. It is far too vague to serve as a helpful sign. At the end of his life, Paul wrote all in Asia had turned against him (2 Timothy 1.15). Was that not apostasy?
6. Paul wrote, "ἡ ἀποστασία" comes and then the man of lawlessness is revealed, the son of destruction" (verse 3). The conjunctive "and" (καὶ) is a resultant temporal conjunction with the sense "and then." This sense is also supported by verses 7-8.

Parallelism of the Appearance of The Man of Sin 2 Thessalonians 2		
Passage	Part 1	Part 2
v. 3	a) Let no one in any way deceive you, for it will not come unless [ἐὰν μὴ] ἡ ἀποστασία comes first [πρῶτον],	b) and [καὶ] the man of lawlessness is revealed, the son of destruction,
vv. 7-8	[7] For the secret [μυστήριον] of lawlessness is already at work; only he who now restrains *will do so* until [ἕως] he is taken out of the way.	[8] Then [καὶ τότε] that lawless one will be revealed whom the Lord will slay with the breath of His mouth and bring to an end by the appearance of His coming;

Verse 3a and verse 7 are parallel and verse 3b and verse 8 are parallel. They describe the advent of the Antichrist. Once ἡ ἀποστασία, "the departure," occurs, the "man of lawlessness is revealed." After "he who now restrains is removed" the "lawless one is revealed." Verse 3 has the temporal indicators, ἐὰν μὴ "unless" or "until" and πρῶτον "first" in addition to καὶ. As noted above, Paul always used πρῶτος in its primary sense: "first in order or succession." Verses 7 and 8 have the temporal indicators ἕως "until" and καὶ τότε "and then."

What did Paul mean by "he who now restrains?" The Holy Spirit permanently indwells believers. He is God's "down payment" (ἀρραβών) of salvation (2 Corinthians 1.22, 5.5; Ephesians 1.13-14). God's removal of believers by the Rapture means the Holy Spirit in believers will be removed from the earth. This action removes the restraint upon evil that believes provide.[83] How long the world will be without a human witness of God or a restraint of evil is unknown. Hopefully, some will soon believe in Christ after the Rapture. But even if that occurs quickly, the influence of believers upon the earth will be greatly reduced.

---

[83] The Holy Spirit Himself remains since, as God, He is omnipresent.

Two key points are involved in Paul's statement about the advent of the Antichrist. One is that believers currently restrain evil and prevent the advent of the Antichrist. The second is that God's removal of the Church, the body of Christ, signals a strategic move in God's plan. God has been building His Church for almost 2,000 years. When He completes and removes it, His focus will again shift to Israel to fulfill His prophetic plan and covenant promises (Romans 11.25).

Satan will recognize God's strategic move and quickly engage a counter move. He will prepare his man to deceive the nations to rule the world. The Scriptures are silent about how soon the Antichrist will emerge following the Rapture. He may appear immediately. It may take a generation.[84] A delay would give time for people to forget the Rapture, time for more Jews to move to Israel, and time for Satan to prepare his man. Satan is the great counterfeiter and imitates God. Jesus lived 30 years before He began His ministry. Satan could exercise a similar plan to position his man to become the Beast.

In 2 Thessalonians 2.5, Paul wrote, "Do you not remember that while I was still with you, I was telling you these things?" To what things did Paul refer? Paul wrote:

> 1 Now as to the times and the epochs, brethren, [you] have no need of anything to be written to [you]. 2 For [you yourselves] know full well that the day of the Lord will come just like a thief in the night. 3 While **they** are saying, Peace and safety! then destruction will come upon **them** suddenly like labor pains upon a woman with child, and **they** will not escape (1 Thessalonians 5.1-3).

The third person pronouns, "they," "them" "those" (noted in **bold)** refer to unbelievers. In contrast, Paul cited believers with first and second person pronouns, "you," "we," "us" (noted in [brackets]):

---

84 What Satan knows is not known to us. Paul provided insight into this matter with his declaration about the "secret of iniquity" in 2 Thessalonians 2.7. This will be examined shortly.

> 4 But [you, brethren], are not in darkness, that the day
> would overtake [you] like a thief; 5 for [you] are all sons of
> light and sons of day. [We] are not of night nor of darkness;
> 6 so then let [us] not sleep as **others** do, but let [us] be alert
> and sober. 7 For **those who sleep** do their sleeping at night,
> and **those who get drunk** get drunk at night. 8 But since
> [we] are of the day, let [us] be sober, having put on the
> breastplate of faith and love, and as a helmet, the hope of
> salvation. 9 For God has not destined [us] for wrath, but for
> obtaining salvation through our Lord Jesus Christ, 10 who
> died for [us], so that whether [we] are awake or asleep, [we]
> will live together with Him. 11 Therefore encourage [one
> another] and build up [one another], just as [you] also are
> doing (1 Thessalonians 5.4-11).

Paul revealed believers will not experience the Tribulation and revealed the timetable of the Rapture and the advent of the Beast:

1. Believers of Paul's gospel who have died, followed by believers still alive, will be raised and transformed to meet the Lord in the air.
2. The Church's departure removes the restraint to the Beast's advent—the Holy Spirit in believers.
3. Satan will begin to prepare to reveal the Beast. God's program to fulfill the prophesied Day of the Lord will move to center stage.

Paul's many attestations believers will not suffer the Tribulation (Romans 5.9-10; 1 Thessalonians 1.10, 5.3-9) along with the grammatical and textual evidence of ἡ ἀποστασία, "the departure," confirms the Church will not experience the Day of the Lord.

The Son of Perdition

The Scriptures name two individuals ὁ υἱὸς τῆς ἀπωλείας, "the son of perdition" or "the son of destruction." They are Judas Iscariot (John 17.12) and the Antichrist (2 Thessalonians 2.3). Judas was indwelt by Satan.[85] Judas was not demon possessed; he was devil-possessed. Jesus declared, "ὑμῶν εἷς διάβολός ἐστιν" (John 6.70). The Lord used the word διάβολός not δαιμόνιον. Most translations read, "one of you is a devil." In this case, the anarthrous noun is definite: "one of you is *the* Devil."

Paul wrote the "son of perdition" opposes and exalts himself above every god or object of worship and seats himself in the Temple ἀποδεικνύντα ἑαυτὸν ὅτι ἔστιν θεός "showing himself that he is God" (2 Thessalonians 2.3-4). The word ἀποδεικνύντα is a present active participle, he "keeps showing himself as God." Peter used this word to persuade the Jews that Jesus was the Messiah on the day of Pentecost (Acts 2.22). Jesus had performed miracles, wonders, and signs to prove He was the Christ. The Antichrist will imitate these signs and deceive the world (Matthew 24, 4-5, 11, 24).

Jesus revealed the key sign to identify the Antichrist will be the "abomination of desolation" (Matthew 24.15) and commanded the Jews in Judea to flee to the mountains when they saw it. The "abomination of desolation" is the Beast's entering the Holy of Holies and declaring himself to be God (2 Thessalonians 2.4). He will likely place an image of himself upon the mercy seat, between the cherubim.[86] The world will worship him and his image (Revelation 13.14-15, 14.9, 11, 15.2, 16.2, 19.20, 20.4; 2 Thessalonians 2.5).

---

[85] Satan is vanquished in heaven and thrown to earth at the midpoint of the Tribulation. No longer having access to heaven (Revelation 12.9), he will possess the Beast. Revelation 13 and 17 reveal this occurs when the Beast is assassinated and rises from the dead (Revelation 13.3-4, 14). This is the meaning of the Beast, who "was and is not and will come" Revelation 17.8 and Revelation 17.11. The Beast is the seventh king. When he rises from death he rises with the power of Satan and is indwelt by him as the eighth king. In the first 3 ½ years of the Tribulation, the Beast is merely a man. In the last 3 ½ years he is more—he is a man possessed by Satan.

[86] The mercy seat represents the throne of God. The Beast will symbolically assert he is God (Isaiah 14.13-14).

<table>
<tr><th colspan="4">Advents of the Messiah</th></tr>
<tr><th colspan="2">Revealed by the Prophets</th><th colspan="2">Revealed by Paul</th></tr>
<tr><td>1st</td><td>Suffer and Serve</td><td rowspan="2">N
E
W</td><td rowspan="2">Rapture: Church Removed from God's Judgment</td></tr>
<tr><td>2nd</td><td>Judge, Establish Kingdom, and Rule</td></tr>
</table>

Throughout the Old Testament, the prophets warned of the "Day of the Lord" (יוֹם יְהוָה).[87] during which God will pour His wrath upon the nations for their evil, which will climax in the world's worship of the Antichrist. It will be a day of "wrath," "darkness," "gloom," and wailing" and is the subject of the book of Revelation. [88]

Jesus described this day in his dissertation upon end-time events and echoed the horrors of this time:

> [21] For then there will be a great tribulation, such as has not occurred since the beginning of the world until now, nor ever will. [22] Unless those days had been cut short, no life would have been saved; but for the sake of the elect those days will be cut short (Matthew 24.21-22).

During this period, the Lord will judge Israel (Jeremiah 30.7) and the nations for unbelief and rejection of Christ. The judgment will end with Christ's return. He will destroy His enemies (Matthew 24.30; Revelation 19.11-19), establish His earthly kingdom, and reign upon David's throne (Luke 1.32).

---

[87] See Isaiah 2.12-21; 13.9-13; 26.20-21; 34.1-2, 8; Ezekiel 30.1-8; Joel 1.13-16; 2.1-3, 11; 2.23-32; 3.12-18; Amos 5.18-20; Obadiah 1.15-17; Zephaniah 1.7-18; 2.1-3; Zechariah 12.2-10; 14.1-20; Malachi 4.1-3; Matthew 24; Acts 2.20; Romans 2.5; 1 Thessalonians 5.2; 2 Thessalonians 2.2; 2 Peter 3.10.

[88] The prophets did not disclose that Christ would have two advents. One could only conclude from prophecy that the Messiah would come. The apostles thought God would initiate the Day of the Lord and return to establish His earthly kingdom shortly after His resurrection.

The Day of Christ

Paul taught a day unrevealed by the prophets, by Jesus in His earthly ministry, or by the Twelve, he called the "day of Christ" or the "day of the Lord Jesus" (1 Corinthians 1.8; 5.5; 2 Corinthians 1.14; Philippians 1.6, 10; 2.16). He also called it "that day" in his last letter.[89] It is unique to Paul and in stark contrast to the "day of the Lord." The "day of Christ" is a day of deliverance (the Rapture) in which Christ returns for His body, the Church. Included in this day is the judgment of believer's works for rewards (1 Corinthians 3.13-15).

The Day of Christ
11 Do this, knowing the time, that it is already the hour for you to awaken from sleep; for now salvation is nearer to us than when we believed. 12The night is almost gone, **and the day is near**. Therefore let us lay aside the deeds of darkness and put on the armor of light (Romans 13.11-12).
4 I thank my God always concerning you for the grace of God which was given you in Christ Jesus, 5 that in everything you were enriched in Him, in all speech and all knowledge, 6 even as the testimony concerning Christ was confirmed in you, 7 so that you are not lacking in any gift, awaiting eagerly the revelation of our Lord Jesus Christ, 8 who will also confirm you to the end, blameless in **the day of our Lord Jesus Christ** (1 Corinthians 1.4-8).
Each man's work will become evident; for **the day** will show it because it is revealed with fire, and the fire itself will test the quality of each man's work (1 Corinthians 3.13).
1 It is actually reported that there is immorality among you, and immorality of such a kind as does not exist even among the Gentiles, that someone has his father's wife. 2 You have become arrogant and have not mourned instead, so that the one who had done this deed would be removed from your midst. 3 For I, on my part, though absent in body but present in spirit, have already

[89] The phrase "the day of the Lord" as "that day" is clearly different from "that day," the "day of Christ." Context determines the definition. The "day of the Lord" is God's wrath; the "day of Christ" is God's deliverance.

judged him who has so committed this, as though I were present. 4 In the name of our Lord Jesus, when you are assembled, and I with you in spirit, with the power of our Lord Jesus, 5 to deliver such a one to Satan for the destruction of his flesh, so that his spirit may be saved in **the day of the Lord Jesus.** (1 Corinthians 5.1-5).
3 I thank my God in all my remembrance of you, 4 always offering prayer with joy in my every prayer for you all, 5 in view of your participation in the gospel from the first day until now. 6 *For I am* confident of this very thing, that He who began a good work in you will perfect it until **the day of Christ Jesus** (Philippians 1.3-6).
8 For God is my witness, how I long for you all with the affection of Christ Jesus. 9 And this I pray, that your love may abound still more and more in real knowledge and all discernment, 10 so that you may approve the things that are excellent, in order to be sincere and blameless until **the day of Christ**; (Philippians 1.8-10)
14 Do all things without grumbling or disputing; 15 so that you will prove yourselves to be blameless and innocent, children of God above reproach in the midst of a crooked and perverse generation, among whom you appear as lights in the world, 16 holding fast the word of life, so that in **the day of Christ** I will have reason to glory because I did not run in vain nor toil in vain (Philippians 2.14-16).
12 For our proud confidence is this: the testimony of our conscience, that in holiness and godly sincerity, not in fleshly wisdom but in the grace of God, we have conducted ourselves in the world, and especially toward you. 13 For we write nothing else to you than what you read and understand, and I hope you will understand until the end; 14 just as you also partially did understand us, that we are your reason to be proud as you also are ours, in **the day of our Lord Jesus** (2 Corinthians 1.12-14).
16 The Lord grant mercy to the house of Onesiphorus, for he often refreshed me and was not ashamed of my chains; 17 but when he was in Rome, he eagerly searched for me and found me— 18 the Lord grant to him to find mercy from the Lord on **that day**—and you know very well what services he rendered at Ephesus (2 Timothy 1.16-18).
6 For I am already being poured out as a drink offering, and the time of my departure has come. 7 I have fought the good fight, I have finished the course, I have kept the faith; 8 in the future

there is laid up for me the crown of righteousness, which the Lord, the righteous Judge, will award to me on **that day**; and not only to me, but also to all who have loved His appearing. (2 Timothy 4.6-8).

Contrasting the Two Days

The Day of Christ	The Day of the Lord
For the Church	For Rejectors of Christ
Deliverance and Reward	Terror and Judgment
A Heavenly Hope	An Earthly Despair
Eagerly Anticipated	Feared and Dreaded
Occurs in the Air	Occurs on Earth

The Day of Christ is the Rapture, the great day of the Church. It is the day God gives all who have believed Paul's gospel immortal, resurrection bodies. Believers who are alive will be delivered from the presence of indwelling sin. The Rapture is the final phase of the Church's salvation—glorification, our blessed hope (Titus 2.13).

The Believer's Salvation		
Justification	Past	Deliverance from the Penalty of Sin
Sanctification	Present	Deliverance from the Power of Sin
Glorification	Future	Deliverance from the Presence of Sin

5. Gathering All Things in Christ

Three passages reveal this secret. Paul wrote the Ephesians:

> [9] Having made known unto us the secret [μυστήριον] of his will, according to his good pleasure which he hath purposed in himself: [10] That in the dispensation of the fullness of times he might gather together in one all things in Christ, both which are in heaven, and which are on earth; even in him: (Ephesians 1.9-10).

God revealed to Paul the secret of His will: in the dispensation of the fullness of times, He would gather all things in heaven and earth in Christ. Paul had written the Galatians "But when the fullness of the time came, God sent forth His Son, born of a woman, born under the Law." The word "fullness" is πλήρωμα and means that which is complete. Thus, according to what Paul wrote the Galatians, Christ advent occurred at just the right time.

Paul's language to the Ephesians had an important difference from what he wrote the Galatians. In Ephesians 1.10, he wrote "fullness of *times*" rather than "fullness of *time*." What significance does the singular "time" have in contrast to the plural "times?" The singular "time" referred to God's revealed, prophetic program concerning Israel and the nations: His covenant program. The plural "times" revealed a new program, the Church, the body of Christ. The "fullness of times" includes both programs: God's prophetic program centered upon Israel and His new program, the Church.

The gathering together in one—things in heaven and things on earth—in Christ refers to God's heavenly program, the Church (Ephesians 1.3; Philippians 3.10) and God's earthly program, Israel (Matthew 6.10, 19.28). These two programs are the main components of the "kingdom of God." Both will be gathered together in Christ.[90] This was unknown before Paul because the Church did not exist. Concerning God's program with Israel and His program with Gentiles, Paul exclaimed:

> 32 For God hath concluded them all in unbelief, that he might have mercy upon all. 33 O the depth of the riches both of the wisdom and knowledge of God! how unsearchable are his judgments, and his ways past finding out! 34 For who hath known the mind of the Lord? or who hath been his counsellor? 35 Or who hath first given to him, and it shall be recompensed unto him again? 36 For of him, and through

---

[90] The phrases, "kingdom of God" and "kingdom of heaven" of the Gospels, refer to the earthly kingdom God promised Israel. When Paul used the phrase the "kingdom of God," he meant God's overall rule and reign of heaven and earth, not the earthly kingdom.

> him, and to him, are all things: to whom be glory forever. Amen (Romans 11.33-36).

Interwoven in this secret of gathering both Israel and the Church in Christ is the revelation Paul wrote the Colossians:

> [2] That their hearts might be comforted, being knit together in love, and unto all riches of the full assurance of understanding, to the acknowledgement of the secret [μυστήριον] of God, and of the Father, and of Christ; [3] In whom are hid all the treasures of wisdom and knowledge (Colossians 2.2-3).

And finally, Paul wrote the Philippians that Christ will "subdue all things unto himself." The word "subdue" is the aorist active infinitive of ὑποτάσσω, "to subject," "arrange under."

> [20] For our conversation is in heaven; from whence also we look for the Saviour, the Lord Jesus Christ: [21] Who shall change our vile body, that it may be fashioned like unto his glorious body, according to the working whereby he is able even to subdue all things unto himself (Philippians 3.20-21).

6. The Secret of Godliness

Paul wrote Timothy:

> And without controversy great is the secret [μυστήριον] of godliness: God was manifest in the flesh, justified in the Spirit, seen of angels, preached unto the Gentiles, believed on in the world, received up into glory (1 Timothy 3.16).

This verse reads like a creedal statement or hymn. It summarized Christ's earthly ministry and included Paul's commission as the Apostle of the Gentiles. The word "godliness" is εὐσέβεια and means, "piety," "reverence," "holiness." What did Paul mean by the secret of godliness?

While God had revealed through His prophets that He would establish His kingdom on earth and that Israel would be preeminent among the nations, specifics about the Messiah were sketchy. Peter wrote:

> [10] Of which salvation the prophets have enquired and searched diligently, who prophesied of the grace that should come unto you: [11] Searching what, or what manner of time the Spirit of Christ which was in them did signify, when it testified beforehand the sufferings of Christ, and the glory that should follow. [12] Unto whom it was revealed, that not unto themselves, but unto us they did minister the things, which are now reported unto you by them that have preached the gospel unto you with the Holy Ghost sent down from heaven; which things the angels desire to look into (1 Peter 1.10-12).

Moses told the nation, "The Lord your God will raise up unto you a Prophet from the midst of you, of your brethren, like unto me; unto him you shall hearken" (Deuteronomy 18.15). In Psalm 2, David wrote God would establish His Messiah as King in Jerusalem and that He would rule the nations (Psalm 2.2, 6-8). Jeremiah wrote God would raise a Righteous Branch from the house of David to reign as King over the earth. He would execute justice and be called "The LORD our righteousness" (Jeremiah 23.5-6). Isaiah wrote of a virgin or maiden who would have a Son called Immanuel (Isaiah 7.14) and described His rule in Isaiah 9.6-7 and 11.1-5. And in Isaiah 53, the prophet revealed the sufferings of the Messiah.

Thus, Paul wrote, "God was manifest in the flesh." But how these prophecies concerning the Messiah would transpire was not known. Many were cryptic and vague. It is clear from Luke's account (Luke 1-2) that the Jews expected a conquering Messiah who would free them from the bondage of Gentiles. But Christ conducted an altogether different ministry from what they expected. Indeed, John the Baptist, of whom the Lord said there was no greater prophet (Matthew 11.11), asked Jesus, "Are you he that should come, or do we look for another" (Matthew 11.3)? The details of Christ's ministry, other than His rule, were veiled in secrecy. Especially recondite was His work regarding sin.

Paul wrote Christ was "justified in the Spirit." Both Jews and Gentiles condemned Him. The Jews demanded Pilate crucify Him and Pilate granted their demand due to political pressure. Christ was certainly *not* justified by men. But He was justified by God. Paul wrote:

> And declared to be the Son of God with power, according to the spirit of holiness, by the resurrection from the dead (Romans 1.4).

The Holy Spirit justified Christ when He rose from the dead.

All of God's creation has an interest in Christ's work: mankind as well as the angelic host (1 Peter 1.12). The angels understand they are engaged in a great drama, a great war, and that God is revealing His plan which will end in great glory. Angels announced His birth to the shepherds, appeared to both Mary and Joseph, and were present at His tomb following His resurrection (Luke 24.23; John 20.12) and were at His ascension (Acts 1.9-11).

With respect to Gentiles, Isaiah revealed Gentiles would seek the Messiah in the kingdom (Isaiah 11.10, 49.22; Zechariah 8.20-23) and He would rule them (Isaiah 42.1; cf. Psalm 2). Israel would serve as a "light to the Gentiles" (Isaiah 42.6, 49.6, 60.3) and the Light of Israel was the Messiah (Isaiah 60.1). The Messiah would bless Israel and Israel would serve as a priestly nation and mediator to bless Gentiles. But when Israel rejected and crucified her Messiah and refused to repent, even after He rose from the dead, God could not establish His kingdom and Israel could not serve as the source of blessing to Gentiles. By God's grace, God commissioned Paul to exercise that role as proxy Israel.

Paul's statement of "preached unto the Gentiles" may have referred to Jesus' limited interaction with Gentiles. But the more probable meaning is Paul referred to his own commission from Christ as "the apostle of the Gentiles." Paul wrote earlier in his letter:

> [3] For this is good and acceptable in the sight of God our Savior; [4] Who will have all men to be saved, and to come unto the knowledge of the truth. [5] For there is one God, and one mediator between God and men, the man Christ Jesus; [6] Who gave himself a ransom for all, to be testified in due time. [7] Whereunto I am ordained a preacher, and an apostle, (I speak the truth in Christ, and lie not;) a teacher of the Gentiles in faith and verity (1 Timothy 2.3-7).

The "secret of godliness" was *how* God had and was fulfilling His plan to Israel and to Gentiles in light of Israel's rejection of the Messiah. God had kept the specifics secret but revealed to Paul the secret of the Church, how Christ had died for the entire human race, and how He was blessing Gentiles.

7. The Secret of Iniquity

> [6] And you know what restrains him now, so that in his time he will be revealed. [7] For the secret [μυστήριον] of lawlessness is already at work; only he who now restrains *will do so* until he is taken out of the way (2 Thessalonians 2.6-7).

Paul wrote his second letter to the Thessalonians to repair the damage of false teachers teaching that the trials they were experiencing was the Day of the Lord (the Tribulation). Someone had forged a letter using Paul's name but Paul had taught them that members of the Church, the body of Christ, would not experience the Day of the Lord, the Tribulation (1 Thessalonians 1.10, 5.9).

Paul reminded the Thessalonians that the Antichrist, cannot appear until after the Rapture (2 Thessalonians 2.1-5). Paul described this personage as ὁ ἄνθρωπος τῆς ἁμαρτίας, ὁ υἱὸς τῆς ἀπωλείας, "the man of sin, the son of destruction (or perdition)." Jesus had warned of false Christs (Matthew 24.5, 15, 24-25; John 5.43) and the Antichrist is the final, false Christ, the key personage described in

Revelation.[91] His appearance was *not* a secret. What, therefore, did Paul mean by his expression, τὸ γὰρ μυστήριον ἤδη ἐνεργεῖται (present middle indicative) τῆς ἀνομίας, "for the secret of lawlessness is already working?"

To answer this question requires understanding how God is unfolding His plan. God knows all events, real or potential. He will accomplish His plan but His foreknowledge accommodates man's will. The Messiah had to die but the Jews of Jesus' day had a choice to accept or reject Jesus as the Messiah. Jesus told them:

> 37 O Jerusalem, Jerusalem, that kills the prophets, and
> stones them which are sent unto you, how often would I
> have gathered your children together, even as a hen gathers
> her chickens under her wings, and you would not!
> 38 Behold, your house is left unto you desolate. 39 For I say
> unto you, You shall not see me henceforth, till you shall
> say, Blessed is he that cometh in the name of the Lord
> (Matthew 23.37-39).

Jesus told the Jews He wished to gather them (unto Himself into the kingdom) but "you would not." They could have had their King and kingdom but they refused. God accommodates human will.

God also keeps strategic parts of His plan hidden. Luke wrote:

> 31 Then he took unto him the twelve, and said unto them,
> Behold, we go up to Jerusalem, and all things that are
> written by the prophets concerning the Son of man shall be
> accomplished. 32 For he shall be delivered unto the Gentiles,
> and shall be mocked, and spitefully entreated, and spit on:
> 33 And they shall scourge him, and put him to death: and the
> third day he shall rise again. 34 And they understood none
> of these things: and this saying was hid from them, neither
> knew they the things which were spoken (Luke 18.31-34).

---

[91] The particle, ἀντί, that constitutes ἀντίχριστος may mean "against" or "instead of." The Antichrist will be both: he will be against Christ and a substitute of Christ: a false Christ.

Jesus told His disciples what was going to happen to Him. He was going to be killed and rise from the dead on the third day. Did they understand this? Were they waiting for Him at the tomb? The record in the Gospels is clear. They had no idea He was going to rise from the dead (John 20.9). Why did they not know? The text tells us: "this saying was hid from them, neither knew they the things which were spoken." Who hid it from them? God did. We do not know how this works but the Scriptures reveal God does it. Satan did not understand Christ's death would lead to his defeat. He possessed Judas to betray Christ so He would be killed. He thought Christ's death would be his victory. Satan had no idea Christ would rise from the dead. Satan knows some of the Scriptures (Matthew 4.1-10) but God hides other portions.[92]

When Paul wrote, "the secret of iniquity is already working" he meant Satan's plan regarding the "man of sin" was in place. This man's advent into human history was not a secret. What was secret was *when* he would come. Paul revealed that secret—he cannot appear until *after the Rapture*. Satan does not know when God will complete His Church. But when it occurs, it will signal Satan his man can emerge to rule and institute Satanic worship. Since Satan does not know when the Rapture will occur, it is reasonable he must continually be preparing for this event. Paul thought the Rapture would occur in his lifetime.[93]

---

[92] Governments employ encryption, misinformation, deception to hide sensitive information. God does this with far greater sophistication to hide His secret plans.

[93] The Twelve and Paul thought the Lord would return in their lifetime (Mathew 3.2, 4.17; Acts 2.17; Romans 13.11-12, 16.20; 1 Corinthians 7.29; Philippians 4.5; 1 Thessalonians 4.15, 17; Hebrews 10.25, 37; James 5.7-9; 1 Peter 4.7; 1 John 2.18, 28; Revelation 1.1, 3, 22.20). Paul thought the Lord would return for His Church (Rapture) and Paul wrote the Philippians he hoped for the ἐξανάστασιν τὴν ἐκ νεκρῶν "out resurrection from the dead" (Philippians 3.11). He coined the word ἐξανάστασις to express his own personal hope. It is a synonym of ἁρπάζω, the Rapture. Paul and the other apostles thought God would fulfill His prophetic plan (Tribulation, 2nd Advent) shortly. But Jesus stated He would not return until the Jewish nation repented (Matthew

Had the Jews accepted Christ, the Tribulation would have taken place. In this potential scenario, Nero could have fulfilled the role of the Antichrist. Since we do not know what Satan understands about God's prophetic plan, we cannot know the details of Satan's preparations. Paul only revealed that the "secret of lawlessness is already at work." But it is clear from what Paul wrote that the potential existed in Paul's lifetime for the advent of the Beast.

8. Other Secrets

If one steps back and reflects on Paul's theology the conclusion is that *all of it was secret*. Pauline theology is not in the prophets, in the Gospels, or in the writings of Peter, James, John, or Jude. In addition to the secrets examined above, Paul revealed other secrets. They do not have the specific word μυστήριον attached to them but they were secrets nevertheless. They include the believer's heavenly citizenship, relationship to the Mosaic Law, the grace of God, and the nature of man.

Heavenly Citizenship

The idea of believers dying and going to heaven is not found in the Old Testament. Old Testament saints had no such hope. The dead went to the grave, the abode of the dead, Sheol (שְׁאוֹל). The righteous had the hope of resurrection, to live again on the earth. In the midst of his suffering, Job wrote of this hope, "Even after my skin is destroyed, yet from my flesh I shall see God (Job 19.26)."

Jesus' narrative of the rich man and Lazarus provides insight into Jewish theology regarding life after death (Luke 16.19-31). In this account, the rich man was in torment and Lazarus in paradise, known as Abraham's bosom. Both abodes were in the earth. Between these abodes lay a great gulf which prevented passage from one realm to the other (Luke 16.26). When the Jews asked Jesus for a sign, He gave the sign of Jonah and declared that as

---

23.37-39). They refused and this opportunity finally ended when Titus' legions destroyed the Temple and Jerusalem.

Jonah was three days and nights in the sea creature, He would be three days and nights in the "heart of the earth" (Matthew 12.40). When Jesus died, He went where Lazarus abode, to the paradise side of "hell" as well as to the torment side.[94]

When Lazarus, the brother of Mary and Martha died, Jesus spoke with Martha about his death. Martha told the Lord that had He been there He could have prevented his death. Jesus replied that her brother would rise from the dead (John 11.23). Martha agreed and replied, "I know that he will rise again in the resurrection on the last day" (John 11.24). The hope of believing Jews was resurrection and life on earth, not in heaven.

Paul revealed a new hope to believers of his gospel. The hope of members of the Church, the body of Christ, is resurrection and life in *heaven*. This was a *secret*. No one knew this before Paul. When a believer dies today, he does not go to Abraham's bosom but to heaven. Paul wrote the Corinthians:

> [6] Therefore we are always confident, knowing that, while we are at home in the body, we are absent from the Lord: [7] (For we walk by faith, not by sight:) [8] We are confident, I say, and willing rather to be absent from the body, and to be present with the Lord (2 Corinthians 5.6-8).

To be present with the Lord means to be in heaven, His location until He returns (Psalm 110.1). Paul wrote that God has blessed members of His body with "all spiritual blessings" (Ephesians 1.3) and that believers have been raised with Christ (Ephesians 2.6; Colossians 1.3). Positionally, members of the Church, alive or dead, are in Christ and enjoy heavenly citizenship (Philippians 3.20). This was unknown before Paul.

---

[94] The Apostles' Creed states, "He descended into hell." Jesus went to the place of the righteous dead, to paradise, as He promised the thief on the cross, "Today, you will be with Me in paradise" (Luke 23.43 cf. Luke 16.19-31). He also went to the place of torment (Tartarus) and proclaimed victory to the fallen angels incarcerated there (1 Peter 3.18-20; Ephesians 4.8-10).

In His earthly ministry, the Lord told his disciples to pray, "Thy kingdom come, thy will be done on earth, as it is in heaven (Matthew 6.10). He promised the Twelve they would sit on twelve thrones ruling the twelve tribes of Israel (Matthew 19.28). Their hope was earthly, not heavenly. Thus, the hope and destiny of Israel is earthly, while the hope and destiny of the Church, the body of Christ, is heavenly. These destinies are eternal.

When Paul used the phrase, "kingdom of God," he did not mean the kingdom of God on earth. He meant God's kingdom which encompasses all creation and the programs in it (Romans 14.17; 1 Corinthians 4.20, 6.9-10, 15.24, 50; Galatians 5.21; Ephesians 5.5; Colossians 1.13, 4.11;1 Thessalonians 2.12; 2 Thessalonians 1.5; 2 Timothy 4.1, 18). God's two major programs, Israel and the Church, along with the righteous angelic host, who operate in both programs, compose the kingdom of God.

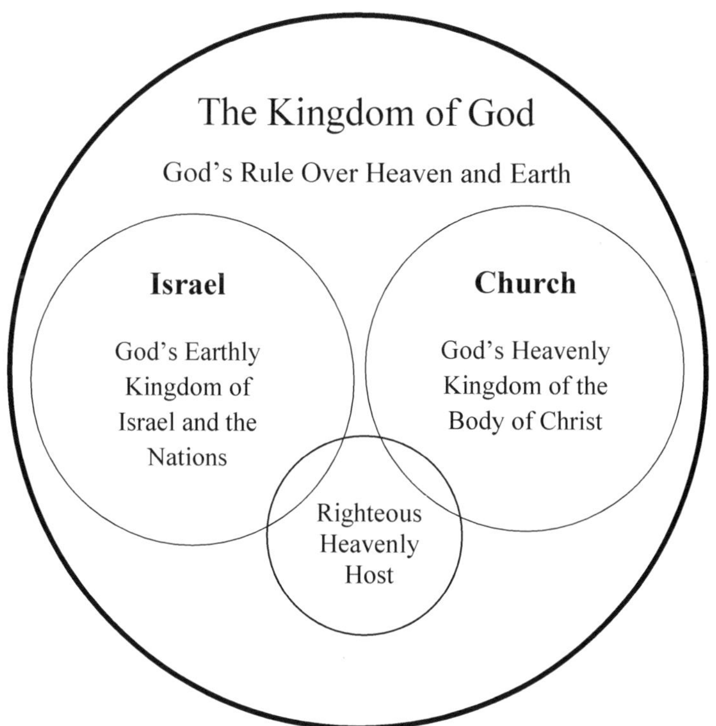

Under Grace, Not Law

God's moral law existed long before He gave Moses the Law.[95] But when God gave the Law to Moses on Mount Sinai He established something new. He gave the Jewish people written laws to govern their civil, ceremonial, moral, and spiritual life to Him.[96] The Mosaic Law was an exclusive covenant of Israel. It was to Israel alone (Ephesians 2.11-13).

Paul wrote that the Church, the body of Christ, was a new and different creation from Israel and that the Church was not under the administration of the Mosaic Law. Paul wrote the Romans:

> 12 Let not sin therefore reign in your mortal body, that you should obey it in the lusts thereof. 13 Neither yield your members as instruments of unrighteousness unto sin: but yield yourselves unto God, as those that are alive from the dead, and your members as instruments of righteousness unto God. 14 For sin shall not have dominion over you: for you are not under the law, but under grace. 15 What then? shall we sin, because we are not under the law, but under grace? God forbid (Romans 6.12-15).

Paul *upheld* God's moral law but revealed members of the Church, the body of Christ, are *not under the administration* of the Mosaic Law. This was *new*. It was a *secret* Paul revealed to the Church.

When Paul wrote that believers are not under Law but under grace, he was explaining a *governing* principle. The Jewish people were governed by the Mosaic Law. Every aspect of their life and relationship with God was governed by the Law. But Paul wrote that *grace* governs the Church.

He continued his dissertation in the next chapter of Romans:

---

[95] The moral law is eternal, based on the holiness and character of God.
[96] The Mosaic Law goes far beyond the Ten Commandments. It included moral, ceremonial, and civil laws and governed Israel's national life. Maimonides cataloged 613 laws.

> [4] Wherefore, my brethren, you also are become dead to the law by the body of Christ; that you should be married to another, even to him who is raised from the dead, that we should bring forth fruit unto God. [5] For when we were in the flesh, the motions of sins, which were by the law, did work in our members to bring forth fruit unto death. [6] But now we are delivered from the law, that being dead wherein we were held; that we should serve in newness of spirit, and not in the oldness of the letter (Romans 7.4-6).

The moral purpose of the Mosaic Law was to reveal sin. While it was "holy, righteous, and good" (Romans 7.12), it had no power over sin. Paul revealed a totally new operation. He wrote, "But now (νυνὶ δὲ) we have been delivered (κατηργήθημεν, aorist passive indicative) from the Law."[97] God has delivered members of the Church, the body of Christ, those who have believed Paul's gospel from the bondage of the Mosaic Law to serve God "in newness of Spirit and not in the oldness of the letter."[98] This was a fundamental change in governance. The believer in Christ is under new management: Grace, not Law.

The governor in this new administration is the Holy Spirit. Paul continued his dissertation in Romans 8:

> [1] There is therefore now no condemnation to them which are in Christ Jesus. [2] For the law of the Spirit of life in Christ Jesus hath made me free from the law of sin and death. [3] For what the law could not do, in that it was weak through the flesh, God sending his own Son in the likeness of sinful

---

[97] It is clear Paul meant the Mosaic Law by his statement, "What shall we say then? Is the law sin? God forbid. Nay, I had not known sin, but by the law: for I had not known lust, except the law had said, You shall not covet" (Romans 7.7).

[98] Peter stated the Mosaic Law was a "yoke upon the neck" (ζυγὸν ἐπὶ τὸν τράχηλον, Acts 15.10). Paul warned the Galatians that the Judaizers wished to enslave them with the Mosaic Law (ἵνα ἡμᾶς καταδουλώσωνται, Galatians 2.4), that the Law was slavery (δουλείαν, Galatians 4.24), and commanded them not to be entangled by this "yoke of bondage" ζυγῷ δουλείας ἐνέχεσθε, Galatians 5.1).

> flesh, and for sin, condemned sin in the flesh: [4]That the righteousness of the law might be fulfilled in us, who walk not after the flesh, but after the Spirit (Romans 8.1-4).

The problem with the Law was not the Law. *We* are the problem. We have a fallen nature inherited from Adam which is bent towards sin. It, by nature, *cannot* obey God. It can try but will always *fail.*

The Galatians: The Great Temptation

Paul wrote the Galatians to correct the false teaching the Galatians were receiving that the way to live the Christian life was by following the Mosaic Law. His main point was to instruct how believers are sanctified following justification.[99] He wrote:

> [1] O foolish Galatians, who has bewitched you, that you should not obey the truth, before whose eyes Jesus Christ hath been evidently set forth, crucified among you? [2] This only would I learn of you, Received you the Spirit by the works of the law, or by the hearing of faith? [3] Are you so foolish? having begun in the Spirit, are you now made perfect by the flesh (Galatians 3.1-3)?[100]

At the Jerusalem Council (Acts 15) in 51 A.D., the issue of the gospel and justification by faith alone had been settled. At the end of that contentious meeting, the gospel of the kingdom ended and only Paul's gospel remained. Justification by faith alone in the death and resurrection of Christ was established for all—Jew and Gentile (Acts 15.7-11). Paul wrote the Galatians his account of the meeting (Galatians 2.1-10) and stated that anyone who proclaimed a gospel different from his was cursed (Galatians 1.6-9).

While justification by faith alone in the death and resurrection of Christ had been settled, Jewish legalists knew nothing about Paul's doctrine of sanctification by faith through grace under the power of

---

[99] Justification is God's legal declaration that the one who believes Paul's gospel is righteous (Romans 3.24, 26, 28, 4.5, 5.1).

[100] Paul revealed more about these false teachers in Galatians 4.13-17.

the Holy Spirit. They maintained that while one was justified by faith, the Christian life was to be lived under the administration of the Mosaic Law. As a result, Paul wrote the Galatians, "Are you so foolish? having begun in the Spirit, are you now made perfect by the flesh?" Paul's point was that as they had been justified by faith apart from the Law, they would be sanctified by faith *apart from the Law*. Thus, he wrote, "For I through the Law am dead to the Law, that I might live unto God (Galatians 2.19).

Paul illustrated the difference between being under grace and being under the Law with an example of Abraham's two sons, Ishmael and Isaac (Galatians 4.21-31). Ishmael was born from the bondwoman, Hagar, and represented the Law. Isaac was born of Sarah, the freewoman, and represented grace. Ishmael was a child of the flesh while Isaac was a child of the Spirit. Paul concluded his illustration with the words: "Cast out the bondwoman and her son: for the son of the bondwoman shall not be heir with the son of the freewoman" (Galatians 4.30-31).

Believers of Paul's gospel are not children of the slave woman, Hagar, but children of the free woman, Sarah. To place oneself under the Mosaic Law is to live the Christian life as a slave. One cannot live an obedient Christian life under the administration of the Mosaic Law. It must be expelled even as Sarah ejected Hagar from her household.[101]

As a result, Paul gave the Galatians the following command: τῇ ἐλευθερίᾳ οὖν ᾗ Χριστὸς ἡμᾶς ἠλευθέρωσεν στήκετε καὶ μὴ πάλιν ζυγῷ δουλείας ἐνέχεσθε "Stand fast therefore in the liberty wherewith Christ has made us free, and be not entangled again with the yoke of bondage" (Galatians 5.1). The verb στήκετε is a present active imperative—a command: "keep standing fast." Does this mean the believer has license to sin? Paul addressed this matter with the Romans:

---

[101] Paul wrote that those trying to bring the Galatians under the Law were persecutors like Ishmael who persecuted Isaac. Paul was trying to protect the Galatians from the bondage of the Law to live godly lives in the freedom in Christ (Galatians 5.1).

> [1] What shall we say then? Are we to continue in sin so that grace may increase? [2] May it never be! How shall we who died to sin still live in it? [3] Or do you not know that all of us who have been baptized into Christ Jesus have been baptized into His death (Romans 6.1-3)?[102]

To the Galatians, he wrote:

> [16] But I say, walk by the Spirit, and you will not carry out the desire of the flesh. [17] For the flesh sets its desire against the Spirit, and the Spirit against the flesh; for these are in opposition to one another, so that you may not do the things that you please. [18] But if you are led by the Spirit, you are not under the Law (Galatians 5.16-18).

> [24] Now those who belong to Christ Jesus have crucified the flesh with its passions and desires. [25] If we live by the Spirit, let us also walk by the Spirit. [26] Let us not become boastful, challenging one another, envying one another (Galatians 5.24-26).

How does a believer keep God's moral law? He keeps it by "walking in the Spirit," Paul's metaphor of allowing the Holy Spirit to control one's behavior. As the believer has received life by faith, he is to live by faith under the control of the Holy Spirit (v. 25). The believer of Paul's gospel is under new, superior management: the Holy Spirit, not the Mosaic Law.

Paul wrote that those identified with Christ by the baptism of the Holy Spirit have been identified in His death:

> [6] Knowing this, that our old man is crucified with him, that the body of sin might be destroyed, that henceforth we should not serve sin. [7] For he that is dead is freed from sin (Romans 6.6-7).

Our fallen, Adamic nature has been identified with Christ in His death. What is dead cannot sin. But sin is present! The desire to sin

---

[102] The believer is (βαπτίζω) "baptized," i.e., identified with Christ.

is all too alive! Romans 7 expressed Paul's own frustration with the power of indwelling sin. Paul stated the Mosaic Law had no power over sin and in fact, incited and increased sin (Romans 7.5). He noted an ongoing war exists within the believer between his Adamic nature and his new nature (Romans 7.14-25).

How does one make the sin nature's death a reality? By faith. Everything in the Christian life is by faith. Paul wrote:

> [11] Likewise reckon yourselves to be dead indeed unto sin, but alive unto God through Jesus Christ our Lord. [12] Let not sin therefore reign in your mortal body, that you should obey it in the lusts thereof. [13] Neither yield you your members as instruments of unrighteousness unto sin: but yield yourselves unto God, as those that are alive from the dead, and your members as instruments of righteousness unto God. [14] For sin shall not have dominion over you: for you are not under the law, but under grace (Romans 6.11-14).

The key to victory over sin is to "reckon yourself dead to sin and alive to God through Christ." This is an act of faith. The old nature *feels* very much alive. But Paul says, "reckon it dead."[103]

Paul also emphasized Holy Spirit's work in our sanctification. He wrote:

> [2] For the law of the Spirit of life in Christ Jesus has made me free from the law of sin and death. [3] For what the law could not do, in that it was weak through the flesh, God sending his own Son in the likeness of sinful flesh, and for sin, condemned sin in the flesh: [4] That the righteousness of the law might be fulfilled in us, who walk not after the flesh, but after the Spirit (Romans 8.2-4).

---

[103] The verb "reckon" is λογίζεσθε, the present middle imperative of λογίζομαι. It is a command to consider yourself dead to sin. The verb is an accounting term and in today's vernacular means, "do the math."

Victorious Christian living cannot be achieved through the Mosaic Law. It can only be achieved by faith, through the Holy Spirit. It should impact the believer by this stage that we find none of this kind of language in Peter, James, John, Jude or the Gospels. It was all new.

Believers Under Grace, Not the Mosaic Law		
Romans 3.28; 6.14-15, 7.1-4, 6, 8.2-4; 13.8, 10; 1 Corinthians 9.20-21; Galatians 3.13, 17-18, 23-24, 4.4-5, 5.14, 18, 6.2; Ephesians 2.15		
Justification	Believers are justified by faith alone, apart from the Mosaic Law.	Romans 3.24-26, 4.5, 13-14, 16; 5.1; Galatians 2.16, 21, 3.11; Philippians 3.9
Sanctification	Believers are sanctified by faith through the Holy Spirit, apart from the Mosaic Law.	Romans 6.1, 6-7, 11-14, 7.22-25; Galatians 2.19, 3.2, 5, 5.3-4; Colossians 2.6-7

Use of the Word "Grace"

The significance of Paul's declaration that believers are under grace, not Law (Romans 6.14) is revealed by his use of χάρις, "grace." It defines God's relationship with members of the Church, the body of Christ.

Sources	Passages Using Χάρις	Frequency
Gospels		
Luke 1.30, 2.40, 52, 4.22, 6.32, 33, 6.34, 17.9		8x
John 1.14, 16, 17		4x
Acts	Acts 2.47, 4.33, 6.8, 7.10, 46, 11.23, 13.43, 14.3, 26, 15.11, 40, 18.27, 20.24, 32, 24.27, 25.3, 9	17x
Paul's Epistles		
Romans 1.5, 7, 3.24, 4.4, 16, 5.2, 15, 17, 20, 21, 6.1, 14, 15, 17, 7.25, 11.5, 6, 12.3, 12.6, 15.15, 16.20, 24		25x

1 Corinthians 1.3, 4, 3.10, 10.30, 15.10, 57, 16.3, 23		10x
2 Corinthians 1.2, 12, 15, 2.14, 4.15, 6.1, 8.1, 4, 6, 7, 9, 16, 19, 9.8, 14, 15, 12.9, 13.14;		21x
Galatians 1.3, 6, 15, 2.9, 21, 5.4, 6.18		7x
Ephesians 1.2, 6, 7, 2.5, 7, 8, 3.2, 7, 8, 4.7, 29, 6.24		12x
Philippians 1.2, 7, 4.23		3x
Colossians 1.2, 6, 3.16, 4.6, 18		5x
1 Thessalonians 1.1, 5.28		2x
2 Thessalonians 1.2, 12, 2.16, 3.18		4x
1 Timothy 1.2, 12, 14, 6.21		4x
2 Timothy 1.2, 3, 9, 2.1, 4.22		5x
Titus 1.4, 2.11, 3.7, 15		4x
Philemon 1.3, 25		2x
Hebrews 2.9, 4.16, 10.29, 12.15, 12.28, 13.9, 25		8x
James' Epistle	James 4.6	2x
Peter's Epistles		
1 Peter 1.2, 10, 13, 2.19, 20, 3.7, 4.10, 5.5, 10, 12		10x
2 Peter 1.2, 3.18		2x
John's Epistles		
2 John 1.3		1x
Revelation 1.4, 22.21		2x
Jude's Epistle	Jude 1.4	1x

The chart reveals χάρις is used 159 times in 148 verses in the New Testament. Paul used the word 112 times. If Hebrews is included, it means Paul's writings account for 70% of its use. If one considers that Luke, Paul's constant companion, was undoubtedly influenced by Paul's teachings, and used the word 25 times, then the usage is 86%. Only the Gospels of Luke and John use the word and John used it only 4x. It should also be noted that Peter wrote his letters late in life, by which time he had gained some understanding of Church theology.[104] One can see why Paul is the "apostle of grace"

[104] Shortly before his death, Peter wrote Paul's letters were Scripture but hard to understand (2 Peter 3.14-18). Since Paul wrote that he completed the Scriptures (Colossians 1.25), the New Testament was complete before Paul died.

(Romans 12.3; Ephesians 3.8). Being "under grace" rather than Law was a revolution in how believers are to live before God.

The Nature of Mankind

Paul revealed more about man's nature and constitution than any other writer. Moses revealed mankind was created in God's image (Genesis 1.26-27) and wrote about mankind's Fall and the beginning of sin and death. His account provided a basic understanding of man's problem. The rest of the Bible said little to expound on this basic truth (Psalm 51.5). But Paul elaborated on Adam's sin and revealed that Adam, unlike Eve, sinned willfully (1 Timothy 2.14). He wrote the Romans:

> Wherefore, as by one man sin entered into the world, and death by sin; and so death passed upon all men, for that all have sinned (Romans 5.12).

Paul wrote that man has inherited a nature in rebellion to God—a sin nature in opposition to God (Romans 1.18-32, 7.14-24). In this state, mankind became an enemy of God (Romans 5.10; Colossians 1.21). Paul revealed the following principle regarding sin:

WE ARE NOT SINNERS BECAUSE WE SIN;
WE SIN BECAUSE WE ARE SINNERS

Sinful behavior is the result of having a nature bent towards sin. Theologically, we sin by doing "what comes naturally."

Man's soul and spirit are indistinguishable in the writings of the Old Testament authors. Paul, however, revealed man is composed of body, soul, and spirit. Man is a tripartite being. This was another truth God revealed that was unknown before Paul. In his letter to the Jews, Paul wrote the Word of God is capable of dividing soul and spirit (Hebrews 4.12).[105] Paul wrote the Thessalonians:

---

[105] The scholarly community almost universally rejects Pauline authorship of Hebrews. But numerous proofs exist which demonstrate Paul wrote Hebrews. This is one of them.

> Now may the God of peace Himself sanctify you entirely; and may your spirit and soul and body be preserved complete, without blame at the coming of our Lord Jesus Christ (1 Thessalonians 5.23).

Completion of the Scriptures

While most of Christendom has been taught the writings of the Apostle John were the last Scriptures written, this is not what the Bible states.

Paul wrote the Colossians:

> 24 Who now rejoice in my sufferings for you, and fill up that which is behind of the afflictions of Christ in my flesh for his body's sake, which is the church: 25 Whereof I am made a minister, according to the dispensation of God which is given to me for you, to fulfil the word of God; 26 Even the secret [μυστήριον] which has been hid from ages and from generations, but now is made manifest to his saints: 27 To whom God would make known what is the riches of the glory of this secret [μυστήριον] among the Gentiles; which is Christ in you, the hope of glory (Colossians 1.24-27).

Paul reaffirmed his office as the Apostle of the Gentiles and reiterated to the Colossians what he had written to the Ephesians: the Church, the body of Christ, was a secret, unknown before him.[106] But also in this passage, Paul proclaimed that his stewardship from God included completing the Scriptures.

When Paul wrote, "to fulfill the word of the God" (verse 25), he did not mean being obedient to his calling and ministry (though he was) but to complete the Scriptures. The Greek text reads: πληρῶσαι τὸν λόγον τοῦ θεοῦ. The word "fulfill" is πληρόω. Paul used this word 24 times. In in every case he used it in the sense of "fill up" or

---

[106] See Ephesians 3.1-11.

"complete."[107] A better rendering of the verse would be, "Whereof I became a minister, according to the dispensation of God which was given to me for you, to complete the word of the God."

The "dispensation" or "stewardship" (οἰκονομία) God gave Paul was to reveal His previously hidden program of the Church, the body of Christ, His program of grace, and the other "secrets."[108] This program was God's last revelation to mankind and He commissioned Paul to complete it. Paul did not write, "to complete the *will* of God" but "to complete the *word* of God." The will of God is revealed in His Word, but the Word is God's written record to mankind.

The Scriptures closed with was Paul's last letter, 2 Timothy. He wrote it shortly before his execution about 67-68 A.D. It is the final testimony of God to the Church, the body of Christ.

When the Scriptures declare something clearly, tradition and opinion must be abandoned. A strong case can be made that all Scripture was completed before 70 A.D. without Colossians 1.25.[109] But Paul's passage seals the deal. It is not debatable for one who believes the Scriptures.

Summary of God's Program of the Church

To understand the Church, to understand ecclesiology, one must recognize:

---

[107] See Romans 1.29, 8.4, 13.8, 15.13-14, 19; 2 Corinthians 7.4, 10.6; Galatians 5.14; Ephesians 1.23, 3.19, 4.10, 5.18; Philippians 1.11, 2.2, 4.18-19; Colossians 1.9, 25, 2.10, 4.12, 17; 2 Thessalonians 1.11;2 Timothy 1.4

[108] Paul used the word οἰκονομία three other times: his stewardship of the gospel of grace (1 Corinthians 9.17), the revelation of the dispensation of the fulness of times of gathering all things in Christ (Ephesians 1.10), and his stewardship of the grace of God (Ephesians 3.2). It is a synonym for his commission to reveal God's secrets.

[109] See Robinson, John A. T. 1976. *Redating the New Testament*. Philadelphia: Westminster Press.

ALL CHURCH DOCTRINE IS FOUND IN PAUL'S LETTERS

God began a new program, the Church, the body of Christ, with His salvation and commission of Paul. Two thousand years before this, God had begun a new program, Israel, with Abraham. God gave Moses the Mosaic Law to govern Israel and gave the nation covenant promises by the prophets. Paul combined the roles of Abraham, Moses, and the prophets for the Church. He was the Church's founder, revealed the Church operated under grace, and revealed the secrets which disclosed God's plan for the Church. As God's creation of the Jewish people through Abraham had been a secret, God's creation of the Church through Paul was a secret.

All Church doctrine is found in Romans through Philemon. Romans through Philemon is TO us. The rest is FOR us.

Major Differences in God's Programs	
Israel	Church
Earthly	Heavenly
Under Law	Under Grace
Established by Covenant	Established by Grace
Revealed Through Prophecy	Revealed through Secrets

	Israel	Church
Vehicle	Covenants (Prophetic Theology)	Secrets (Paul's Theology)
Corporate Destiny	Eternal Earthly Kingdom	Eternal Heavenly Kingdom
Individual Destiny	Priests of God	Joint-Heirs with Christ
Prophetic Destiny	Day of the Lord	Rapture

For the Scriptures to make sense we must let them lay out as they are. When men force one area of Scripture onto another area, mix Israel and the Church, law and grace, salvation by faith alone and salvation by faith and works, the gospel of the kingdom and the gospel of the grace of God, the apostleship of the Twelve and Paul's apostleship, the prophetic plan of Israel and Paul's revelations to the Church, the body of Christ, contradiction and confusion results. God is the same throughout all generations. But His methods of dealing with men change. God is sovereign. He does as He pleases. Dealing solely with Gentiles, choosing Israel, creating the Church, and returning to Israel is His prerogative. To understand the Scriptures and to become obedient to God one must allow God to be God and let the Scriptures mean what they say.

Chapter 4
Israel: Program Two Redux

For I say unto you, You shall not see me henceforth, till you shall say, Blessed is he that cometh in the name of the Lord (Matthew 23.39).

And this gospel of the kingdom shall be preached in all the world for a witness unto all nations; and then shall the end come (Matthew 24.14).

For then shall be great tribulation, such as was not since the beginning of the world to this time, no, nor ever shall be (Matthew 24.21).

Israel failed to accept its Messiah, Jesus of Nazareth, in His first appearance. They would not repent and believe He was the Christ. But the nation will have another chance and in the Day of the Lord, the Tribulation, the nation will recognize Jesus for who He is and repent.

In Paul's great illustration of the olive tree in Romans 11, he used the example of a cultivated olive tree to illustrate God's two programs of Israel and Gentiles. The olive tree represented God's place of blessing (the Abrahamic Covenant). God broke off the "natural branches" of the tree, Israel, (Romans 11.21) because of unbelief (Romans 11.17, 20) and God grafted "wild branches," Gentiles, into the tree in their place (Romans 11.17, 24).

The "natural branches" and "wild branches" are two programs: Israel and Gentiles. As the principal beneficiaries of the "natural branches" were believing Jews, the principal beneficiaries of the "wild branches" are members of the Church, the body of Christ. Both believing Jews and Gentiles constitute the Church but the vast majority of the Church are Gentiles.

Paul explained that at the present time national Israel has been partially hardened or blinded due to unbelief—their rejection of the Messiah. This blindness was a secret (μυστήριον). God had revealed nothing in the prophets that Israel would be judicially blinded for a period in which He would engraft Gentiles into the place of blessing formerly enjoyed by Israel. This design became a reality because of Israel's unbelief. As noted above, God's plan is fixed but accommodates human will. It has flexibility.

Paul wrote that Israel's blindness was partial and would continue until "the fullness of the Gentiles" (τὸ πλήρωμα τῶν ἐθνῶν).[1] The "fullness" is the completion of the Church, the body of Christ. Once complete, God will remove it with the Rapture and initiate the Day of the Lord (1 Thessalonians 4.13-18; 1 Corinthians 15.51-54). At the end of the Tribulation, the Lord will return to earth and establish His kingdom (Matthew 6.10).

The Scriptures are unclear as to whether a gap of time will occur between God's removal of the Church (the Rapture) and the advent of the Beast. It is possible the Beast will be revealed immediately. It is also possible a significant period of time will elapse before his advent and he makes the "covenant with many" (Daniel 9.27) that begins the Tribulation clock, i.e., Daniel's 70th week.

Any statement about the timing of the Lord's return is speculative. However, Hosea's prophecy (Hosea 5.14-6.3) provides a guideline for the Lord's return. While He did not provide specifics, the Lord did give signs to serve as indicators for the time of His return.

As noted in the examination of the covenants, the Jews having their homeland is essential to their fulfillment. The northern kingdom fell to the Assyrians in 722 B.C. and the southern kingdom fell to Babylon in 586 B.C. The Romans destroyed the Temple and Jerusalem and the Jews went into dispersion in 70 A.D. When the Jews became a nation in 1948 and took back Jerusalem in 1967, they regained control of their city they had lost 2,000 years ago to Titus' legions and regained control of the land for the first time in

---

[1] The word πλήρωμα means "completion" in Romans 11.25.

2,700 years. Ezekiel's prophecy (Ezekiel 37) and many other prophecies (e.g., Deuteronomy 30.1-4) promised God would restore the Jewish people to their land. Israel's reestablishment in the promised land is a sign God has begun to set the stage for the final days of the age.

Hosea 6: The Three Days of God Towards Israel			
Torn, Wounded	Two Days	2,000 Years	Blinding of Israel (Romans 11.25)
Healed, Bandaged, Revived, Raised	Third Day	1,000 Years (Kingdom)	All Israel Saved (Romans 11.26)

The chart above reveals God working in 1,000-2,000 year increments.[2] As we have seen, God dealt with all mankind for 2,000 years. He then chose Abraham and created the nation of Israel and worked with them for 2,000 years. After that, He called Paul as the Apostle of the Gentiles to found the Church. For the past 2,000 years, God has been calling Jews and Gentiles into the Church, the body of Christ. In light of Hosea's prophecy, the "fullness of the Gentiles" (Romans 11.25) is close.

John's Gospel also provides a confirming picture of Hosea's timetable. John 11 recorded Lazarus' death. Lazarus's sickness and death represented the Jewish nation beginning with Abraham. Jesus stated Lazarus' sickness was not unto death but for the glory of God (John 11.4). As Lazarus was in the tomb four days (John 11.17, 39) the Jewish people have been spiritually dead for 4,000 years. When Jesus learned Lazarus was sick, He delayed coming to him for two days (John 11.6). That delay symbolically constituted 2,000 years—from Abraham to Jesus' 1st Advent. Jesus told His disciples, "Our friend Lazarus has fallen asleep; but I go, so that I may awaken him out of sleep" (John 11.11). Jesus appeared in His 1st

---

[2] Peter declared a day with the Lord is 1,000 years (2 Peter 3.8). God's program with mankind will compose a "week." The "seventh day" will be the Kingdom, a Sabbatic rest and the "eight day" will be the New Heavens and New Earth. "Eight" in Scripture is the number of new beginnings.

Advent to awaken them from sickness. But the nation rejected the Great Physician. Despite their failure. Jesus said of Lazarus, "this sickness is not unto death" (John 11.4). Lazarus' four days in the tomb represented the time from Abraham to the Lord's return when the nation will recognize their Messiah—from 2,000 B.C. until 2,000 A.D. Jesus' calling Lazarus from the grave (John 11.43) and restoring him to life pictured Israel's spiritual birth when the Messiah returns (Isaiah 66.8; Ezekiel 37.1-14; Romans 11.26). Given Peter's accounting of a day being 1,000 years with the Lord, His return is near.

Lazarus' Sickness and Death a Picture of Israel			
"Sick" from Abraham to Christ's Advent	2,000 Years	Lazarus "sick"	2 Days
"Dead" from Abraham to Christ's Return	4,000 Years	Lazarus "dead"	4 Days

Speculative Dating for the Lord's Return

The Lord began His ministry when He was about 30 and ministered for 3 years. He was crucified about 30 A.D. After He rose from the dead, God gave the nation another opportunity to repent and accept Him as King. Had they, the Day of the Lord would have taken place and Christ would have returned and established His kingdom.

Luke recorded Peter's appeal to Israel in two sermons (Acts 2-3). The crisis for the nation after Christ's resurrection occurred when the Sanhedrin stoned Stephen in Acts 7. In Acts 9, Luke revealed the salvation of Saul of Tarsus. Luke recorded three appeals Paul made to the Jews and each appeal resulted with Jewish rejection of Jesus as the Messiah (Acts 13, 18, 28). In 70 A.D., the Roman legions destroyed the Temple, Jerusalem, and dispersed the nation. That event occurred 40 years after the crucifixion. The number forty is frequently used in the Scriptures as a period of testing. The Jews had 40 years to change their mind about Jesus the Messiah. They refused. Thus, the terminal date for God's dealings with national Israel was A.D. 70.

If we begin at A.D. 70 and move forward 2,000 years (2 days in Hosea's prophecy) we arrive at 2070 A.D. According to Hosea's timetable, it is reasonable to speculate the Lord will return by then. But before His return, the Rapture, the Antichrist, and the 7-year Tribulation must take place.

If we assume a 40-year time of testing for Israel and count back from 2070, we arrive at 2030. This would seem a realistic date for the Rapture. Satan invariably counterfeits God and it is reasonable he will imitate the Lord's earthly life with his counterfeit Christ. This would give Satan 30-40 years to prepare his man.

Such a delay would also provide time for the invasion by the Arab-Muslim confederacy against Israel (Ezekiel 38.2-6) which God will destroy (Ezekiel 38.18-23). Iraq (Babylon) is notably absent in this alliance. This defeat of the Arab confederacy will give Iraq/Babylon an opportunity to establish itself as the leader of false religion and financial power revealed in Revelation 17-18.

Jesus repeatedly warned about deception in Matthew 24. A generation with almost no Christian witness will succumb to Satanic deception (2 Corinthians 4.4) and the Beast will emerge as a man with all the answers.

Speculative Timeline of the Lord's Return	
Rapture (Return of Christ for His Body)	2030 A.D.
Deception and Emergence of Antichrist	2030-2063 A.D.
7 Year Tribulation (Day of the Lord)	2063-2070 A.D.
Return of Christ for Israel and the Nations	2070 A.D.

The dating above is speculative. Whatever its merit, our blessed hope draws nigh (Titus 2.13). The clock reads 11:59. With this hope, we should live lives honoring to the Lord, redeeming the time (Romans 13.12).

The Tribulation: The Day of the Lord

King David was the first to reveal the Day of the Lord (Psalm 2). After that, it became a key theme of the prophets. This day, along with the kingdom, were the main themes of Israel's theology (Isaiah 2.12, 13.6, 9; Jeremiah 46.10; Ezekiel 13.5, 30.3; Joel 1.15, 2.1, 11, 31, 3.14; Amos 5.18, 20; Obadiah 1.15; Zephaniah 1.7, 14; Zechariah 14.1; Malachi 4.5; Acts 2.20; 1 Thessalonians 5.2; 2 Peter 3.10; Revelation 1.10). All the prophets wrote about the Day of the Lord. Zephaniah's description was succinct:

> [14] The great day of the LORD is near, it is near, and hastens greatly, even the voice of the day of the LORD: the mighty man shall cry there bitterly.[15] That day is a day of wrath, a day of trouble and distress, a day of wasteness and desolation, a day of darkness and gloominess, a day of clouds and thick darkness, [16] A day of the trumpet and alarm against the fenced cities, and against the high towers. [17] And I will bring distress upon men, that they shall walk like blind men, because they have sinned against the LORD: and their blood shall be poured out as dust, and their flesh as the dung. [18] Neither their silver nor their gold shall be able to deliver them in the day of the LORD's wrath; but the whole land shall be devoured by the fire of his jealousy: for he shall make even a speedy riddance of all them that dwell in the land (Zephaniah 1.14-18).

The Lord called this day the Tribulation, a time of distress such as the world has never experienced. He told His disciples that almost the entire human race will perish (Matthew 24.21-22). During this time, the Lord will exercise His wrath against the human race for its evil. The Lord stated this time will be like the time of Noah (Matthew 24.37-38). Moses wrote of that period, "And God saw that the wickedness of man was great in the earth, and that every imagination of the thoughts of his heart was only evil continually" (Genesis 6.5, 11-12). The picture of God's judgment is that the Lord will crush humanity as a man crushes grapes in a winevat. This is not Charles Wesley's "gentle Jesus meek and mild" but Christ exercising His wrath against man. Isaiah wrote:

> 1 Who is this that cometh from Edom, with dyed garments from Bozrah? this that is glorious in his apparel, travelling in the greatness of his strength? I that speak in righteousness, mighty to save. 2 Why are you red in your apparel, and your garments like him that treads in the winefat? 3 I have trodden the winepress alone; and of the people there was none with me: for I will tread them in mine anger, and trample them in my fury; and their blood shall be sprinkled upon my garments, and I will stain all my raiment. 4 For the day of vengeance is in mine heart, and the year of my redeemed is come. 5 And I looked, and there was none to help; and I wondered that there was none to uphold: therefore mine own arm brought salvation unto me; and my fury, it upheld me. 6 And I will tread down the people in mine anger, and make them drunk in my fury, and I will bring down their strength to the earth (Isaiah 63.1-6).

Jeremiah wrote of this time:

> 30 Therefore prophesy against them all these words, and say unto them, The Lord shall roar from on high, and utter his voice from his holy habitation; he shall mightily roar upon his habitation; he shall give a shout, as they that tread the grapes, against all the inhabitants of the earth. 31 A noise shall come even to the ends of the earth; for the Lord has a controversy with the nations, he will plead with all flesh; he will give them that are wicked to the sword, says the Lord. 32 Thus says the Lord of hosts, Behold, evil shall go forth from nation to nation, and a great whirlwind shall be raised up from the coasts of the earth. 33 And the slain of the Lord shall be at that day from one end of the earth even unto the other end of the earth: they shall not be lamented, neither gathered, nor buried; they shall be dung upon the ground (Jeremiah 25.30-33).

> 4 And these are the words that the Lord spoke concerning Israel and concerning Judah. 5 For thus says the Lord; We have heard a voice of trembling, of fear, and not of peace. 6 Ask now, and see whether a man does travail with child?

> wherefore do I see every man with his hands on his loins, as a woman in travail, and all faces are turned into paleness? [7] Alas! for that day is great, so that none is like it: it is even the time of Jacob's trouble, but he shall be saved out of it (Jeremiah 30.4-7).

For 2,000 years since the cross, God has exercised patience and grace. God's judgment is the culmination of His anger against a Christ-rejecting world which has embraced evil. His patience has ended. He will destroy His enemies. John gave more detail about this judgment in Revelation. He wrote:

> [14] And I looked, and behold a white cloud, and upon the cloud one sat like unto the Son of man, having on his head a golden crown, and in his hand a sharp sickle. [15] And another angel came out of the temple, crying with a loud voice to him that sat on the cloud, Thrust in your sickle, and reap: for the time is come for you to reap; for the harvest of the earth is ripe. [16] And he that sat on the cloud thrust in his sickle on the earth; and the earth was reaped. [17] And another angel came out of the temple which is in heaven, he also having a sharp sickle. [18] And another angel came out from the altar, which had power over fire; and cried with a loud cry to him that had the sharp sickle, saying, Thrust in your sharp sickle, and gather the clusters of the vine of the earth; for her grapes are fully ripe. [19] And the angel thrust in his sickle into the earth, and gathered the vine of the earth, and cast it into the great winepress of the wrath of God. [20] And the winepress was trodden without the city, and blood came out of the winepress, even unto the horse bridles, by the space of a thousand and six hundred furlongs (Revelation 14.14-20).

The One reaping is the Lord Jesus Christ. He is the Son of Man who sits upon the clouds. In the final battle described in Revelation, the battle of Armageddon, the blood will flow for 180 miles at a depth of a horse's bridle (about 5 feet high).[3] This blood will come from

---

[3] The word "furlong" is στάδιον, which was 600 feet.

the hundreds of millions of soldiers packed around Jerusalem who have come to destroy the Jewish people. God will crush them with massive, 100-pound hailstones like grapes in a vat (Revelation 16.21). The melted hailstones, mixed with the blood of these massive armies, accounts for the numbers John described.

The prophet Daniel (Matthew 24.15) related 70 weeks of years in his prophecy in Daniel 9. This prophecy is the foundation for the Tribulation lasting 7 years. The passage reads:

> [24] Seventy weeks are determined upon your people and upon your holy city, to finish the transgression, and to make an end of sins, and to make reconciliation for iniquity, and to bring in everlasting righteousness, and to seal up the vision and prophecy, and to anoint the most Holy. [25] Know therefore and understand, that from the going forth of the commandment to restore and to build Jerusalem unto the Messiah the Prince shall be seven weeks, and threescore and two weeks: the street shall be built again, and the wall, even in troublous times. [26] And after threescore and two weeks shall Messiah be cut off, but not for himself: and the people of the prince that shall come shall destroy the city and the sanctuary; and the end thereof shall be with a flood, and unto the end of the war desolations are determined. [27] And he shall confirm the covenant with many for one week: and in the midst of the week he shall cause the sacrifice and the oblation to cease, and for the overspreading of abominations he shall make it desolate, even until the consummation, and that determined shall be poured upon the desolate (Daniel 9.24-27).

In verse 24, Gabriel the angel revealed to Daniel a timetable of 70 weeks concerning the Jews. This timetable began with the decree to restore and rebuild Jerusalem until the coming of the Messiah. The time comprised 69 weeks. In verse 27, the prophecy shifted to the last week.

The "he" of verse 27 is "the prince or ruler who will come." This individual will make a "one week" covenant with many. In the middle of this "week," he will stop Temple sacrifices and offerings and commit the abomination of desolation (Matthew 24.15).[4]

The weeks in the passage are weeks of years. Leviticus 25.8 reads, שֶׁבַע שַׁבְּתֹת שָׁנִים, i.e., seven Sabbaths of years, seven years seven times or forty-nine years. The normal plural of "week" is שָׁבֻעֹת but Daniel used the masculine ending ִימ "weeks" (שָׁבֻעִים) similar to "years" (שָׁנִימ). This indicated שָׁבֻעִים referred to a multiple of seven years. Verse 27 confirms this: one does not make a covenant with many for seven days. If one compares Daniel with Revelation, the latter has two 42 month periods or 1260 days. These two 3½ year periods equal 7 years (Revelation 11.2-3, 12.6, 13.5).

The Lord spoke extensively in Matthew 24-25 about the Tribulation in response to His disciples' questions about the sign of His coming and the end of the age. Earlier in His ministry, He had spoken about life during this time (Matthew 10). The Lord said:

> [21] And the brother shall deliver up the brother to death, and the father the child: and the children shall rise up against their parents, and cause them to be put to death. [22] And you shall be hated of all men for my name's sake: but he that endures to the end shall be saved. [23] But when they persecute you in this city, flee into another: for verily I say unto you, You shall not have gone over the cities of Israel, till the Son of man be come (Matthew 10.21-23).

The Lord continued:

> [28] And fear not them which kill the body, but are not able to kill the soul: but rather fear him which is able to destroy both soul and body in hell. [29] Are not two sparrows sold for a farthing? and one of them shall not fall on the ground without your Father. [30] But the very hairs of your head are all numbered. [31] Fear ye not therefore, ye are of more value than many sparrows. [32] Whosoever therefore shall confess

---

[4] This indicates the Jews will again be under that Mosaic Law with a Temple offering animal sacrifices (cf. Matthew 24.40).

> me before men, him will I confess also before my Father which is in heaven. 33 But whosoever shall deny me before men, him will I also deny before my Father which is in heaven. 34 Think not that I am come to send peace on earth: I came not to send peace, but a sword. 35 For I am come to set a man at variance against his father, and the daughter against her mother, and the daughter in law against her mother in law. 36 And a man's foes shall be they of his own household. 37 He that loves father or mother more than me is not worthy of me: and he that loves son or daughter more than me is not worthy of me. 38 And he that takes not his cross, and follows after me, is not worthy of me. 39 He that finds his life shall lose it: and he that loses his life for my sake shall find it. 40 He that receives you receives me, and he that receives me receives him that sent me. 41 He that receives a prophet in the name of a prophet shall receive a prophet's reward; and he that receives a righteous man in the name of a righteous man shall receive a righteous man's reward. 42 And whosoever shall give to drink unto one of these little ones a cup of cold water only in the name of a disciple, verily I say unto you, he shall in no wise lose his reward (Matthew 10.28-42).

Read in the context of the Day of the Lord, these passages are clear. Because of the Antichrist’s deception, family members will betray one another and Jews who are faithful to the Lord will be hated by all. The Lord warned, “he that endures to the end shall be saved” (Matthew 10.22; 24.13) and later told the seven Jewish assemblies in Revelation 2-3 the same thing.

The Lord counseled not to fear those who can kill the body—the Antichrist and those in league with him—but to fear the One who can destroy body and soul in hell—God. Throughout the passage, He issued many warnings about remaining faithful to Him. The great temptation during the Tribulation will be to accept the mark of the Beast and worship him as God. Those who do are doomed (Revelation 13.8, 14.9-11, 19.20). Almost everyone who refuses to take the Beast’s mark will be put to death. This is what the Lord meant when He stated, “He that finds his life shall lose it: and he that loses his life for my sake shall find it." Most will lose their lives. But they will gain life eternal. Jesus called this period, the last 3 ½ years, the "great tribulation." He said that the world had never witnessed such a time and that if He did not return not a single human would survive (Matthew 24.21-22).

How "Near" is the Day of the Lord?

God has revealed what He will do, but *when* He will do it is shrouded in secrecy. The prophetic record of the Old Testament seemed to indicate God's advent, wrath, and kingdom on earth would occur in short order. In the Zephaniah passage quoted above, the prophet declared the Day of the Lord was "near." Zephaniah wrote in the 7th century B.C. What did he mean by "near?"

The earliest prophecy to declare the nearness of the Day of the Lord was Joel (Joel 1.15, 2.1, 3.14). Joel lived in the 9th century B.C. This "nearness" (קָרוֹב)[5] of the Day of the Lord was echoed by other prophets: Isaiah (8th century B.C., Isaiah 13.6), Zephaniah (7th century B.C.), Ezekiel (6th century B.C., Ezekiel 30.3), Obadiah (6th century B.C., Obadiah 1.15). Zephaniah wrote it was not only near but coming "very quickly" (וּמַהֵר מְאֹד). By the time of Jesus, over 800 years had elapsed since Joel. How did the Jews understand this prophecy and how are we to understand its meaning?

"Nearness" in the Gospels

John the Baptist began his ministry declaring the kingdom of God was "near" (Matthew 3.2). Shortly afterward, the Lord proclaimed the same message (Matthew 4.17) and commanded His disciples to proclaim it (Matthew 10.7). The Scriptures indicate the Twelve, as well as Paul, thought the Lord would return in their lifetime after His ascension. Were they wrong to think this? Consider the following passages:

---

[5] The word קָרוֹב means near in place, time, or personal relationship.

> Repent, for the kingdom of heaven is at hand (Matthew 3.2)
>
> From that time Jesus began to preach and say, Repent, for the kingdom of heaven is at hand (Matthew 4.7).
>
> And as you go, preach, saying, The kingdom of heaven is at hand (Matthew 10.7).
>
> And saying, The time is fulfilled, and the kingdom of God is at hand; repent and believe in the gospel (Mark 1.15).
>
> And heal those in it who are sick, and say to them, The kingdom of God has come near to you. (Luke 10.9)
>
> Even the dust of your city which clings to our feet we wipe off in protest against you; yet be sure of this, that the kingdom of God has come near (Luke 10.11).

The words used in the above passages for "near" or "at hand" are ἐγγίζω (verb) or ἐγγύς (adverb). They mean to draw or come near in time or place. The straightforward meaning of these passages was the long-anticipated kingdom of God was at hand. It was. The King was present in the person of the Lord Jesus Christ. He was ready to establish His kingdom for Israel.

This "nearness" was even more tantalizing by the following statements of the Lord:

> Truly I say to you, there are some of those who are standing here who will not taste death until they see the Son of Man coming in His kingdom (Matthew 16.28, cf. Mark 9.1; Luke 9.27).

It is obvious the Lord has not returned and the kingdom of God is not presently on the earth. Wolves and lambs are not reclining together (Isaiah 11.6) and the Lord is not ruling in Jerusalem (Zechariah 8.3). What then, are we to make of His statements?

A fuller answer will develop but let us note that in each Gospel, an account of Jesus' Transfiguration immediately followed these passages. Peter, James, and John witnessed the Lord's glory which He will have in His return. To see the King glorified was to see the kingdom. Peter, James, and John witnessed a "preview" of His return. The Transfiguration fulfilled the prophecy based on Jewish disobedience, but a fulfillment remains for Jewish obedience.

The Lord also said these things would come upon "this generation:"

> 34 Therefore, behold, I am sending you prophets and wise men and scribes; some of them you will kill and crucify, and some of them you will scourge in your synagogues, and persecute from city to city, 35 so that upon you may fall the guilt of all the righteous blood shed on earth, from the blood of righteous Abel to the blood of Zechariah, the son of Berechiah, whom you murdered between the temple and the altar. 36 Truly I say to you, all these things will come upon this generation (Matthew 23.34-36).

> 32 Now learn the parable from the fig tree: when its branch has already become tender and puts forth its leaves, you know that summer is near; 33 so, you too, when you see all these things, recognize that He is near, right at the door. 34 Truly I say to you, this generation will not pass away until all these things take place (Matthew 24.32-34; cf. Mark 13.18-30; Luke 21.29-32).

Jesus declared "this generation" would not end until the Day of the Lord occurred and He returned. The word "generation" is γενεά. Depending on context, γενεά means a race of people, people living during a particular time, or an age. The most straightforward meaning of the word in this context is that it means "people living at a particular time." Did He mean the Jews of His day or something else? Before addressing this question, let us consider more passages. Mark wrote:

> 61 But He kept silent and did not answer. Again the high priest was questioning Him, and saying to Him, Are You the Christ, the Son of the Blessed One? 62 And Jesus said, I am; and you shall see the Son of Man sitting at the right

> hand of Power, and coming with the clouds of heaven (Mark 14.61-62).

Did Jesus mean the high priest would live to see His coming? It appeared so. But upon examination, His answer was cryptic.

"Nearness" after the Gospels

The apostles expected the Lord to return in their lifetime. They had no idea this event would not occur or be delayed for 2,000 years. At Pentecost, Peter quoted Joel's prophecy and the prophecy was partially fulfilled (Acts 2.16-21). God gave His Holy Spirit accompanied by prophecy, visions, and dreams. But the signs in heaven and earth of blood, fire, vapor, smoke and the sun being darkened and the moon looking like blood did not occur (Matthew 24.29-31). Nor have they yet.

The apostle John wrote in Revelation:

> The revelation of Jesus Christ, which God gave unto him, to show unto his servants things which must shortly [ἐν τάχει][6] come to pass; and he sent and signified it by his angel unto his servant John: [2] Who bore record of the word of God, and of the testimony of Jesus Christ, and of all things that he saw. [3] Blessed is he that reads, and they that hear the words of this prophecy, and keep those things which are written therein: for the time is at hand [καιρὸς ἐγγύς][7] (Revelation 1.1-3).

> Behold, He is coming with the clouds, and every eye will see Him, even those who pierced Him; and all the tribes of

---

[6] John's prepositional phrase, ἐν τάχει, meant "speedily" or "swiftly." The described events will transpire in a short timeframe.

[7] Sometimes καιρός and χρόνος are used synonymously but καιρός usually meant a specified time as opposed to χρόνος, which tended to convey broader, more conceptual time. Coupled with the adverb ἐγγύς, John thought the Tribulation was "at hand."

> the earth will mourn over Him. So it is to be. Amen (Revelation 1.7).
>
> Nevertheless what you have, hold fast until I come (Revelation 2.25).
>
> I am coming quickly [ταχύ]; hold fast what you have, so that no one will take your crown (Revelation 3.11).
>
> 6 And he said to me, These words are faithful and true; and the Lord, the God of the spirits of the prophets, sent His angel to show to His bond-servants the things which must soon take place [τάχος]. 7 And behold, I am coming quickly [ταχύ]. Blessed is he who heeds the words of the prophecy of this book (Revelation 22.6-7).[8]
>
> And he said to me, Do not seal up the words of the prophecy of this book, for the time is near [ἐγγύς] (Revelation 22.10).
>
> Behold, I am coming quickly [ταχύ], and My reward is with Me, to render to every man according to what he has done (Revelation 22.12).
>
> He who testifies to these things says, Yes, I am coming quickly [ταχύ]. Amen. Come, Lord Jesus (Revelation 22.20).

These passages indicated Jesus would return soon. In His address to the seven Jewish assemblies, He warned the Thyatira and Philadelphia assemblies to hold fast until He came. But God cloaks the timing of His strategic plans in great secrecy. Jesus said about His coming:

> But of that day and hour no one knows, not even the angels of heaven, nor the Son, but the Father alone (Matthew 24.36).

---

[8] The words τάχος (noun) and ταχύ (adjective) mean quickly in speed or shortly in time.

In John's first letter, he wrote:

> Little children, it is the last time: and as you have heard that antichrist shall come, even now are there many antichrists; whereby we know that it is the last time [ἐσχάτη ὥρα] (1 John 2.18).[9]

James, whose letter was the first text of the New Testament, wrote:

> [8] Be also patient; establish your hearts: for the coming of the Lord draws nigh [ἤγγικεν]. [9] Grudge not one against another, brethren, lest you be condemned: behold, the judge stands before the door (James 5.8-9).

Peter, in his first letter to believing Jews scattered abroad wrote:

> [7] That the testing of your faith, being much more precious than of gold that perishes, though it be tried with fire, might be found unto praise and honor and glory at the appearing of Jesus Christ: [8] Whom having not seen, you love; in whom, though now you see him not, yet believing, you rejoice with joy unspeakable and full of glory: [9] Receiving the end of your faith, even the salvation of your souls (1 Peter 1.7-9).
>
> But the end of all things is at hand [ἤγγικεν]: be therefore sober, and watch unto prayer (1 Peter 4.7).[10]

Peter believed the Tribulation was near and encouraged his readers to endure the coming testing which would result in their salvation (verse 9). His words echoed those the Lord had spoken to the

---

[9] John's language, ἐσχάτη ὥρα, indicated he thought the Tribulation and the Lord's return would come soon. John's usual use of ὥρα, (from which we get "hour") indicated a brief or specific span of time but included flexibility for eschatological events (John 1.39, 2.4, 4.6, 4.21, 23, 52-53, 5.25, 28, 35, 7.30, 8.20, 11.9, 12.23, 27, 13.1, 16.2, 4, 21, 25, 32, 17.1, 19.14, 27; Revelation 3.3, 10, 9.15, 11.13, 14.7, 15, 17.12, 18.10, 17, 19).

[10] James' and Peter's "draws nigh," ἤγγικεν is a perfect, active, indicative—"has drawn near."

Twelve on the Mount of Olives, in which He revealed what would happen before His return.

Paul's letter to the Hebrews revealed he too believed the Lord would soon return:

> Not forsaking the assembling of ourselves together, as the manner of some is; but exhorting one another: and so much the more, as you see the day approaching [ἐγγίζουσαν τὴν ἡμέραν] (Hebrews 10.25).

> 36 For you have need of patience, that, after you have done the will of God, you might receive the promise. 37 For yet a little while, and he that shall come will come, and will not tarry (Hebrews 10.36-37).

Paul revealed the Rapture will occur before the Day of the Lord and is different from Christ's 2nd Advent. Did Paul think the Rapture was near? The answer is a resounding "yes." He described the order of the event:

> 15 For this we say unto you by the word of the Lord, that we which are alive and remain unto the coming of the Lord shall not prevent them which are asleep. 16 For the Lord himself shall descend from heaven with a shout, with the voice of the archangel, and with the trump of God: and the dead in Christ shall rise first: 17 Then we which are alive and remain shall be caught up together with them in the clouds, to meet the Lord in the air: and so shall we ever be with the Lord. 18 Wherefore comfort one another with these words (1 Thessalonians 4.16-18).

Paul's use of "we" in verses 15 and 17 indicated he believed he would live to experience the Rapture. Paul also expressed this hope in Philippians 3.11, "if by any means I might attain to the out-resurrection from the dead" (εἴ πως καταντήσω εἰς τὴν ἐξανάστασιν τῶν νεκρῶν).

To the Corinthians, Paul wrote:

> [4] I thank my God always on your behalf, for the grace of God which is given you by Jesus Christ; [5] That in everything you are enriched by him, in all utterance, and in all knowledge; [6] Even as the testimony of Christ was confirmed in you: [7] So that you come behind in no gift; waiting for the coming of our Lord Jesus Christ: [8] Who shall also confirm you unto the end, that you may be blameless in the day of our Lord Jesus Christ.

Paul's encouraging words to the Corinthians, "waiting for the coming our Lord Jesus Christ" indicated he thought the Lord would come soon.

Not until the end of his life did Paul understand that he would not experience the Rapture:

> [6] For I am now ready to be offered, and the time of my departure is at hand [ἐφέστηκεν].[11] [7] I have fought a good fight, I have finished my course, I have kept the faith: [8] Henceforth there is laid up for me a crown of righteousness, which the Lord, the righteous judge, shall give me at that day: and not to me only, but unto all them also that love his appearing (2 Timothy 4.6-8).

The Gospels and Acts reveal why the Lord did not return and why the kingdom of God was not established. The Lord stated He would return and establish His kingdom *when Israel repented and recognized Him as their Messiah.* He told the nation:

> [37] Jerusalem, Jerusalem, who kills the prophets and stones those who are sent to her! How often I wanted to gather your children together, the way a hen gathers her chicks under her wings, and you were unwilling. [38] Behold, your house is being left to you desolate! [39] For I say to you, from

---

[11] Paul used the word ἐφίστημι on two other occasions, 1 Thessalonians 5.3 and 2 Timothy 4.2. Here, the verb is a perfect active indicative and should be translated, "has arrived."

> now on you will not see Me until you say, Blessed is He who comes in the name of the Lord (Matthew 23.37-39)!

This will occur at the end of the Tribulation. Zechariah described this event:

> [8] In that day shall the Lord defend the inhabitants of Jerusalem; and he that is feeble among them at that day shall be as David; and the house of David shall be as God, as the angel of the Lord before them. [9] And it shall come to pass in that day, that I will seek to destroy all the nations that come against Jerusalem. [10] And I will pour upon the house of David, and upon the inhabitants of Jerusalem, the spirit of grace and of supplications: and they shall look upon me whom they have pierced, and they shall mourn for him, as one mourns for his only son, and shall be in bitterness for him, as one that is in bitterness for his firstborn (Zechariah 12.8-10).

The context of the passage is the Day of the Lord, specifically when the armies of the nations of the world will occupy Israel to assault Jerusalem (Revelation 16.14-21; cf. Zephaniah 3.8; Zechariah 14.2). This will be the Beast's strategic move to destroy every Jew. Zechariah described the Lord's response: "Then shall the LORD go forth, and fight against those nations, as when he fought in the day of battle" (Zechariah 14.3). The Jews will recognize Him, repent, and "all Israel will be saved" (Romans 11.26).

Making Sense of "Nearness"

Israel is the focus of prophecy. Had the nation repented, "this generation" would have been the Jews of Jesus' day. Since they refused, "this generation" refers to a future generation who will repent. They are the "other sheep" to whom Jesus referred in John 10.19. If the nation had repented, Jesus' words, "some of those who are standing here who will not taste death until they see the Son of Man coming in His kingdom" would have meant the Jews of His day would have witnessed His actual return, not just Peter, James, and John's Transfiguration preview (Matthew 17.1-9 Mark 9.2-8

Luke 9.28-26). The same is true of the high priest whom Jesus addressed at His trial. Had the nation repented, the high priest would have lived to witness His return in glory. But the high priest *will* see Jesus' return for John wrote, "Behold, He is coming with the clouds, and every eye will see Him, even those who pierced Him" (Revelation 1.7).

What are we to make of the Old Testament prophets who declared the Day of the Lord was "near?" The only reasonable answer is to interpret the language in terms of God's perspective. Time is a property of matter. But God is Spirit and eternal. Eternity is not a long-time. Eternity is the absence of time—non-time—timelessness. Time does not exist in eternity. It has no meaning. As mortal, physical creatures bound by the laws of nature, such a state is incomprehensible. God accommodates time but does so from His perspective. The Psalmist recorded a prayer of Moses: "For a thousand years in Your sight are like yesterday when it passes by, or as a watch in the night" (Psalm 90.4). Echoing the Psalmist, Peter wrote, "But do not let this one fact escape your notice, beloved, that with the Lord one day is like a thousand years, and a thousand years like one day" (2 Peter 3.8). Joel first proclaimed the day of the Lord was near 2,800 years ago. That was less than three days ago if you have a God watch. But this is language of accommodation. For God, past, present, and future are all "now."

What would have happened had Israel repented? Had the nation repented, Jesus would have gone to the cross. This was foreordained (Genesis 3.15; Isaiah 53.1-12; 1 Corinthians 15.1-4). He had to die for mankind's sins. He had to rise from the dead (Psalm 16.10). The Day of the Lord would have taken place and one of the Julio-Claudian Caesars (probably Nero) would have become the Antichrist. The Lord would have returned and set up His kingdom. It *could* have happened. But the Lord knew it wouldn't due to His foreknowledge. Nevertheless, God gave Israel every opportunity. They had a choice.

Would the Church have come into being if Israel had repented? Had Israel repented there would have been no need for the Church. Gentiles would have been blessed by Israel according to God's prophetic plan, according to the Abrahamic Covenant (Genesis 12.1-3) and God's other covenants. But God, in His grace and mercy, did not initiate the Tribulation. Instead, Instead, He saved Saul of Tarsus and created the Church, the body of Christ. God delayed His judgment to create a new program through which He could bless Gentiles—in spite of Jewish rejection of the Messiah.

Some argue this means the Church was an "afterthought" or "Plan B" of God. Such analysis reveals a lack of understanding of God's sovereignty. God operates so His purposes will be accomplished but gives man freedom to choose within His plan. He knew Israel would reject Him but gave the nation a choice. He also knew He would save Paul to become the Apostle of the Gentiles. This was no more of an "afterthought" than God's choosing Abraham to create the Jewish people after dealing with all mankind for the first 2,000 years. God gives man free will and though man disobeys, God reveals His grace is greater than man's sin. Paul exclaimed:

> [33] Oh, the depth of the riches both of the wisdom and knowledge of God! How unsearchable are His judgments and unfathomable His ways! [34] For who has known the mind of the LORD, or who became His counselor? [35] Or who has first given to Him that it might be paid back to him again? [36] For from Him and through Him and to Him are all things. To Him be the glory forever. Amen (Romans 11.33-36).

The Book of Revelation

Revelation is a confusing book to most people despite the many commentaries written about it. The reason most commentaries fail to enlighten the book's contents is because they violate one or more of the three basic principles of sound Biblical interpretation: 1) acceptance of the Scriptures as God-breathed (θεόπνευστος), 2) correct placement of the text within the framework of God's progressive revelation, and 3) maintaining a sound and consistent hermeneutic or interpretative method. The book is not difficult if one adheres to these principles. Doing so means one must understand the book is about Israel and the nations in the Day of the Lord. The Church is not present in it.

The title of the book comes from its first three words, Ἀποκάλυψις Ἰησοῦ Χριστοῦ, "the revelation of Jesus Christ." This prepositional phrase is both an objective and a subjective genitive: the revelation John received revealed Jesus Christ (objective genitive) and was from Jesus Christ (subjective genitive). John called it the Day of the Lord.[12]

Revelation begins with Jesus warning seven Jewish assemblies (ἐκκλησία) to remain faithful to Him (Revelation 2-3). Those who do are promised eternal life. Throughout these warnings, Jesus repeated His words to the Jews in His earthly ministry, "He that has an ear, let him hear." The Lord's great warning is to remain faithful to Him, to overcome, i.e., not to worship the Beast and take His mark.[13] These addresses contain no Church language for Revelation concerns the Day of the Lord. Paul made it clear that before it begins the Lord will return for His Church and taken it to heaven (Romans 5.9-10; 1 Thessalonians 1.10; 5.9). Revelation is the fulfillment of God's prophetic program which concerns Israel and the nations.

---

[12] Most translations render John's adjectival expression, ἐν τῇ κυριακῇ ἡμέρᾳ as "on the "Lord's day" (Revelation 1.10). The majority view is this is "Sunday." Such a meaning is highly unlikely. John recorded the events of the Day of the Lord (Isaiah 2.12; 13.6, 9; Ezekiel 13.5, 30.3; Joel 1.15, 2.1, 11, 31; 3.14; Amos 5.18, 20; Obadiah 1.15; Zephaniah 1.7, 14; Zechariah 14.1; Malachi. 4.5 cf. Revelation 6.17; 16.14). Also, the idea the Lord's day was Sunday is not found in the Scriptures and is not found in Church literature until long after John wrote Revelation. A better rendering is, "I was in the Spirit on the Day of the Lord."

[13] The "mark of the Beast" is a physical sign (Revelation 14.9) of allegiance to the Antichrist. Those who take this mark worship the Beast, believing he is the Messiah. All who take his mark are doomed and will suffer eternally in the Lake of Fire (Revelation 14.9-11).

Israel is the centerpiece about which all action occurs in the book.[14] It is the time of "Jacob's trouble" (Jeremiah 30.7). But God's promise of salvation is also in the verse, "he shall be saved out of it." Jacob will repent and become Israel. The Lord will return for His people (Matthew 23.37-39) and Israel, as Loammi, will become Ammi.[15] Anticipating this end, Paul wrote, "And so all Israel shall be saved: as it is written, There shall come out of Sion the Deliverer, and shall turn away ungodliness from Jacob (Romans 11.26; Isaiah 66.8). This will be the repentance John the Baptist and Peter expected.

---

[14] Jesus addressed 7 Jewish assemblies in Revelation 2-3. Revelation 7 describes God's sealing 12,000 from each of the twelve tribes of Israel for a total of 144,000. They are sealed to be God's special servants during this time of distress. The Church, the body of Christ, is not in Revelation.

[15] God declared Israel had become Loammi (לֹא עַמִּי), "not My people" (Hosea 1.9). When the nation repents and returns to the Lord, it will become Ammi, עַמִּי "My people" (2 Samuel 8.10, 10-11; Isaiah 51.16; Jeremiah 31.33; Ezekiel 11.20, 36.28; Zechariah 13.9).

Chapter 5
The Kingdom: Program Four

> *And the LORD shall be king over all the earth: in that day shall there be one LORD, and his name one (Zechariah 14.9).*

> *Thy kingdom come. Thy will be done in earth, as it is in heaven (Matthew 6.10).*

In God's second program, Israel, God revealed He would establish His kingdom upon the earth. We have noted several passages but hundreds of prophetic passages in the Old Testament spoke of this earthly kingdom. The fulfillment of the prophecies to restore Israel to its land and establish the kingdom with the Messiah ruling on David's throne was the great hope of godly Jews (Luke 1.32).

Despite this John the Baptist and Jesus' ministry in which He performed hundreds of miracles, the Jewish nation refused to accept Jesus of Nazareth as their Messiah. Instead, they plotted with Rome and had Him crucified. This was Israel's darkest day, the nation's greatest sin. But Peter and the other disciples, after they saw the resurrected Lord, regained hope that the nation would repent and Lord would return and establish His kingdom.

Peter, having witnessed the coming of the Holy Spirit at Pentecost, expected the rest of God's prophetic promises to occur shortly. In Acts 3, he told the people:

> 19 Repent therefore, and be converted, that your sins may be blotted out, when the times of refreshing shall come from the presence of the Lord. 20 And he shall send Jesus Christ, which before was preached unto you: 21 Whom the heaven must receive until the times of restitution of all things, which God hath spoken by the mouth of all his holy prophets since the world began (Acts 3.19-21).

The "times of refreshing" and the "restitution of all things" referred to the kingdom. Peter told the Jews that if they would repent, Jesus would return and establish the kingdom of God on earth. He expected it to happen. Moses had spoken of this promise 1,500 years before Peter:

> 1 And it shall come to pass, when all these things are come
> upon you, the blessing and the curse, which I have set
> before you, and you shalt call them to mind among all the
> nations, whither the Lord thy God hath driven you, 2 And
> shalt return unto the Lord thy God, and shalt obey his voice
> according to all that I command you this day, you and thy
> children, with all thine heart, and with all thy soul; 3 That
> then the Lord thy God will turn thy captivity, and have
> compassion upon you, and will return and gather you from
> all the nations, whither the Lord thy God hath scattered you.
> 4 If any of thine be driven out unto the outmost parts of
> heaven, from thence will the Lord thy God gather you, and
> from thence will he fetch you: 5 And the Lord thy God will
> bring you into the land which thy fathers possessed, and
> you shall possess it; and he will do you good, and multiply
> you above thy fathers. 6 And the Lord thy God will
> circumcise thine heart, and the heart of thy seed, to love the
> Lord thy God with all thine heart, and with all thy soul, that
> you mayest live (Deuteronomy 30.1-6).

The Kingdom in the Gospels

The central message of the Gospels was the proclamation of the nearness of the kingdom of God upon the earth. This good news was the message of John the Baptist and the Lord continued it throughout His ministry. It was the message of the prophets which Jews understood.[1] After the Pharisees attributed Jesus' power to Satan (Matthew 12.24), He changed the way He spoke about the kingdom. He told the Pharisees that if He expelled demons by the Holy Spirit then the kingdom of God had come upon them

---

[1] The word "kingdom" (βασιλεία) is found in 120 verses in the Gospels.

(Matthew 12.28) and warned that a word spoken against the Holy Spirit would not be forgiven (Matthew 12.31-32). Heretofore, He had spoken openly and plainly concerning the kingdom. Now, He began to teach the kingdom through parables to hide the message.

Confused by His new approach, the disciples asked Him why He now taught in parables. Matthew wrote:

> [10] And the disciples came, and said unto him, Why speak
> unto them in parables? [11] He answered and said unto them,
> Because it is given unto you to know the secrets [τὰ
> μυστήρια] of the kingdom of heaven, but to them it is not
> given. [12] For whosoever hath, to him shall be given, and he
> shall have more abundance: but whosoever hath not, from
> him shall be taken away even that he hath. [13] Therefore
> speak I to them in parables: because they seeing see not;
> and hearing they hear not, neither do they understand.
> [14] And in them is fulfilled the prophecy of Esaias, which
> says, By hearing you shall hear, and shall not understand;
> and seeing you shall see, and shall not perceive: [15] For this
> people's heart is waxed gross, and their ears are dull of
> hearing, and their eyes they have closed; lest at any time
> they should see with their eyes and hear with their ears, and
> should understand with their heart, and should be
> converted, and I should heal them. [16] But blessed are your
> eyes, for they see: and your ears, for they hear. [17] For verily
> I say unto you, That many prophets and righteous men have
> desired to see those things which you see, and have not
> seen them; and to hear those things which you hear, and
> have not heard them (Matthew 13.10-17).

Most have been taught Jesus used parables to communicate to uneducated, rural people with simple, earthy stories. This is exactly wrong. Jesus taught in parables to *conceal truth* about the kingdom.

The Revelation of the Kingdom

The first intimation of divine kingship in the Bible was the appearance of the mysterious Melchizedek, "King of

Righteousness" (Genesis 14.18). The passage states he was "King of Salem," i.e., Jerusalem.[2] Melchizedek, in addition to being a king, was a priest, the "priest of the Most High (כֹּהֵן לְאֵל עֶלְיוֹן). He brought "bread and wine" and blessed Abraham on behalf of the Most High God. Melchizedek's appearance was God's earliest disclosure of kingship and His plan for the Messiah to be a High Priest to secure salvation. Five hundred years later, God revealed Israel's destiny as a nation of priests:

> [5] Now therefore, if you will obey my voice indeed, and keep
> my covenant, then you shall be a peculiar treasure unto me
> above all people: for all the earth is mine: [6] And you shall
> be unto me a kingdom of priests, and a holy nation. These
> are the words which you shall speak unto the children of
> Israel (Exodus 19.5-6).

Isaiah wrote the following concerning Israel in the Messianic kingdom:

> [2] And the Gentiles shall see your righteousness, and all
> kings your glory: and you shall be called by a new name,
> which the mouth of the Lord shall name. [3] You shall also
> be a crown of glory in the hand of the Lord, and a royal
> diadem in the hand of thy God (Isaiah 62.2-3).

Peter, writing to Jewish believers (1 Peter 1.1), recognized this fact:

> You also, as lively stones, are built up a spiritual house, a holy priesthood, to offer up spiritual sacrifices, acceptable to God by Jesus Christ (1 Peter 2.5).

> [9] But you are a chosen generation, a royal priesthood, a holy
> nation, a peculiar people; that you should shew forth the
> praises of him who hath called you out of darkness into his
> marvelous light; [10] Which in time past were not a people,

---

[2] Melchizedek is מֶלֶךְ "king" and צֶדֶק "righteousness." "Salem" is שָׁלֵם, the same as "shalom," i.e., "peace." Melchizedek is "King of Righteousness" and "King of Peace."

> but are now the people of God: which had not obtained mercy, but now have obtained mercy (1 Peter 2.9-10).

Peter anticipated Jewish believers of his generation to fulfill God's destiny for them. Believing Israel would be "a holy priesthood," "a royal priesthood," a "holy nation," a "crown of glory," and a "royal diadem" of God.

From Moses until Samuel, Israel had no king other than God Himself. They were ruled by judges and were different from their surrounding nations. Dissatisfied in being different from their neighbors, they complained to Samuel and demanded a king:

> 4 Then all the elders of Israel gathered themselves together,
> and came to Samuel unto Ramah, 5 And said unto him,
> Behold, you are old, and your sons walk not in your ways:
> now make us a king to judge us like all the nations. 6 But
> the thing displeased Samuel, when they said, Give us a king
> to judge us. And Samuel prayed unto the LORD. 7 And
> the LORD said unto Samuel, Hearken unto the voice of the
> people in all that they say unto you: for they have not
> rejected you, but they have rejected me, that I should not
> reign over them. 8 According to all the works which they
> have done since the day that I brought them up out of Egypt
> even unto this day, wherewith they have forsaken me, and
> served other gods, so do they also unto you. 9 Now therefore
> hearken unto their voice: howbeit yet protest solemnly unto
> them, and show them the manner of the king that shall reign
> over them (1 Samuel 8.4-9).

God told Samuel the people had rejected Him, not Samuel. He instructed him to tell the people what having a king meant but not to oppose them. As a result, the people chose Saul, of the tribe of Benjamin, as their first king (1 Samuel 11.15-12.1, 13). His reign began well but ended in failure due to disobedience.[3]

---

[3] Saul was tall, handsome and to all appearances a splendid choice as king (1 Samuel 9.2). God would have established Saul's line forever

God chose David, the shepherd boy of Judah, as Israel's second king. He was not tall and impressive like Saul but revealed his zeal for God in killing the Philistine giant, Goliath (1 Samuel 17.26, 37, 45-47). God made a covenant with David in which He established an eternal Davidic dynasty (2 Samuel 7.12-16). The prophecy will reach its final fulfillment in the person of the Lord Jesus Christ who will reign forever.

The Beginning of the Kingdom

Despite Israel's failure, in the final days of the Tribulation, when the world's armies have gathered to destroy the Jews, they will repent and the Lord will return to the Mount of Olives (Acts 1.9-11). Zechariah described this event:

> [2] For I will gather all nations against Jerusalem to battle; and the city shall be taken, and the houses rifled, and the women ravished; and half of the city shall go forth into captivity, and the residue of the people shall not be cut off from the city. [3] Then shall the LORD go forth, and fight against those nations, as when he fought in the day of battle. [4] And his feet shall stand in that day upon the mount of Olives, which is before Jerusalem on the east, and the mount of Olives shall cleave in the midst thereof toward the east and toward the west, and there shall be a very great valley; and half of the mountain shall remove toward the north, and half of it toward the south (Zechariah 14.2-4).

The Lord told His disciples:

> [29] Immediately after the tribulation of those days shall the sun be darkened, and the moon shall not give her light, and the stars shall fall from heaven, and the powers of the heavens shall be shaken: [30] And then shall appear the sign of the Son of man in heaven: and then shall all the tribes of the earth mourn, and they shall see the Son of man coming

---

but he disobeyed God by failing to wait for Samuel and taking on the office of priest in offering a burnt offering (1 Samuel 13.10-14).

> in the clouds of heaven with power and great glory (Matthew 24.29-30).

When the Lord returns, *all* His angels come with Him.[4] Heaven will be left vacant and the entire heavenly host, hundreds of millions of angels, will accompany the Lord in His return. What a day! Daniel, interpreting Nebuchadnezzar's dream, stated the Lord would return as a "stone cut without hands" to crush the kingdoms of the world and establish an eternal kingdom (Daniel 2.44-45). The nations of the world will mourn when they see the Lord returning (Matthew 24.30) for they will understand the Judge has come and they are doomed. Israel will mourn also but in repentance and thanksgiving for the Deliverer has returned to save them (Zechariah 12.10). One of the first things the King will do will be to separate those who will enter the kingdom and those who will go to judgment.[5]

> [31] When the Son of man shall come in his glory, and all the holy angels with him, then shall he sit upon the throne of his glory: [32] And before him shall be gathered all nations: and he shall separate them one from another, as a shepherd divides his sheep from the goats: [33] And he shall set the sheep on his right hand, but the goats on the left. [34] Then shall the King say unto them on his right hand, Come, you blessed of my Father, inherit the kingdom prepared for you from the foundation of the world (Matthew 25.31-34).

The Nature of the Kingdom

The kingdom will be a golden age. God will restore the earth to its original splendor and the human race will enjoy unprecedented blessings. God will fulfill His covenant promises to Israel. The phrase, בַּיּוֹם, "in that day," used for God's judgment, also refers to that time when God will bless Israel and the nations by establishing

---

[4] All angels come with the Lord in His 2nd Advent. They can leave heaven because Satan and the fallen angels were expelled from heaven at the mid-point of the Tribulation (Revelation 12.7-9).

[5] Matthew 24.40-41 and Luke 17.35-36 refer to this separation. Believers enter the kingdom and unbelievers go to judgment.

His kingdom on earth, in which the Messiah will rule (cf. Isaiah 2.17, 4.1-2, 10.27, 11.10-11, 12.1, 4, etc.

Covenants	Fulfilled in the Messianic Kingdom
Abrahamic	Jews will serve as priests and bless Gentiles (Exodus 19.5-6; Isaiah 2.2-3; Zechariah 8.20-23; Revelation 20.6).
Land	Israel's borders will be established by the Mediterranean, Nile, and Euphrates rivers (Genesis 15.18).
Mosaic	The Mosaic and Sabbatic covenants Law will be kept through the power of the Holy Spirit promised in the New Covenant (Ezekiel 36.24-28, 37.4-14; Jeremiah 31.31-36; Joel 228-29).
Sabbatic	
Davidic	Jesus Christ will reign and rule as King over Israel and the nations (Zechariah 14.9).
New	The Holy Spirit will empower the Jews to keep the Law and the Sabbath.

Government

The Lord Jesus Christ will rule Israel and the nations and fulfill the Davidic Covenant (Matthew 6.10; Psalm 2.6, 8). His rule is described as a "rod of iron" and all nations will serve Him (Exodus 15.16-18; Psalm 2, 72, 93, 95, 99; Isaiah 9.6-7, 11.1-5, 12.1-6, 24.23; 31.1, 42.1-12, 51.4-5, 60.1-3; Daniel 7.13-14, 21-27; Micah 4.7; Zechariah 6.12-15, 9.10, 14.9, 16-19; Revelation 12.5, 19.15). He will not allow injustice (Isaiah 40.10-11) and the earth will finally enjoy peace.[6] War will no longer exist and crime will be minimal (Isaiah 2.4, 40.2; Zechariah 14.11). His capital will be Jerusalem (Jeremiah 3.17; Zechariah 14.16-17).

Abundance

Earth will realize its destiny of Edenic splendor and become incredibly fertile and productive (Psalm 72, Isaiah 2, 4.2, 27.6, 29.17, 30.23-25, 34.26-31, 35.1-2, 41.18-20, 51.3, 65.21-22;

---

[6] The kingdom will be a 1,000 year Sabbath. Utopia will be realized.

Jeremiah 31.12-14; Ezekiel 34.14-15, 36.8-11, 30, 35-36; Amos 9.13; Zechariah 14.8). A new river will flow from Jerusalem, from the Temple (Joel 3.18). Part of it will go to the Mediterranean and another part will go to the Dead Sea, which will be revived from death (Zechariah 14.8; Ezekiel 47.8). The inequities of our present world will disappear (Isaiah 40.4-5).

Peace and Joy

The earth will be full of peace, joy, and rejoicing (Psalm 29, 72, 96, 97, 98, 100; Isaiah 2, 32.16-18, 35, 34.25, 40.9-11, 52.9-10; Jeremiah 23.3-4; Micah 4.3-5). The animal kingdom will enjoy peace (Isaiah 11.6-9, 65.25; Ezekiel 34.25; Hosea 2.18).

Spiritual Life and Removal of Sin

Through the indwelling Holy Spirit, the Lord will enable Israel to keep the Mosaic Law (Ezekiel 36.25-27, 37.1-14; Zechariah 13.1-2, 14.20-21). God had promised them if they were obedient He would bless them. This will occur. The Temple will be the focal point of worship (Haggai 2.6-9; Ezekiel 40-48).

Every Jew a Priest

God's intention was that every Jew would serve as a priest to represent Him to Gentiles (Exodus 19.5-6; Isaiah 62.3; 1 Peter 2.5, 9). This privilege is fulfilled in the kingdom (Isaiah 61.6-9; Zechariah 8.20-23).

Israel Restored to its Land

God promised He would gather the Jewish people from the nations of the world and reestablish them in their homeland (Isaiah 11.10-12, 66.8; Jeremiah 31.7-8, 10, 31-34; Ezekiel 34.13, 36.24, 28, 37.15-28; Amos 9.14-15; Zechariah 10.8-12, 14.11). He will establish the borders He revealed to Abraham (Genesis 15.18) and Israel will be the greatest nation on earth (Deuteronomy 7.13-14, 28.1, 11, 13; Micah 4.6-8) with Jerusalem as the capitol of the world (Jeremiah 3.17; Isaiah 2.2-4; Psalm 48.1-2, 125.1-2) .

Life and Health

The inhabitants in the kingdom will enjoy long life and health (Deuteronomy 7.15; Isaiah 35.5-6; Ezekiel 34.16. Death will exist but life spans will be greatly extended, probably back to what they were before the Flood (Isaiah 65.20).

Duration of the Kingdom

The earthly kingdom is the *introductory* phase of the kingdom of God on earth. It will last 1,000 years (Revelation 20.1-5) and is but a preview of the glory God will create with a New Heaven and a New Earth which will remain for eternity (Isaiah 51.6, 65.17, 66.22; Revelation 21-22).

Rebellion at the End of the Kingdom

Satan has been incarcerated for a 1,000 years during the kingdom (Revelation 20.1-3). During this time, humanity has enjoyed unprecedented peace and prosperity. But at the end of this period, Satan will be freed. He will again deceive the nations and orchestrate a great rebellion against God (Revelation 20.7-8). This is almost incomprehensible but it will be God's final demonstration that mankind's problem is not the environment, education, wealth, or anything external; the problem lies within. God will quickly destroy this revolt (Revelation 20.9) and sentence Satan to the Lake of Fire forever (Revelation 20.10).

Judgment at the End of the Kingdom

After this, the Lord Jesus Christ will judge humanity. Those who have been in hell are resurrected and judged according to their works (Revelation 20.11-13). Men's good works will be shown to insufficient to meet God's standard of righteousness. The book of life will be examined to see if anyone's name is in it. The Lake of Fire consumes Hell and everyone who is not found in the book of life will be sent to the Lake of Fire (Revelation 20.14-15).

Chapter 6
Eternity: Program Five

And I saw a new heaven and a new earth: for the first heaven and the first earth were passed away; and there was no more sea (Revelation 21.1).

And God shall wipe away all tears from their eyes; and there shall be no more death, neither sorrow, nor crying, neither shall there be any more pain: for the former things are passed away (Revelation 21.4).

God's final program is eternity. The Scriptures reveal little about this program. It begins with God creating a New Heavens and a New Earth and extends God's kingdom into its main phase after the Messiah's 1,000-year reign following His return. The primary revelation of eternity is from the last two chapters of the book of Revelation. Like the previous chapters of Revelation, these chapters are all Jewish.

New Heavens and New Earth

The earliest references to the New Heavens and New Earth are from Isaiah, who wrote in the 8th century B.C. Isaiah wrote:

> For, behold, I create new heavens and a new earth: and the former shall not be remembered, nor come into mind (Isaiah 65.17).
>
> For as the new heavens and the new earth, which I will make, shall remain before me, says the LORD, so shall your seed and your name remain (Isaiah 66.22).

These verses reveal the following:

1. God will create new heavens and a new earth and the former heavens and earth will not be remembered.

2. The new heavens and new earth will exist forever, even as the Jewish people and nation.

What did God mean by His statement that the former heavens and earth will not be remembered? The word "remember" is זָכַר, the normal word for recollection or remembrance (Genesis 8.1, 9.15-16, 19.29, 30.22; Isaiah 12.4, 17.10, 19.17, 43.18, 25-26, etc.). It seems unreasonable the former heavens and earth *cannot* be remembered. The more probable meaning is the new heavens and new earth will be so intense, real, and beautiful, that the former will pale in significance. They will seem like a shadow or dream—a faint and long-forgotten reality, a dim memory, lost in the glory of eternity.[1]

John wrote he saw the new heavens and new earth and the sea no longer existed (Revelation 21.1). In his vision, John said the New Jerusalem came down from heaven onto the earth and that a great voice declared, "Behold, the tabernacle (σκηνή) of God is with men."[2] John wrote:

> [3] And I heard a great voice out of heaven saying, Behold, the tabernacle of God is with men, and he will dwell with them, and they shall be his people, and God himself shall be with them, and be their God. [4] And God shall wipe away all tears from their eyes; and there shall be no more death, neither sorrow, nor crying, neither shall there be any more pain: for the former things are passed away (Revelation 21.3-4).

---

[1] C. S. Lewis developed this idea in *The Great Divorce*. In the novel, a group in hell takes a bus to heaven but cannot endure it for it is too intensely real to enjoy. Plato's Theory of Ideas or Forms expressed a similar idea, illustrated with his Cave. Those in the Cave thought they saw reality but only saw the shadows of real objects.

[2] God instructed Moses how to build the earthly tabernacle and its implements (Exodus 25.9). The tabernacle was a "shadow of heavenly things" (Hebrews 8.5) and represented God's heavenly throne complex. In the New Heavens and New Earth, the New Jerusalem will be the heavenly tabernacle.

The Millennial Kingdom was a golden age. God greatly extended lifespans, disease was rare, crime was rare, and war did not exist. But death, disease, and crime did exist. In the New Heavens and Earth they will cease entirely. There will be no death, no disease, or sorrow.

The One who spoke to John was the Lord Himself:

> [5] And he that sat upon the throne said, Behold, I make all things new. And he said unto me, Write: for these words are true and faithful. [6] And he said unto me, It is done. I am Alpha and Omega, the beginning and the end. I will give unto him that is athirst of the fountain of the water of life freely. [7] He that overcomes shall inherit all things; and I will be his God, and he shall be my son (Revelation 21.5-7).

The Lord's identification of Himself as Alpha and Omega echoes His statement in the beginning of the book (Revelation 1.8, cf. 22.13). He and His words are "faithful and true" (Revelation 19.8, 22.6) for He is the Word of God (Revelation 19.11). Those "athirst" will partake of the fountain of life and he who "overcomes shall inherit all things" (Revelation 21.6-7). This is the language the Lord used in His addresses to the seven Jewish assemblies in Revelation 2-3.

The New Jerusalem is identified as the Bride of Christ and those whose names are in the Lamb's book of life inhabit the city. (Revelation 21.9-10).[3] John then went on the describe the city. The

---

[3] John described the New Jerusalem "prepared as a bride adorned for her husband" (Revelation 21.2). This is a figure and governs the later reference of Revelation 21.9-10. The "bride" is Israel, believing Jews who looked for "heavenly" Jerusalem (Hebrews 11.16; 12.22). "Wife" and "bride" are terms associated with Israel. The "wife" is associated with the Millennium; the "bride" with eternity. Jerusalem is associated only with Israel and is the complement of Israel, not the actual bride. The Church is only called "the body of Christ," not "the bride of Christ" (1 Corinthians 12.13; Ephesians 1.22-23; Colossians 1.18) and Christ is its Head. The Church is of the bridegroom, not the bride.

city is immense. Its dimensions are 1,500 miles in every direction, 1,500 miles wide, long, and high (Revelation 21.15-16). In appearance, it was like crystal clear jasper stone, transmitting light (Revelation 21.11). John also stated the city was pure gold, but like glass (Revelation 21.18) as were its streets (Revelation 21.21). The source of the light was the glory of God. There is no need for the sun or moon for light (Revelation 21.23). The city contained no Temple because the Lord God Almighty, the Lamb, are the Temple (Revelation 21.22).

Regarding New Jerusalem's wall, John stated it was 144 cubits high,[4] was of jasper, and had 12 gates, each of which was named for a tribe of Israel (Revelation 21.12). Three gates were on each side, in the same arrangement as how the 12 tribes camped around the Tabernacle (Revelation 21.13; Numbers 2). The wall was built upon 12 foundations, each of which was named after one of the 12 apostles (Revelation 21.14). Each foundation was a different precious stone: jasper, sapphire, chalcedony, emerald, sardonyx, sardius, chrysolite, beryl, topaz, chrysoprasus, jacinth, amethyst (Revelation 21.20). Each gate was a pearl, always open, with an angel attending it (Revelation 21.12, 21, 25).

From the throne of God, a river of water of life flowed and on each side of it was the tree of life. The trees produced twelve different fruits, one each month and its leaves were for the healing of the nations (Revelation 22.1-2). In addition, the Lord revealed the following to John:

> [3] And there shall be no more curse: but the throne of God and of the Lamb shall be in it; and his servants shall serve him: [4] And they shall see his face; and his name shall be in their foreheads. [5] And there shall be no night there; and they need no candle, neither light of the sun; for the Lord God giveth them light: and they shall reign for ever and ever (Revelation 22.3-5).

---

[4] This is a height of 216 feet high at a minimum.

Revelation ends with these encouraging words to Jews and Jesus' assurance that He will come quickly (Revelation 22.20):[5]

> And the Spirit and the bride say, Come. And let him that hears say, Come. And let him that is athirst come. And whosoever will, let him take the water of life freely (Revelation 22.17).

Where is the Church?

John made no mention of the Church in his description of the New Heavens and Earth. The reason is simple: John was an apostle of Israel, not an apostle of the Church. He wrote to Jews who had been saved believing the gospel of the kingdom.

God has not revealed the Church's role in eternity. It remains secret. What God has revealed about the destiny of the Church, the body of Christ, is the following:

1. Members receive eternal, resurrection bodies at the Rapture (1 Corinthians 15.51-54; 1 Thessalonians 4.13-18).
2. Members have heavenly citizenship (Ephesians 2.6; Philippians 3.20).
3. Members are children of God, heirs of God, and joint-heirs of Christ (Romans 8.16-17).
4. Members will rule the world and govern angels (1 Corinthians 6.2-3).[6]

---

[5] Jesus' statement of coming "quickly" echoed His words to the 7 Jewish assemblies in Revelation 2.5, 16, 3.11, 22.7, 12. When He does return, He will come speedily. But He cannot come, however, until the Jewish nation repents, as He stated in Matthew 23.37-39).

[6] The word "judge" is κρίνω. It has a range of meanings but most often translated judge, rule, govern. The Hebrew word used most often for κρίνω in the LXX is שָׁפַט as in Genesis 31.53; Exodus 2.14; Psalm 7.8, etc. It was used for Israel's judges, the nation's rulers before they had a king. Jesus told the Twelve they would occupy 12 thrones "judging," i.e., "ruling" (κρίνω) the 12 tribes of Israel (Matthew 19.28). Members

Paul also revealed,

> [7] But we speak the wisdom of God in a secret [μυστήριον], even the hidden wisdom, which God ordained before the world unto our glory: [8] Which none of the princes of this world knew: for had they known it, they would not have crucified the Lord of glory. [9] But as it is written, Eye has not seen, nor ear heard, neither have entered into the heart of man, the things which God hath prepared for them that love him (1 Corinthians 2.9).

What God has planned for those who have trusted Him, who love Him, is beyond comprehension. *Beyond comprehension.* Think about that!

---

of the Church, the body of Christ, will rule the world and angels. God has not revealed what other responsibilities members of His body will have.

Appendix 1:

The Scriptures God-Breathed

Inspiration is the work of God the Holy Spirit in superintending God's revelation to mankind. The Bible is a book but more than a book. It sets itself apart from other books in the same way Jesus' feeding the 5,000 is set apart from an ordinary meal. It is supernatural. Through it we learn answers to questions and secrets that lie beyond our ken: who God is, how heaven and the earth came into being, how we came into being, how sin and death originated, our place in God's plan, and how God will conquer sin and death and sum up all things in Christ.

Necessity of Revelation

Revelation is necessary for two reasons. The first is God is inaccessible to the creature. He is wholly other. According to the Scriptures:

> [15] He is the blessed and only Sovereign, the King of kings and Lord of lords, [16] who alone possesses immortality and dwells in unapproachable light whom no man has seen or can see (1 Timothy 6.15-16).

The second reason is that because of Adam's sin, our relationship with God has been broken. We enter the world spiritually dead, separated from God (Ephesians 2.1). Apart from believing the gospel (1 Corinthians 15.1-4), one remains spiritually dead, separated from God, devoid of spiritual understanding (1 Corinthians 2.14).

Even though sin has separated us from God, God has given each person the capacity to perceive Him. Every person knows God exists. The physical universe, nature, reveals God. God has also given each person a conscience. Every person knows right from wrong. Those who do not perceive God have actively suppressed knowledge of Him. God Paul wrote the Romans,

> [19] Because that which is known about God is evident within them for God made it evident to them. [20] For since the creation of the world His invisible attributes, His eternal power and divine nature, have been clearly seen, being understood through what has been made, so that they are without excuse (Romans 1.19-20).

Theologians call our ability to perceive God through nature and conscience general revelation. But one needs more than general revelation for salvation and understanding God's plan. This is special revelation. God has provided this information in the Scriptures. God has revealed Himself to all every person will account to Him (John 1.9; Romans 1.19-20; Colossians 1.23; Titus 2.11).

The Scriptures and the Son

The Scriptures are called the Word of God. The second person of the Trinity, God the Son, is also called the Word of God. He is the author of the Scriptures even though human beings wrote the words. Peter wrote:

> [10] Of which salvation the prophets have enquired and searched diligently, who prophesied of the grace that should come unto you: [11] Searching what, or what manner of time the Spirit of Christ which was in them did signify, when it testified beforehand the sufferings of Christ, and the glory that should follow (1 Peter 1.10-11).

John wrote, "the testimony of Jesus is the spirit of prophecy" (Revelation 19.10). John revealed that Jesus is the Word of God in His 1st and 2nd Advents. In his Gospel, he wrote:

> And the Word became flesh and dwelt among us, and we beheld his glory, glory as of the only begotten from the Father, full of grace and truth (John 1.14).

In Revelation, John identified Christ in his 2nd Advent:

> And He is clothed with a robe dipped in blood; and His name is called The Word of God (Revelation 19.13).

Jesus and the Scriptures are both divine and human. Jesus is the God-Man, wholly God and wholly man. While on earth He was God but His deity was largely veiled. Paul wrote:

> [5] Have this attitude in yourselves which was also in Christ Jesus, [6] who, although He existed in the form of God, did not regard equality with God a thing to be grasped, [7] but emptied Himself, taking the form of a bond-servant, and being made in the likeness of men (Philippians 2.5-7).

> [13] Who has delivered us from the power of darkness, and has translated us into the kingdom of his dear Son: [14] In whom we have redemption through his blood, even the forgiveness of sins: [15] Who is the image of the invisible God, the firstborn of every creature: [16] For by him were all things created, that are in heaven, and that are in earth, visible and invisible, whether they be thrones, or dominions, or principalities, or powers: all things were created by him, and for him: [17] And he is before all things, and by him all things consist (Colossians 1.13-17).

Anyone who looked at Jesus saw a man. He did not glow or have a halo around Him. He looked like an ordinary human being. But in the transfiguration, Peter, James, and John saw Him glorified. In the same way, the Scriptures appear as ordinary writings, no different from any other. But they are more—as Jesus was more than man. As Jesus, the Living Word, is both divine and human, the Scriptures, the written Word, are divine and human. Human beings were the scribes of God's Word. But behind them is God Himself. The Word is God-breathed, with the same breath God gave Adam to live (Genesis 2.7). His breath is life.

The Scriptures Expired or Exhaled

The Scriptures, New and Old Testaments, claim inspiration. The classic text for inspiration, 2 Timothy 3.16-17, reads:

> [16] All scripture is given by inspiration of God, and is profitable for doctrine, for reproof, for correction, for instruction in righteousness: [17] That the man of God may be perfect, thoroughly furnished unto all good works.

The word translated "inspired" is θεόπνευστος. Our word "inspiration" comes from the Latin "inspirare" which means "breath into." This is not what the Greek word means. The word θεόπνευστος is formed by combining Θεός "God" and πνέω "to breathe or blow." It means "God-breathed" or "God-blown." One cannot help but think of Jesus' words in John 3.8 where He used πνέω:

> The wind blows where it wishes and you hear the sound of it, but do not know where it comes from and where it is going; so is everyone who is born of the Spirit (John 3.8).

A similar passage is John 6.63:

> It is the Spirit who gives life; the flesh profits nothing; the words that I have spoken to you are spirit and are life.

A person who speaks *expires* air. Speaking requires breathing out, not breathing in. When Jesus spoke, His words were the Holy Spirit. The written Word is the breath of God.

The word θεόπνευστος is a *hapax legomenon* (ἅπαξ λεγόμενον)—that which is spoken once. It occurs only here in the New Testament and is not found in Greek classical literature. Paul coined the word to describe the divine nature of God's written word. A better rendering would be "All Scripture is *expired* by God." The Word of God is "expired," not "inspired."[1] A more accurate translation of 2 Timothy 3.16-17 is the following:

> 16 All (or every) Scripture is God-breathed (expired or exhaled by God) and profitable for doctrine, for proof,[2] for correction, for training in righteousness in order 17 that the man of God may be complete, having been furnished for every good work.

In Stephen's account of Jewish history before the Sanhedrin he declared concerning Moses:

> This is the one who was in the congregation in the wilderness together with the angel who was speaking to him on Mount Sinai, and who was with our fathers; and he received living oracles to pass on to you (Acts 7.38).

The expression "living oracles" (λόγια ζῶντα) conveys the sense "living words or utterances." Hebrews 4.12 reads, "the word of God is alive." The word ζωή should be translated "living" or "alive." This word (from which we get words such as zoology) carries the sense of the vitality or capacity of life. It is the same word Jesus used in John 6.63 by which He conveyed the concept that the words He speaks are spirit and life. Jesus said, "'Εγώ εἰμι . . . ἡ ζωή" "I am the life" (John 14.6).[3] The noun with definite article emphasizes the identity or source of life: Jesus is the source of life, i.e., "THE Life."

Genesis 2.7 reads:

---

[1] Warfield, B. B. "Inspiration." *The International Standard Bible Encyclopedia*, Eerdmans, 1982, p. 840. Warfield analyzed θεόπνευστος and corrected its mistranslations.

[2] The verse has a textual variant: ἔλεγχον, "proof" or ἐλεγμόν, "reproof." The former is more likely. See Hebrews 11.1. A parallel is set up with ἔλεγχον: doctrine/proof and correction/training. The word ἐλεγμόν is not found elsewhere.

[3] The word ζωή is distinguished from another Greek word for life–βίος (from which we get words such as biology). The word βίος carries the sense of the manner, means, or duration of life, i.e., "lifetime."

> Then the LORD God formed man of dust from the ground and breathed into his nostrils the breath of life; and man became a living being.

The breath of God (נְשָׁמָה) gave life to man. The Scriptures are the breath or the life of God in written form. Jesus reminded Satan of this by quoting Deuteronomy 8.3:

> It is written, Man shall not live on bread alone but on every word that proceeds out of the mouth of God (Matthew 4.4).

Mankind's original life came from the breath of God. Spiritual life begins with God's making our spirits alive when we believe the gospel. Paul called this creative act the "new man" (Ephesians 4:24; Colossians 3:10). The believer's life is maintained and strengthened by the outbreathing of God in the form of the Scriptures. The Word of God proceeds from the mouth of God. It is the very breath of God.

Paul wrote to the Hebrews and testified to this truth:

> For the word of God is alive and powerful and sharper than any two-edged sword, piercing even unto the division of soul and spirit, of both joints and marrow and able to judge the thoughts and intents of the heart (Hebrews 4.12).

Peter revealed something of the mechanics of how the Scriptures are God-breathed:

> But know this first of all, that no prophecy of Scripture is of one's own interpretation, for no prophecy was ever made by an act of human will, but men moved by the Holy Spirit spoke from God (2 Peter 1.21).

The Scriptures come into existence through divine will, not man's will. Men were the vehicles, the scribes, of God's declarations. Peter stated men were "moved" (φέρω means "bear" or "carry") by the Holy Spirit. The Holy Spirit "bore" or "conveyed" men along as they wrote God's words. In the genius of God, men retained their individuality and personality in conveying God's words. Many Old

Testament statements describe the Scriptures coming into being. The Old Testament has over 2,000 expressions such as "the LORD said", "the word of the LORD came saying" etc.

Jesus appealed constantly to the Scriptures to validate His message. Most of the time, He used the phrase, "It is written." He declared the Scriptures could not be broken (John 10.35) and that it was easier for the universe to cease than for one stroke of the letter of Scripture to fail (Luke 16.17).

The Mosaic Law governed Jewish society beginning with Moses. While Moses was the agent of the Law, God was its author. The Scriptures reveal God Himself wrote on the tablets of stone. Some of them are the following:

> Now the LORD said to Moses, Come up to Me on the mountain and remain there, and I will give you the stone tablets with the law and the commandment which I have written for their instruction (Exodus 24.12).
>
> When He had finished speaking with him upon Mount Sinai, He gave Moses the two tablets of the testimony, tablets of stone, written by the finger of God (Exodus 31.18).
>
> 15 Then Moses turned and went down from the mountain
> with the two tablets of the testimony in his hand, tablets
> which were written on both sides; they were written on one
> side and the other. 16 The tablets were God's work, and the
> writing was God's writing engraved on the tablets. (Exodus
> 32.15-16).
>
> 11 You came near and stood at the foot of the mountain, and
> the mountain burned with fire to the very heart of the
> heavens: darkness, cloud and thick gloom. 12 Then the Lord
> spoke to you from the midst of the fire; you heard the sound
> of words, but you saw no form—only a voice. 13 So He
> declared to you His covenant which He commanded you to
> perform, that is, the Ten Commandments; and He wrote

> them on two tablets of stone. [14] The Lord commanded me at that time to teach you statutes and judgments, that you might perform them in the land where you are going over to possess it. (Deuteronomy 4.11-14).

> These words the LORD spoke to all your assembly at the mountain from the midst of the fire, of the cloud and of the thick gloom, with a great voice, and He added no more. He wrote them on two tablets of stone and gave them to me (Deuteronomy 5.22).

David authored most of the Psalms. How did David describe his work?

> [1] Now these are the last words of David. David the son of Jesse declares, The man who was raised on high declares, the anointed of the God of Jacob, and the sweet psalmist of Israel, [2] The Spirit of the Lord spoke by me, and His word was on my tongue. [3] The God of Israel said, the Rock of Israel spoke to me, He who rules over men righteously, Who rules in the fear of God (2 Samuel 23.1-3).

Other declarations by God's servants include the following:

> So Balaam said to Balak, Behold, I have come now to you! Am I able to speak anything at all? The word that God puts in my mouth, that I shall speak (Numbers 22.38).

Balaam told Balak that God put His words into his mouth. The following Scriptures reveal the same:

> [10] Then the word of the LORD came to Samuel, saying, [11] I regret that I have made Saul king, for he has turned back from following Me and has not carried out My commands. And Samuel was distressed and cried out to the LORD all night (1 Samuel 15.10-11).

> [11] Now the word of the LORD came to Solomon saying, [12] Concerning this house which you are building, if you will walk in My statutes and execute My ordinances and keep

> all My commandments by walking in them, then I will carry out My word with you which I spoke to David your father (1 Kings 6.11-12).

> [22] But the word of God came to Shemaiah the man of God,
> saying, [23] Speak to Rehoboam the son of Solomon, king of
> Judah, and to all the house of Judah and Benjamin and to
> the rest of the people, saying, [24] 'Thus says the LORD, You
> must not go up and fight against your relatives the sons of
> Israel; return every man to his house, for this thing has
> come from Me. So they listened to the word of the LORD,
> and returned and went their way according to the word of
> the LORD (1 Kings 12.22-24).

> [3] It came about the same night that the word of God came
> to Nathan, saying, [4] Go and tell David My servant, Thus
> says the LORD, You shall not build a house for Me to dwell
> in (1 Chronicles 17.3-4).

> [1] Moreover, the word of the LORD came to me saying, [2]
> And you, son of man, thus says the Lord GOD to the land
> of Israel, An end! The end is coming on the four corners of
> the land (Ezekiel 7.1-2).

God told Jeremiah He had known him before He formed him in the womb and that in the womb He consecrated and appointed him to be a prophet. When Jeremiah protested he did not know how to speak as a prophet, God touched his mouth and told him He would put His words into his mouth.

> [4] Now the word of the LORD came to me saying, [5] Before
> I formed you in the womb I knew you, And before you
> were born I consecrated you; I have appointed you a
> prophet to the nations. [6] Then I said, Alas, Lord GOD!
> Behold, I do not know how to speak, because I am a youth.
> [7] But the LORD said to me, Do not say, I am a youth,
> because everywhere I send you, you shall go, and all that I
> command you, you shall speak. [8] Do not be afraid of them,
> for I am with you to deliver you, declares the LORD. [9] Then

> the LORD stretched out His hand and touched my mouth, and the LORD said to me, Behold, I have put My words in your mouth (Jeremiah 1.4-9).

Jeremiah revealed his humanity in his complaint to God about his message. He wished to be silent but could not. God's word was like an uncontrollable fire burning in his bones. He declared:

> [7] O LORD, You have deceived me and I was deceived; You have overcome me and prevailed. I have become a laughingstock all day long; Everyone mocks me. [8] For each time I speak, I cry aloud; I proclaim violence and destruction, because for me the word of the LORD has resulted in reproach and derision all day long. [9] But if I say, I will not remember Him or speak anymore in His name, then in my heart it becomes like a burning fire shut up in my bones; And I am weary of holding it in, and I cannot endure it (Jeremiah 20.7-9).

God assured Jeremiah He would be with him. This assurance is similar to the words the Lord spoke to His disciples:

> [19] But when they hand you over, do not worry about how or what you are to say; for it will be given you in that hour what you are to say. [20] For it is not you who speak, but it is the Spirit of your Father who speaks in you (Matthew 10.19-20).

Paul wrote the Thessalonians:

> And for this reason we also constantly thank God that when you received from us the word of God's message, you accepted it not as the word of men, but for what it really is, the word of God, which also performs its work in you who believe (1 Thessalonians 2.13).

Jesus and the Scriptures

The strongest testimony the Scriptures are God-breathed, inviolable, trustworthy, and truthful is from Jesus. He said:

> [17] Do not think that I came to abolish the Law or the Prophets; I did not come to abolish, but to fulfill. [18] For truly I say to you, until heaven and earth pass away, not the smallest letter or stroke shall pass away from the Law, until all is accomplished (Matthew 5.17-18).

> Heaven and earth shall pass away, but my words shall not pass away (Matthew 24.35).

Jesus referred to the Hebrew letter "yod" (י) with the Greek word ἰῶτα (iota) and the word κεραία, the projection or horn part of a Hebrew letter, the smallest written points of the text. Jesus was saying that not just the words but the tiniest letters and parts of letters of the Scriptures are inspired. An even more arresting statement is Jesus' statement that physical universe will cease to exist but the Scriptures will continue. Indeed, it was by the word of God that the universe came into existence. The Psalmist wrote,

> By the word of the LORD the heavens were made, and by the breath of His mouth all their host (Psalm 33.6).[4]

In His confrontation with the Jews in John 10, Jesus declared, "the Scripture cannot be broken." This is as clear a statement as can be made regarding the inerrancy and inviolability of Scripture. Jesus had a larger scope in view than just the Torah for His quote, "Has it not been written in your Law . . . ?" came from Psalm 82. The "Law" was a metonymy for all the Scriptures.

When the Sadducees presented Jesus with the situation of the seven brothers and one woman and asked Him whose wife she would be

---

[4] The origin of the universe is simple. God simply spoke.

in the resurrection, Jesus replied by citing the authority of the Scriptures and pointed to a direct quote from God:

> [29] You are mistaken, not understanding the Scriptures, or the power of God. [30] For in the resurrection they neither marry, nor are given in marriage, but are like angels in heaven. [31] But regarding the resurrection of the dead, have you not read that which was spoken to you by God, saying, [32] I am the God of Abraham, and the God of Isaac, and the God of Jacob? He is not the God of the dead but of the living (Matthew 22.29-32).

When Jesus began His ministry, Satan tempted Him with three specific temptations. To each one, the Lord responded, "it is written" (Matthew 4.1-11; Luke 4.1-13). Jesus appealed to the Scriptures. The written word was authoritative and inerrant.

Jesus was keenly attuned to the inseparable link between His ministry and the fulfillment of the Scriptures. At his arrest, He declared:

> Have you come out with swords and clubs to arrest Me, as against a robber? Every day I was with you in the temple teaching, and you did not seize Me; but this has happened that the Scriptures might be fulfilled (Mark 14.49).

Many attacks have been leveled against the Word of God. These are attacks upon God Himself for the Scriptures represent God and His character. The first attack came in the garden of Eden from Satan, the source of all attacks against God. He said to the woman, "Indeed, has God said, 'You shall not eat from any tree of the garden?'" Satan's manipulative conversation left Eve confused. Was God telling the truth or withholding a blessing? Satan deceived her and she believed his lie. Satan's strategic objective is to confuse mankind regarding God's goodness by doubting the Word of God. Jesus declared those who oppose Him and His Word have the Devil for their father. He told the Jews:

> [43] Why do you not understand what I am saying? It is because you cannot hear My word. [44] You are of your father the devil, and you want to do the desires of your father. He was a murderer from the beginning, and does not stand in the truth, because there is not truth in him. Whenever he speaks a lie, he speaks from his own nature; for he is a liar, and the father of lies (John 8.43-44).

Several significant Biblical events that have been vigorously attacked from skeptics. But Jesus confirmed them in His earthly ministry. Some of them are the following:

1. Creation of Adam and Eve

> [4] And He answered and said, Have you not read, that He who created them from the beginning made them male and female, [5] and said, For this cause a man shall leave his father and mother, and shall cleave to his wife; and the two shall become one flesh (Matthew 19.4-5)?

2. Mosaic authorship of the Pentateuch

> And Jesus said to him, See that you tell no one; but go, show yourself to the priest, and present the offering that Moses commanded, for a testimony to them (Matthew 8.4).

> But he said to him, If they do not listen to Moses and the Prophets, neither will they be persuaded if someone rises from the dead (Luke 16.31).

> For Moses said, Honor your father and your mother'; and, He who speaks evil of father or mother, let him be put to death (Mark 7.10).

> He said to them, Because of your hardness of heart, Moses permitted you to divorce your wives; but from the beginning it has not been this way (Matthew 19.8).

> Now He said to them, These are My words which I spoke to you while I was still with you, that all things which are

> written about Me in the Law of Moses and the Prophets and the Psalms must be fulfilled (Luke 24.44).
>
> Do not think that I will accuse you before the Father; the one who accuses you is Moses, in whom you have set your hope. For if you believed Moses, you would believe Me; for he wrote of Me. But if you do not believe his writings, how will you believe My words (John 5.45-47)?
>
> Did not Moses give you the Law, and yet none of you carries out the Law (John 7.19)?

3. The Flood

> [37] For the coming of the Son of Man will be just like the days of Noah. [38] For as in those days which were before the flood they were eating and drinking, they were marrying and giving in marriage, until the day that Noah entered the ark, [39] and they did not understand until the flood came and took them all away; so shall the coming of the Son of Man be (Matthew 24.37-39).

4. Existence and destruction of Sodom and Gomorrah

> [23] And you, Capernaum, will not be exalted to heaven, will you? You shall descend to Hades; for if the miracles had occurred in Sodom which occurred in you, it would have remained to this day. [24] Nevertheless, I say to you that it shall be more tolerable for the land of Sodom in the day of judgment, than for you (Matthew 11.23-24).

5. Jonah and the great sea creature

> For just as Jonah was three days and three nights in the belly of the sea monster, so shall the Son of Man be three days and tree nights in the heart of the earth (Matthew 12.40).

6. Daniel a prophet

> [15] Therefore, when you see the abomination of desolation which was spoken of through Daniel the prophet, standing in the holy place (let the reader understand), [16] then let those who are in Judea flee to the mountains (Matthew 24.15-16).

7. Existence of a literal Satan and demons

> Then Jesus said to him, Begone, Satan! For it is written, You shall worship the Lord your God, and serve Him only (Matthew 4.10).

> Simon, Simon, behold, Satan has demanded permission to sift you like wheat (Luke 22.31).

> [6] And seeing Jesus from a distance, he ran up and bowed down before Him; [7] and crying out with a loud voice, he said, What do I have to do with You, Jesus, Son of the Most High God? I implore You by God, do not torment me! [8] For He had been saying to him, Come out of the man, you unclean spirit! And He was asking him, What is your name? [9] And he said to Him, My name is Legion; for we are many (Mark 5.6-9).

> Then He will also say to those on His left, Depart from Me, accursed ones, into the eternal fire which has been prepared for the devil and his angels (Matthew 25.41).

> [17] But He knew their thoughts, and said to them, Any kingdom divided against itself is laid waste; and a house divided against itself falls. [18] And if Satan also is divided against himself, how shall his kingdom stand? For you say that I cast out demons by Beelzebul. [19] And if I by Beelzebul cast out demons, by whom do your sons cast them out? Consequently, they shall be your judges. [20] But if I cast out demons by the finger of God, then the kingdom of God has come upon you (Luke 11.17-20).

8. Existence of a literal hell

> And do not fear those who kill the body, but are unable to kill the soul; but rather fear Him who is able to destroy both soul and body in hell (Matthew 10.28).

> And I also say to you that you are Peter, and upon this rock I will build My church; and the gates of Hades shall not overpower it (Matthew 16.18).

> You serpents, you brood of vipers, how shall you escape the sentence of hell (Matthew 23.33)?

> [23] And in Hades he lifted up his eyes, being in torment, and
> saw Abraham far away, and Lazarus in his bosom. [24] And
> he cried out and said, Father Abraham, have mercy on me,
> and send Lazarus, that he may dip the tip of his finger in
> water and cool off my tongue; for I am in agony in this
> flame (Luke 16.23-24).

Textual Considerations

Before leaving this subject, we would be remiss in not addressing the subject of the text itself. Determining the Biblical text is the work of textual critics. No autographs or original manuscripts exist. The Aleppo Codex is the oldest Hebrew Bible and was created in Tiberias, Israel, around 930 A.D., by scribes called Masoretes. The Leningrad Codex is the oldest complete Hebrew Bible and dates to about 1008 A.D. and was penned in Cairo. These were the oldest copies until the discovery of the Dead Sea scrolls in 1947. The Jews were meticulous copyists and developed numerous techniques to ensure the integrity of the text. The Dead Sea scrolls, written about 250-68 B.C., confirmed the accuracy of the text.

The Hebrew Bible had also been translated into Greek by scholars between 300-100 B.C. and was a sound translation. It was called the Septuagint (LXX) because 70 scholars attended the work. Most quotations of the Old Testament in the New Testament are from the Septuagint.

With regard to the New Testament, several thousand Greek and Latin manuscript copies (papyri, uncials, minuscules, lectionaries, Latin manuscripts) exist and are categorized into three families: Alexandrian, Byzantium, and Western. The earliest are dated in the 2nd and 4th centuries A.D. While these manuscripts have hundreds of thousands of variant readings, they are of little consequence and pose no problem for any major doctrine. Essentially, we have 105% of text. The textual critic's task is to determine the correct 100%. The text is 99% correct.

Conclusion

Several theories of inspiration exist which try to explain its mechanics but ultimately, this is unknowable. Is this a problem? Many mysteries exist in nature. Who understands how God created the universe? What is life? How does the mind work? How does mind interact with the body? How do birds unerringly fly thousands of miles? What is the nature of light? These are mysteries. Jesus referred to such mysteries in the natural world when He said,

> The wind blows where it wishes and you hear the sound of it, but do not know where it comes from and where it is going; so is everyone who is born of the Spirit (John 3.8).

We do not know where the wind comes from much less how the Holy Spirit operates. The Bible declares every Scripture is God-breathed. The proof of the Bible is prophecy. Hundreds of fulfilled prophecies confirm the Bible. No other holy book has this testimony. The Bible is the Word of God, written by the Alpha and the Omega, the One who inhabits eternity. Those who abandon this truth are uncertain travelers on a hopeless road with only darkness ahead.

Charting God's Programs

The following chart shows the books of the Bible associated with God's specific programs. The first eleven chapters of Genesis concern God's dealings with mankind, prior to His call of Abraham. The remaining chapters of Genesis through Malachi concern Israel in its role as God's covenant people, the conduit of God's blessing of the nations. The Gospels continued God's prophetic program and are Old Testament books which fit snugly next to Malachi. The book of Acts is transitional. Luke wrote it to explain why the kingdom of the prophets and Gospels did not come upon the earth. Hebrews is also transitional. Paul admonished the Jews not to fail as their ancestors had at Kadesh-Barnea. He proclaimed that Jesus was the Christ who fulfilled the Old Testament types. The letters of James, Peter, John, and Jude were written to Jews who had believed the gospel of the kingdom to encourage and admonish them about life in God's prophetic program. The books of Romans through Philemon, the Pauline corpus, contain all Church doctrine. They reveal God's new program—of the Church, the body of Christ.

Scriptures Associated with God's Programs

Mankind	Israel (Prophetic Program)		Church (Secret Program)
Genesis 1-11	Genesis 12-Malachi	Matthew Mark Luke John James 1 Peter 2 Peter 1 John 2 John 3 John Jude Revelation[5] ------- Acts and	Romans 1 Corinthians 2 Corinthians Galatians Ephesians Philippians Colossians 1 Thessalonians 2 Thessalonians 1 Timothy 2 Timothy Titus Philemon ------- Hebrews[6]

[5] Revelation 21-22 describe God's eternal program related to Israel.
[6] Acts and Hebrews belong primarily to God's prophetic program but are a bridge to God's secret program, the Church.

Appendix 2:

Sound Interpretation (Hermeneutics)

> Scripture speaketh after the most grossest maner: be diligent therefore that thou be not deceaued with curiousness.
>
> God is a spirit and all his wordes are spirituall. His literal sense is spirituall.
>
> Thou shalt understand, therefore, that the scripture hath but one sense, which is the literal sense. And that literal sense is the root and ground of all, and the anchor that never faileth, whereunto if thou cleave, thou canst never err or go out of the way. And if thou leave the literal sense, thou canst not but go out of the way. Neverthelater, the scripture useth proverbs, similitudes, riddles, or allegories, as all other speeches do; but that which the proverb, similitude, riddle, or allegory signifieth, is ever the literal sense, which thou must seek out diligently: as in the English we borrow words and sentences of one thing, and apply them unto another, and give them new significations.[1]
>
> It shall greatly helpe ye to understande Scripture, If thou mark Not only what is spoken or wrytten, But of whom, And to whom, With what words, At what time, Where, To what intent, With what circumstances, Considering what goeth before And what followeth. [2]

---

[1] Lewis, C. S. *English Literature in the Sixteenth Century Excluding Drama*, Oxford, Clarendon Press, 1954, p. 186. These quotes are from Tyndale's *Parable of the Wicked Mammon* and *The Obedience of a Christian Man*. By "gross," Tyndale meant "plain," "evident," or "obvious." Lewis' comments on William Tyndale (1494-1536) are the finest brief analysis of the great Reformer and his views of the Gospel.

[2] Pearson, George, ed. *Remains of Coverdale, Bishop of Exeter*. Parker Society. Cambridge, University Press, 1846, p. 15. This statement is

Hermeneutics is the art and science of interpretation. The key factors for a hermeneutic are rigor and consistency. How we approach language is foundational to how we determine meaning. Language is of two sorts: figurative or literal.[3] The best way to understanding this subject is probably by examining specific examples. Consider the following passage from Matthew:

> Now after Jesus was born in Bethlehem of Judea in the days of Herod the king, magi from the east arrived in Jerusalem, saying, ... (Matthew 2.1).

This is a simple, historical statement. The normal, obvious meaning is Jesus was born in a place called Bethlehem (a real, geographical place) when Herod (a historical person who reigned in a recorded time) was king (a real position) over Judea (a real, geographical place). By means of such a statement, Matthew rooted Jesus' birth in a real place in a real time. Contrast Matthew's literal statement with the following by Jesus in the Gospel of John:

> Truly, truly, I say to you, I am the door of the sheep (John 10.7).

We understand Jesus was not saying He was a wooden door of a sheep pen. We understand He was using a figure of speech.[4] Even though He used a metaphor, Jesus communicated a *literal* truth. As a wooden door is the entrance to a sheep pen, Jesus is the entrance to salvation. Jesus was not talking about animals, i.e. sheep, but human beings—Jews.

Communication is *literal*. Think about daily conversations. We talk about going to dinner, watching a movie, what our children are doing, projects, what we're reading, what's happening at church, in politics, in sports, our job etc. These communications are literal. Were it not so, we would find it impossible to communicate. We regularly employ conventions in speech. A new car is called a "nice

---

from Myles Coverdale's (1488-1569) Prologue to the Translation of the Bible.

[3] Like Tyndale, by "literal" I mean "normal" speech.

[4] John tells us it was a figure of speech (John 10.6).

set of wheels." We use expressions such as, "She's the apple of his eye." We understand we're talking about a whole car and not just its wheels. We know someone's eye does not have an apple in it but that the apple represents an object of appeal. Figurative language is, in most cases, readily understood by its context. It can also be identified by the kind of literature. Poetry lends itself to figurative language. What is essential to remember is figurative language communicates *literal* truth. Isaiah penned the poetic line:

> All flesh is grass, and all its loveliness is like the flower of the field (Isaiah 40.6).

The literal truth is not that flesh *is* grass—that makes no sense—but that we are mortal. Isaiah conveyed literal truth through figurative language.

Most difficulties in interpreting the Scriptures arise from neglecting context. The guiding principle of sound interpretation is to take a passage literally—in its normal sense—as Tyndale instructed. Without such discipline, interpretation becomes so elastic it can mean almost anything. The result is erroneous or ridiculous interpretations. The interpreter must ask the same questions of Coverdale: To whom was a passage written? What did it mean to its audience? When was it written? Under what circumstances was it written? What was the historical context? How does the passage compare with other passages the writer has written and with passages of other writers? Other questions pertinent to interpretation include: What light do the original languages shed on the passage? Do cognate languages offer insight? What customs were in place? Are idioms or conventions present? Does archaeology shed linguistic or historical light on the passage? Interpreters must consider these factors to determine meaning.

An illustrative example of interpretive confusion can be seen with the subject of David's throne. Because a normal hermeneutic has been abandoned, a theological controversy exists as to whether Jesus will occupy David's throne literally in a future day or whether He now occupies it figuratively or symbolically in heaven. A normal reading of the Davidic Covenant (2 Samuel 7:8-17) indicates God promised to establish the throne of David forever upon the earth. We know from history that no son of David has occupied Israel's throne since the time of Nebuchadnezzar. We also know Mary and Joseph were members of the tribe of Judah and descendants in the royal line of David. The angel Gabriel announced to Mary that God would give her son the throne of David. He said:

> [32] He will be great, and will be called the Son of the Most High; and the Lord God will give Him the throne of His father David; [33] and He will reign over the house of Jacob forever; and His kingdom will have no end (Luke 1.32-33).

A normal reading of the prophecy is that God would give Mary's son, Jesus, the Davidic throne and He would reign over the house of Jacob forever. The kingdom meant only one thing to a Jew: God's kingdom on earth. Everything in this covenant promise was *Jewish.* How would Mary have understood the words of the angel? She would have remembered the Davidic covenant and the prophecies that had been made that promised Israel a Messiah-King who would reign on earth.

The context indicates Gentiles or the Church were *not* in view. Jesus was a Jew. He was from the tribe of Judah and his ancestor was King David. Jesus did not occupy David's throne during his life on earth. Is He sitting on it now? Can one visit Jerusalem and find Jesus reigning? The answer is obvious. Jesus is not in Jerusalem but is seated at the right hand of his *Father's throne* (Psalm 110:1). Therefore, the prophetic promise awaits fulfillment. A future day remains in which Jesus will rule from Jerusalem on David's throne and fulfill God's promise to David as reiterated to Mary (Daniel 7:14; Zechariah 14:9; Isaiah 9:6-7, 16:5; Jeremiah 33:17, 20-22, etc.).

Some maintain David's throne is symbolic and that Christ is now reigning over the Church and this fulfills the Davidic covenant. They mold the Scriptures to fit their theological viewpoint and have abandoned literal interpretation.

The Davidic Covenant was prophecy. How were other prophecies associated with Jesus fulfilled? Were they fulfilled literally or figuratively? Was Jesus born in Bethlehem? Were Jesus' garments parted? Did soldiers cast lots for them? Was He crucified with thieves? Was He betrayed for 30 pieces of silver? Did His disciples forsake Him? Did Jesus die for our sins? Did He rise from the dead? To accept a non-literal hermeneutic means all these fulfillments are in jeopardy. Some maintain Jesus did not *literally* rise from the dead but rose in the hearts of believers. And why not? What interpretive discipline exists in a non-literal hermeneutic to prevent this conclusion? There is none. How can anyone maintain Jesus is now occupying the *Davidic* throne in heaven? David was never promised a heavenly throne. Such an interpretation is impossible unless one abandons a literal hermeneutic.

Another example of interpretive confusion regards the events that took place at Pentecost as recorded in Acts. At Pentecost, Peter told his audience they had crucified their Messiah (Acts 2.22-23, 36). His words convicted them and they asked what they should do. Peter told them to repent and be baptized for the forgiveness of sins and that they would receive the promise of the Holy Spirit (Acts 2.38). He then declared:

> For the promise is for you and your children, and for all who are far off, as many as the Lord our God shall call to Himself (Acts 2.39).

In Peter's second sermon he spoke similar words:

> And likewise, all the prophets who have spoken, from Samuel and his successors onward, also announced these days. It is you who are the sons of the covenant which God made with your fathers, saying to Abraham, And in your seed all the families of the earth shall be blessed (Acts 3.24-25).

The great challenge of this passage is not to read future revelation, e.g., Paul, into the passage. Peter's audience Jewish. Peter only addressed Jews. Pentecost was a Jewish feast day. It concerned

Jews, national Israel, not Gentiles or the Church. How could anything at Pentecost concern the Church, the body of Christ, when Peter only addressed Jews and had no contact with a Gentile until Acts 10, several years later? The answer should be obvious. What happened at Pentecost concerned Israel. The coming of the Holy Spirit was a fulfillment of God's promise to national Israel (Jeremiah 31; Ezekiel 36). It had *nothing* to do with the Church, the body of Christ.

Paul declared the Church, the Body of Christ, was a secret God had revealed to him (Ephesians 2.11-22; 3.3-9; Colossians 1.26-27).[5] In this new entity, no distinction exists between Jew and Gentile. Peter knew only God's prophetic program in which Gentiles were to be blessed *through* Israel. His knowledge of the Church, the body of Christ, came much later, from the Apostle Paul. To force later revelation and Church doctrine onto the early chapters of Acts is to abandon sound interpretive principles.

Maintaining a literal hermeneutic has been a challenge throughout history. Allegorical interpretation influenced Christian interpretation of Scripture by way of Greek philosophy. Allegorical interpretation came into existence largely to solve a Greek scholarly dilemma. The Greeks had an established religious heritage from Hesiod and Homer. When philosophers and scholars began to reject their religious heritage, it created a social problem. They could not reject the writings of the earlier Greek poets due to their popularity. To preserve Hesiod and Homer in an intellectually acceptable form, scholars allegorized their religious heritage. The stories of the gods were not to be taken *literally* but figuratively or allegorically. This new hermeneutic proclaimed that a greater meaning lay beyond the literal sense.

Adopting the hermeneutical methods applied to pagan texts, scholars, primarily from Alexandria, began to influence Biblical

---

[5] Paul stated the Church, the body of Christ, was a secret (μυστήριον) and revealed several other secrets God gave to him (Romans 11:25, Romans 16:25; 1 Corinthians 2:7, 13:2, 14:2, 15:51; Ephesians 1:9, 3:3, 4, 3:9, 5:32, 6:19; Colossians 1:26, 27, 2:2, 4:3; 2 Thessalonians 2:7; 1 Timothy 3:9, 16).

interpretation. While Rome was the political center of the ancient world, Alexandria was a leading intellectual and cultural center. It had the greatest library in the world and scholars flocked to it. A large Jewish population resided there and later, a great Christian population. Jewish intellectuals and scholars wished to reconcile the Scriptures with Greek philosophy and adopted an allegorical hermeneutic. Influenced by these scholastic trends, Christian intellectuals began to do the same. This interpretive tradition dominated Christian scholarship until the Reformation. The man probably most responsible for introducing allegorical interpretation into the Christian church was Origen (c. 185-254), who sought to harmonize Christian theology with the teachings of Plato.

Augustine, the Bishop of Hippo (354-425), incorporated Origen's methodology and devised a unified theology. His ideas influenced Christian interpretation for a millennium. Augustine originally had held to a literal eschatological (doctrine of last things) view of the kingdom—as had most of the earliest Church fathers. But he abandoned this view as he systematized his theology under an allegorical hermeneutic. Because of this methodology, many reject a normal reading of the Scriptures that God will establish a literal kingdom on earth in which Christ will physically reign on earth. They thus view the kingdom as our present Church age.

As early as the 2nd second century A.D., some had begun to teach that the Church had replaced Israel since the Jews had rejected their Messiah.[6] As such, God's promises to Israel were being fulfilled figuratively by the Church. Throughout the Middle Ages, this idea became cemented as orthodox theology. This remains the predominant view in Christendom even though it is built upon hermeneutical sand.

---

[6] For example, Justin Martyr (c. 100-165) wrote in *Dialogue with Trypho*, "For the true spiritual Israel, and descendants of Judah, Jacob, Isaac, and Abraham (who in uncircumcision was approved of and blessed by God on account of his faith, and called the father of many nations), are we who have been led to God through this crucified Christ, as shall be demonstrated while we proceed." Theologians call this supersessionism.

When the Reformers emerged, they reasserted a literal interpretation in soteriology (the doctrine of salvation). As a result, they recovered and rediscovered justification by faith alone. The bywords of the Reformation were *sola Scriptura, sola gratia, sola fide*—the Scriptures alone, grace alone, faith alone.

But old habits and traditions die hard. The Reformers failed to apply their methodology to other realms of theology: e.g., eschatology and ecclesiology. They were under tremendous pressures in reestablishing the Scriptures and what they achieved was remarkable. But since that time, little progress has been made to establish a unified hermeneutical rigor into all areas of theology. Most scholars, pastors, and theologians fail to apply a consistent, literal hermeneutic to the Scriptures. This has resulted in the confusion about the difference between Israel and the Church and misunderstanding prophecy.

Appendix 3:

Means of Perception (Epistemology)

> *And without faith it is impossible to please Him, for he who comes to God must believe that He is and that He is a rewarder of those who seek Him (Hebrews 11.6).*

Epistemology: How We Know What We Know

God has given mankind three means of perception to understand the external world. They are reason, experience, and faith. Reason derives knowledge about the external world through logic and intellect. Experience gains knowledge about the visible world through the senses: taste, touch, sight, smell, and hearing. Faith gains knowledge that is beyond reason and experience by trusting authority.

Science deals with knowledge gained through our senses and reason and operates primarily through the scientific method. By the scientific method, one observes the world and formulates a hypothesis or theory. The hypothesis or theory is tested through experimentation. The results are analyzed and interpreted to confirm or deny the theory. New conclusions are drawn and the process begins again. In the scientific method, a theory is validated if data is observed and reproduced. If the data is not observed or cannot be repeated, a theory falls outside the realm of science.

Scientific knowledge is extremely valuable but it occupies only a small subset of knowledge. For example, all historical knowledge falls outside of science. A scientist cannot form a theory and run an experiment to determine if Julius Caesar crossed the Rubicon, what year he crossed the Rubicon, or even if there was a Julius Caesar. Historical knowledge is based upon authority. Historical knowledge requires trust in historical records. Most knowledge is non-scientific. Many people have never been to India but believe it exists. The reason is trust. They trust atlases, satellites, newspapers, television, radio, the internet, and testimonies of people who have been there. It is knowledge based on faith. Learning begins by faith. A child learns language by a parent saying "dog." The child then says, "dog." He learns based on authority. A child in school continues to learn based upon the authority of the teacher and textbooks.

Means of Perception	
Reason	Trusts Logic and Intellect
Experience	Trusts Senses
Faith	Trusts Authority

What is Faith?

Faith, like reason and the senses, is a means of *perception*. Paul defined faith in his letter to the Hebrews:

> Now faith is the assurance of things hoped for, the conviction of things not seen. For by it the men of old gained approval (Hebrews 11.1).

The Bible declares no one can please God apart from faith (Hebrews 11.6). The definition above states faith is the means of perception which apprehends unseen reality. Faith understands that which is not visible, that which is unknowable through reason and the senses. Faith, trust, and believe mean the same thing. In theology, faith means believing God, believing the Bible. Through such perception, men and women achieved God's approval. Why is faith so important to God?

What is Biblical Faith?

A vast difference exists between these two propositions:

Statement		Meaning of Statement
1.	I believe in God	Mental Assent
2.	I believe God	Personal Trust

The first proposition is a statement of mental assent. It means one believes God exists. The second proposition is a statement of personal trust. When one declares he believes God it means he *trusts* God. It means one believes what God has said. This is Biblical faith. Biblical faith is personal trust of God and what He has said. Believing God is obeying God (cf. Deuteronomy 9.23; Romans 16.26).

What's Special About Faith?

Answering this question is complex. It goes to the heart of the problem God had to solve to save the human race. Adam and Eve's disobedience caused them to die spiritually (immediately) and physically (later). God told Adam that eating from the Tree of the Knowledge of Good and Evil: (מוֹת תָּמוּת) "dying you will die". When Adam disobeyed, he plunged the human race into a condition of sin and death (Genesis 2.17; 1 Corinthians 15.22; Ephesians 2.1-3). Tragic as this was, as soon as man sinned, God began His redemptive plan (Genesis 3.15). Because the penalty of sin is death (Genesis 2.17; Romans 6.23; Ephesians 2.1-2) man could not save himself. A dead man cannot save himself from death. How then can man be saved?

God's Dilemma

God's character consists of sovereignty, omnipotence, omnipresence, omniscience, veracity, eternal life, righteousness, immutability, justice, and love. God's justice demanded death for sin. God's love for man desired his salvation. God created man in His own image (וַיִּבְרָא אֱלֹהִים אֶת-הָאָדָם בְּצַלְמוֹ, Genesis 1.27) and put His breath of life, (נִשְׁמַת חַיִּים, "breath of lives") into him so he became a living being (Genesis 2.7). Man was God's special creation whom He loved man and desired to live.

Man could live only if someone could satisfy God's justice and pay the penalty for sin. The penalty of sin required death, i.e., the shedding of blood, since the life of the flesh is in the blood (Genesis 9.4; Leviticus 17.14; Deuteronomy 12.23; John 6.53-54; Hebrews

9.22). As early as Genesis 3.21, God revealed this truth when He provided animal skins to clothe Adam and Eve. For hundreds of years God taught mankind that sin required a blood sacrifice (Hebrews 9.22). The Jews formally incorporated this truth under the Mosaic Law in their Levitical sacrifices. And though most of the world rejected God's revelation they retained the fundamental knowledge of the necessity of animal sacrifices. But animal deaths could not atone for sin (Hebrews 10.1). They were but shadows.

Solving mankind's problem of sin and death required someone who was sinless, another "Adam," to pay his penalty of sin (1 Corinthians 15.22, 45). This "new Adam" was the Lord Jesus Christ (1 Corinthians 15.45). As God, He stepped out eternity, became a man, and died to pay man's sin. Theologians call His work redemption, reconciliation, justification, atonement, propitiation, etc. Each of these theological terms describes an aspect of Christ's salvific work. Christ's resurrection was the physical proof He had satisfied the justice of God.

Since man is born spiritually dead, to regain spiritual life required the work of another. Man's dependence on this work, the work of Christ, is expressed by faith. By trusting God, man apprehends God's salvation. That is why faith is essential.

Faith Throughout History

Faith has always been required for salvation. Hebrews 11 is an account of Old Testament believers who lived victorious lives by faith. In Romans 1.7, Paul quoted Habakkuk:

> For in it the righteousness of God is revealed from faith to faith; as it is written, But the just shall live by faith (Habakkuk 2.4).

Paul and Faith

While salvation has always been by faith, Paul received and revealed a new doctrine about faith. He began his great treatise of Romans with the following introduction:

> 1 Paul, a bond-servant of Christ Jesus, called as an apostle,
> set apart for the gospel of God, 2 which He promised
> beforehand through His prophets in the holy Scriptures, 3
> concerning His Son, who was born of a descendant of
> David according to the flesh, 4 who was declared the Son
> of God with power by the resurrection from the dead,
> according to the Spirit of holiness, Jesus Christ our Lord, 5
> through whom we have received grace and apostleship to
> bring about the obedience of faith among all the Gentiles
> for His name's sake, 6 among whom you also are the called
> of Jesus Christ (Romans 1.1-6).

Paul identified himself as God's chosen apostle and defined his mission: to proclaim the gospel—that Christ died for us and rose from the dead—and bring about "the obedience of faith" among the Gentiles. Prior to Paul, God's attention had been on Jew only (with a few exceptions). But the ascended Lord commissioned Paul as "the apostle of the Gentiles" (Romans 11.13; 2 Timothy 1.11). This was a vast change of God's program—something that had not occurred since God called Abraham, 2,000 years before. What did Paul mean by the phrase "obedience of faith" (εἰς ὑπακοὴν πίστεως)? The phrase is a genitive of apposition and means "obedience, which is faith," or "obedience, namely, faith."

Before Paul, faith and works were inseparably linked. Salvation required faith *and* works.[1] God revealed nothing in the Old Testament about salvation by faith *alone*. The Mosaic Law required a sinner to bring a sacrifice to the priest. That was a work. If a person reasoned, "I believe God will cover my sin but I'm not going to bring an animal" he could not be forgiven because he refused to obey God by performing the work God demanded. If one reasoned, "I will bring the sacrifice but do not believe it will cover my sin," he could not be forgiven for he had no faith in the sacrifice. To experience God's forgiveness under the Law, one had to bring a sacrifice for sin (a work) in obedience to the Law and exercise faith.

---

[1] The exception was Abraham. Abraham was saved apart from works, by faith alone and Paul used him to demonstrate his doctrine of salvation by faith alone (Romans 4.1-5).

God pounded this into the Jews for hundreds of years. The believing Jews in Jerusalem were adamant that Paul's converts could not be saved apart from works. They insisted they must be circumcised and keep the Mosaic Law to be saved (Act 15.1, 5). And why not? This is how it had been for 1,500 years.

Paul fought this view—not because he was in rebellion to Judaism or the Mosaic Law—but because he had received a new revelation from God. The gospel the risen Christ revealed to Paul was a gospel of salvation by faith alone in the death and resurrection of Christ (1 Corinthians 15.1-4). This revelation became such a source of contention that it precipitated the need for the Council of Jerusalem in 51 A.D.

Paul received his gospel directly from the ascended Lord. He had not consulted with the Twelve or anyone else (Galatians 1.1, 11-12). Because of this, he set his feet like a bulldog and would not give an inch. Paul's gospel required no works or Law keeping. It was salvation by faith alone: faith + 0. Paul declared that anyone who believed his gospel was saved (1 Corinthians 15.2), became a member of the body of Christ, the Church, (1 Corinthians 12.13; Ephesians 1.22-23; Colossians 1.18), and was free from the Mosaic Law (Romans 6.14, Galatians 5.18; Ephesians 2.15). Thus, "obedience of faith" according to Paul's gospel meant salvation by faith *alone*. Paul wrote the Galatians with this dire warning:

> [6] I am amazed that you are so quickly deserting Him who called you by the grace of Christ, for a different gospel; [7] which is really not another; only there are some who are disturbing you and want to distort the gospel of Christ. [8] But even if we, or an angel from heaven, should preach to you a gospel contrary to what we have preached to you, he is to be accursed! [9] As we have said before, so I say again now, if any man is preaching to you a gospel contrary to what you received, he is to be accursed! (Galatians 1.6-9).

Paul wrote these words *after* the Council of Jerusalem. At the Council, Peter had declared:

> [10] Now therefore why do you put God to the test by placing upon the neck of the disciples a yoke which neither our fathers nor we have been able to bear? [11] But we believe that we are saved through the grace of the Lord Jesus, in the same way as they also are (Acts 15.10-11).

After much arguing, Peter finally spoke and made an astonishing declaration: Jews now had to be saved as Gentiles. This was a watershed event. From that time forward, one could *only* be saved by believing Paul's gospel—salvation by faith alone (faith + 0) in Christ's death and resurrection. Anyone who taught otherwise was accursed (Galatians 1.6-9). Paul could not have written such strong words until *after* the issue of salvation had been settled at the Council.

What Peter had declared was almost incomprehensible to the Jew. They had been under the authority of the Mosaic Law for 1,500 years. Jesus had ministered under the Law. But Peter, under the direction of the Holy Spirit recognized Paul's gospel had now superseded the "gospel of the kingdom."[2]

Life is a Gift

God is the source of life. One can do nothing to merit life. God owes man nothing (Romans 4.2, 4-5). We come His way or not at all (Matthew 7.13-14; John 14.6). Salvation is based upon trust and obedience to what God has revealed. If God declared salvation was by doing 10 jumping jacks, a person who trusted God would do 10 jumping jacks. At the present time, God has revealed men and

---

[2] God prepared Peter for this critical moment 14 years earlier. Foreseeing the crisis Paul would face, God commanded Peter to visit the Gentile, Cornelius. As Peter began his message the Holy Spirit came upon Cornelius and the others with him. Peter and the six Jewish believers with him were stunned. Gentiles had received the Holy Spirit. This had occurred without out baptism, works, Law-keeping, circumcision, etc. (Acts 10.44-48). It was a faith + 0 event: a total shock.

women are saved by believing Paul's gospel (1 Corinthians 15.1-4).

Paul wrote:

> [23] for all have sinned and fall short of the glory of God, [24] being justified as a gift by His grace through the redemption which is in Christ Jesus (Romans 3.23-24).
>
> [4] Now to the one who works, his wage is not credited as a favor, but as what is due. [5] But to the one who does not work, but believes in Him who justifies the ungodly, his faith is credited as righteousness (Romans 4.4-5).
>
> For the wages of sin is death, but the free gift of God is eternal life in Christ Jesus our Lord (Romans 6.23).
>
> [15] But the free gift is not like the transgression. For if by the transgression of the one the many died, much more did the grace of God and the gift by the grace of the one Man, Jesus Christ, abound to the many. [16] The gift is not like that which came through the one who sinned; for on the one hand the judgment arose from one transgression resulting in condemnation, but on the other hand the free gift arose from many transgressions resulting in justification. [17] For if by the transgression of the one, death reigned through the one, much more those who receive the abundance of grace and of the gift of righteousness will reign in life through the One, Jesus Christ (Romans 5.15-17).
>
> [8] For by the grace you have been saved through the faith; and that not of yourselves, it is the gift of God; [9] not as a result of works, so that no one may boast (Ephesians 2.8-9).

Could anything be simpler? Salvation, eternal life, is a gift given by God simply by trusting Him, by believing the gospel: Christ died for our sins and rose from the dead.

Summary of the Plan of God

Introduction

Once upon a time when there was no time God made a plan.

Everyone loves a good story. And God is the greatest of storytellers. Countless years ago He began a drama that dwarfs all dramas in terms of plot, character, and setting by a near infinite order of magnitude. The stage and scope of God's drama occupy the entire physical universe and all that is beyond—hidden from us. God is the archetypal author who has written a drama with heroes and villains, life and death, triumph and tragedy. In this drama, God has given His creatures the freedom to choose. But as the writer of a novel knows the choices his characters will make, God knows the choices we will make. His goal is to bring glory and honor to Himself so that His creation might rejoice in that glory—for we are heirs of it. In His wisdom, God created his creatures with free will, which allowed the possibility for sin. Despite mankind's failure, God redeemed the human race and this fallen, redeemed creation will be more glorious than the original creation. Those who have trusted Him will receive His accolade, as actors receive applause at the end of the play.

Eternity and Creation

God has existed eternally in perfect harmony. He exists as one in nature or essence and three in person or roles as God the Father, God the Son, and God the Holy Spirit. The Godhead share attributes of sovereignty, omniscience, omnipotence, omnipresence, veracity, eternal life, righteousness, immutability, justice, and love. In eternity past God created sentient beings to serve Him. These were angels—spirit beings with great knowledge and power. He named the preeminent angel Lucifer, the Day Star (Isaiah 14.12). He governed heaven and had the privilege of orchestrating divine worship (Ezekiel 28.11-19). Sometime after God created the angelic host, He created the physical universe (Job 38.7). At some point, Lucifer became displeased with his exalted role. He wanted more than to be the highest and most beautiful creature of God: he wanted to be God. Instead, he became Satan, the adversary of God, a twisted, fallen creature. In his rebellion, he convinced a third of the angels to follow him against God (Revelation 12.3-4). This began sin in the universe, the conflict between good and evil. Instead of millions of wills working in harmony, millions of wills became opposed God.

The Creation of Mankind

The Bible does not reveal how long the angelic creation existed before God created man. And why did God create man? The best answer is He created man to resolve the angelic conflict and the problem of evil. From what the Scriptures indicate, God wished to demonstrate His goodness by having man choose Him for His own sake. This is what faith is all about. The book of Hebrews states it is impossible to please God apart from faith (Hebrews 11.6). The one thing God wishes from us (and the only way we can have a relationship with Him) is our trust. The book of Job is a wonderful microcosm and mini-drama of the larger drama being played out with the human race. When we believe God, when we believe the gospel—that Christ died for our sins and rose from the dead (1 Corinthians 15.1-4)—we agree with God that we are incapable of pleasing or commending ourselves to Him by our own efforts. We are left to trusting and depending on Christ's work on our behalf. This act of faith is a choice of sides. Such an act of faith is a defeat for Satan. When we put our trust in Christ we transfer our allegiance from those in rebellion against God, His enemies, to God.

God created man perfect, without sin, and he enjoyed a perfect relationship with his Creator. Satan, hating God, perceived (rightly) man's creation threatened him and his ambitions. Satan is not only God's greatest enemy, he is mankind's greatest enemy. He wishes to depose God and enslave or destroy the human race. He deceived Eve into eating from the Tree of the Knowledge of Good and Evil—the one tree's fruit God had forbidden Adam to eat (Genesis 2.15-17)—for he discerned this was the best strategy to defeat Adam. He was right. Adam was not deceived but ate anyway (Genesis 3.13; 1 Timothy 2.14). God had warned Adam that the day he ate from the

Tree he would die but Adam likely had no idea of the grave and long-lasting consequences of his act. The couple died immediately—not physically (that came later) but spiritually. Their relationship and communion with God, which they had enjoyed without inhibition ended. Theologians call this the Fall. From this one act, spiritual death passed to all humanity. The Scriptures reveal we are "in Adam" and that his sin imposed a death sentence upon us all (1 Corinthians 15.22). God was merciful, however, and drove Adam and Eve from Eden to prevent them from eating from the Tree of Life, which had the ability to give eternal life (Genesis 3.22). Without this Tree, their bodies weakened until they died physically. Instead, God gave Adam and Eve the promise in Genesis 3.15: a redeemer would come and redeem the loss they had brought upon themselves and the human race.

God's Dealings With Mankind

God's first dealings were with all mankind. Many historical records of ancient man have been lost but archaeological evidence shows ancient man built great civilizations. The pyramids reveal genius architectural skill and technology. In Genesis 6 is the strange account in which the "sons of God" had sexual relations with women and produced men of great strength and power called Nephilim (giants). These sons of God were fallen angels (Genesis 6.2, 4; Job 1.6. 2.1, 38.7) and their activity was a Satanic attempt to corrupt and destroy the human race. It was nearly successful. Our stories of gods, goddesses, demigods, that have passed through mythology and folklore come from their activities. During this time, the earth became so corrupt and violent (Genesis 6.5, 11-12) that God determined He had to destroy most of humanity and began anew to save mankind.

God found one righteous and genetically unpolluted family (Genesis 6.9), the family of Noah. He instructed Noah how to build a great ship, the ark, to survive the flood He would bring. This flood destroyed all humanity except Noah and his immediate family. From Noah's sons, Shem, Japheth, and Ham, and their wives came all the races and nations of the earth. Civilization began again. Instead of spreading forth across the world as God had commanded

(Genesis 1.22, 9.1), the people settled and consolidated at a place called Babel. They attempted to set up a global political and religious government to worship the heavenly host instead of God. This was the beginning of polytheism. The heavenly host are spiritual beings. Some are loyal to God and some disloyal. All of them are created beings and worship of them is forbidden. To preserve the human race, God broke up this rebellious system by confusing mankind's language (Genesis 11.6-9). The language barriers God created divided people and they formed nations. Nationalism is a divine institution which curbs evil through the balance of power of nation states.

God's Dealings With Israel

Humanity as a whole had rejected God. As a result, God began a new program and revealed Himself to one man through whom He would create a new race of people—the Jews. They would be the central actors in His plan to bless the world and defeat evil.

God chose Abram, who became Abraham (Genesis 12.1-5), who responded to God in faith. God made a sovereign covenant with him (the Abrahamic Covenant, Genesis 12.1-3, 15.1-20). The elements of that covenant were that God would make Abraham great, that he and his offspring would be a blessing to mankind, that God would bless those who blessed him and curse him who cursed him, that Abraham would have innumerable offspring (physical and spiritual), and that God would give Abraham and his offspring a land, "from the river of Egypt unto the great river, the river Euphrates" (Genesis 15.18). Satan is committed to defeating this plan and destroying God's agents. This explains why Jews have been the focal point of hatred and persecution throughout history. They are the center of gravity in God's strategic plan since God has declared all spiritual blessings are mediated through the Jews—and one Jew in particular, the Lord Jesus Christ.

Satan has made several attempts but has failed to destroy God's covenant people. His evil plan is still in effect and will reach its apex in the Tribulation (Matthew 24.15-22). Since God's prophetic covenant promises (Abrahamic, Land, Mosaic, Sabbatic, Davidic, and New covenants) remain unfulfilled, Satan's purpose to destroy the Jews continues. If he can destroy the Jews, God's plan would fail. The source of all anti-Semitism is Satan. He is behind the hatred of the Jewish people. One only need look at the nations who vote against Israel in the United Nations to understand who controls the governments of this world.

The Abrahamic Covenant is the foundation for God's other covenants with Israel: the Land, Mosaic, Sabbatic, Davidic, and New Covenant. God promised Abraham these covenants would go through the line of Isaac and later through Jacob, whom God named Israel. For hundreds of years God dealt with Israel, blessing them for obedience and disciplined them for disobedience. God fought for Israel and His greatest victory was delivering them from Egypt. God dispensed the Mosaic Law (Exodus 20.1-17) through Moses and it governed Jewish life for 1,500 years. The Levitical sacrifices "covered" sin until the death and resurrection of Christ—the Lamb slain from the foundation of the world (Revelation 13.8). Christ's death and resurrection defeated the power of sin, death, and Satan. Israel's festivals, Tabernacle and Temple, accessories, and animal sacrifices were pictures of Christ and His work.

John the Baptizer and Jesus in His earthly ministry proclaimed a message of repentance (the gospel of the kingdom) to Israel (Matthew 3.1-2, 4.17). Jesus' first miracle, making wine (wine was a symbol of gladness and blessing) at the wedding of Cana, was a sign of this kingdom. Instead of accepting Jesus as the Messiah, the nation rejected and crucified Him. Despite their rejection, Christ's death satisfied God's justice and God raised him from the dead. Christ had defeated sin and death. Repeated pleas after His resurrection for the nation to repent and accept Jesus as the Messiah by Jesus' disciples were unheeded. The nation continued to harden its heart. After 40 years of testing, in 70 A.D., God judged the nation. The Romans destroyed Jerusalem, the Temple, and scattered the Jews (Diaspora). This status continued for almost 1,900 years, until 1948, when the nation of Israel was reestablished.

God's Creation of the Church (Body of Christ)

While God was working through Jesus' disciples in their ministry to Israel, He also began to work in a new and different way. This change may be compared to the change God made when He called Abraham. National Israel had every opportunity to accept Jesus as the Messiah. But God knew they would reject His Son. Saul, a brilliant Pharisee, became the leader of Israel's continued rejection of Jesus. In his zeal for Judaism, he petitioned and received from the Jewish authorities the power to persecute Jewish believers beyond the borders of Israel (Galatians 1.13-14; Acts 9.1-2, 22.3-5, 26.9-11). Nearing Damascus, the resurrected Jesus revealed Himself to Saul (Paul) and changed his heart (Acts 9.3-8, 22.6-11, 26.12-18). Following that experience, he became as zealous a follower of Christ as he had been His enemy.

God revealed to Paul a new creation, the Church, the body of Christ (Ephesians 1.22-23; Colossians 1.18, 22). For hundreds of years, God had worked exclusively through the Jews—Israel. If one came to God, one came through Israel. But in light of Israel's continued rejection of the Messiah, God created a new program, the Church, which removed the distinction between Jew and Gentile. The Church, the body of Christ, was a "secret." Jesus did not reveal it in His earthly ministry and Peter and the Twelve knew nothing of it.

Almost all early believers in Christ were Jews. But under the ministry of Paul, the majority changed from Jew to Gentile. God commissioned Paul as "the Apostle to the Gentiles" (Romans 11.13; Galatians 2.7-9). God had chosen Peter and Eleven as the apostles of Israel. The risen Lord also revealed to Paul a new gospel, the "gospel of the grace of God" (Acts 20.24) which was wholly different from the "gospel of the kingdom."

Paul wrote that believers of his gospel have been blessed with every spiritual blessing and are positionally seated with Christ in the heaven (Ephesians 1.3) with heavenly citizenship (Philippians 3.20). Members of the Church will one day rule angels (1 Corinthians 6.3) and are joint-heirs with Christ (Romans 8.17). The

Church is the body of Christ and Christ is its Head. Every believer is in a grace relationship with God and indwelt by God the Holy Spirit (1 Corinthians 1.22, 5.5; Ephesians 5.14). When the Church is complete, God will remove it and take it to heaven. This event is known as the Rapture and is the resurrection of the Church. God will then complete His dealings with the nation of Israel.

Israel Redux

Centuries ago, God revealed the future empires on the earth to Daniel—Babylon, Medo-Persia, Greece, and Rome (Daniel 2, 7). He also revealed Israel's future in a timetable of 70 weeks of years. After 69 weeks, the Messiah would be killed (Daniel 9). That is the current status of God's prophetic timetable. One "week" remains.

God did not reveal the Church, the body of Christ in the Old Testament or Gospels. He kept it secret. According to Daniel's timetable, one week (of years) remains in Israel's history before the return of the Messiah. That week is known as the "time of Jacob's trouble" (Jeremiah 30.7) which Jesus called the Tribulation. The events Daniel foretold were expanded in detail by the revelation John received from Jesus, recorded in the book of Revelation. During this period, a false-Christ, the Beast, the Antichrist, will arise and deceive the world. He will be brilliant, charming, and a proponent of peace. He will befriend Israel. But in the middle of the "week" or after 3 ½ years, he will reveal his true nature. He will seat himself in the rebuilt Temple in Jerusalem, in the Holy of Holies, and proclaim he is God. Israel will recognize they have been deceived and that this world ruler is not the true Messiah. At the end of the "week," the Jews will repent and believe that Jesus of Nazareth, the One they crucified, is the Christ. Jesus spoke of this event and said it would signal His return (Matthew 23.37-39).

God will seal and protect 144,000 Jews, 12,000 from each of the twelve tribes, for special ministry during the Tribulation (Revelation 7.4-8). They will proclaim the Messiah and many will come to trust Him. Echoing Isaiah, Paul wrote all Israel will be saved (Romans 11.25-26; Isaiah 66.8). At the end of seven years of terrible tribulation, the armies of the world will surround Israel.

When the Beast has victory in his grasp and hope appears lost for Israel and the world, the Lord Jesus Christ as Lord of Hosts will return to deliver Israel and destroy His enemies (Revelation 19).

God's Kingdom on Earth

For hundreds of years, God's prophets foretold God's kingdom (Isaiah 2.1-11, 11.1-10). God will restore earth to its Edenic splendor and peace and righteousness will characterize this golden age. Warfare will cease and mankind will enjoy the long lifespans which existed before the Flood. God will fulfill His covenant promises to Israel and Jesus will reign from Jerusalem as David's greater Son over the world (Zechariah 14.9).

Israel will possess the land from the Nile, to the Mediterranean, to the Euphrates. God will write His laws onto hearts with the New Covenant. During these 1,000 years, Satan will be incarcerated (Revelation 20.1-3) but at its end, God will free him. Even though mankind has enjoyed perfect environment without war, disease, poverty, and crime, Satan will convince many to rebel against God. God will destroy them and execute His final judgment upon Satan. He will incarcerate him in the Lake of Fire for eternity, which the Beast and False Prophet already occupy.

God will then judge those who have rejected Christ (John 5.22; Revelation 20.11-15) according to their works. Having rejected Christ's work, their own works will be all they have to commend themselves. These will be insufficient to meet God's righteousness. God will then open the Book of Life to see if their names can be found. They will not be. The Lord Jesus Christ will consign them in the Lake of Fire forever.

A New Beginning

After the final judgment, God will create a New Heaven and a New Earth—a new universe (Revelation 21.1-4). How it will be different from our present universe in its physical laws or properties is not known. What is known is it will be wonderful beyond comprehension. Death will have vanished. Sun and moon will no longer exist as sources of light for God's glory will light the earth. The New Jerusalem will descend from heaven and reside upon the earth. It will be immense, measuring 1,500 miles in each dimension. The Temple will be gone. Reality will have entirely replaced shadow. The Tree of Life, unseen since Eden, will reappear. God will have become fully victorious and all possibility of sin or evil will have ceased. Those who have trusted Christ will begin a new adventure of love, righteousness, and peace. All will love and adore God from a free and willing heart. John revealed a heavenly scene that gives some indication of the glory of heavenly worship:

> And round about the throne were four and twenty seats: and upon the seats I saw four and twenty elders sitting, clothed in white raiment; and they had on their heads crowns of gold. And out of the throne proceeded lightnings and thunderings and voices: and there were seven lamps of fire burning before the throne, which are the seven Spirits of God. And before the throne there was a sea of glass like unto crystal: and in the midst of the throne, and round about the throne, were four beasts full of eyes before and behind. And the first beast was like a lion, and the second beast like a calf, and the third beast had a face as a man, and the fourth beast was like a flying eagle. And the four beasts had each of them six wings about him; and they were full of eyes within: and they rest not day and night, saying,
>
> > Holy, holy, holy, LORD God Almighty, which was, and is, and is to come.
>
> And when those beasts give glory and honor and thanks to him that sat on the throne, who lives for ever and ever, the four and twenty elders fall down before him that sat on the throne, and worship him that lives for ever and ever, and cast their crowns before the throne, saying,
>
> > Thou art worthy, O Lord, to receive glory and honor and power: for thou hast created all things,

> and for thy pleasure they are and were created (Revelation 4.4-11).

> And I beheld, and I heard the voice of many angels round about the throne and the beasts and the elders: and the number of them was ten thousand times ten thousand, and thousands of thousands; saying with a loud voice,
>
> > Worthy is the Lamb that was slain to receive power, and riches, and wisdom, and strength, and honor, and glory, and blessing.
>
> And every creature which is in heaven, and on the earth, and under the earth, and such as are in the sea, and all that are in them, heard I saying,
>
> > Blessing, and honor, and glory, and power, be unto him that sits upon the throne, and unto the Lamb for ever and ever.
>
> And the four beasts said,
>
> > Amen.
>
> And the four and twenty elders fell down and worshipped him that lives for ever and ever (Revelation 5.11-14).

God’s story ends as all good stories end. And they lived happily ever after….

The End…of the beginning…

and the Beginning of that which has no end.

94868408R00161

Made in the USA
Columbia, SC
02 May 2018